HISTORY OF ECONOMIC THEORY

THEORY

ADAM SMITH, JEAN-BAPTISTE SAY,
AND J.R. McCULLOCH

CONTENTS

CONTENTS

An Inquiry into the Nature and Causes of the Wealth of Nations. Book II: Of the Nature, Accumulation, and Employment of Stock

Adam Smith; 1776

In that rude state of society, in which there is no division of labour, in which exchanges are seldom made, and in which every man provides everything for himself, it is not necessary that any stock should be accumulated, or stored up beforehand, in order to carry on the business of the society. Every man endeavours to supply, by his own industry, his own occasional wants, as they occur. When he is hungry, he goes to the forest to hunt; when his coat is worn out, he clothes himself with the skin of the first large animal he kills; and when his hut begins to go to ruin, he repairs it, as well as he can, with the trees and the turf that are nearest it.

But when the division of labour has once been thoroughly introduced, the produce of a man's own labour can supply but a very small part of his occasional wants. The far greater part of them are supplied by the produce of other men's labour, which he purchases with the produce, or, what is the same thing, with the price of the produce, of his own. But this purchase cannot be made till such time as the produce of his own labour has not only been completed, but sold. A stock of goods of different kinds, therefore, must be stored up somewhere, sufficient to maintain him, and to supply him with the materials and tools of his work, till such time at least as both these events can be brought about. A weaver cannot apply himself entirely to his peculiar business, unless there is beforehand stored up somewhere, either in his own possession, or in that of some other person, a stock sufficient to maintain him, and to supply him with the materials and tools of his work, till he has not only completed, but sold his web. This accumulation must evidently be previous to his applying his industry for so long a time to such a peculiar business.

As the accumulation of stock must, in the nature of things, be previous to the division of labour, so labour can be more and more subdivided in proportion only as stock is previously more and more accumulated. The quantity of materials which the same number of people can work up, increases in a great proportion as labour comes to be more and more subdivided; and as the operations of each workman are gradually reduced to a greater degree of simplicity, a variety of new machines come to be invented for facilitating and abridging those operations. As the division of labour advances, therefore, in order to give constant employment to an equal number of workmen, an equal stock of provisions, and a greater stock of materials and tools than what would have been necessary in a ruder state of things, must be accumulated beforehand. But the number of workmen in every branch of business generally increases with the division of labour in that branch; or rather it is the increase of their number which enables them to class and subdivide themselves in this manner.

As the accumulation of stock is previously necessary for carrying on this great improvement in the productive powers of labour, so that accumulation naturally leads to this improvement. The person who employs his stock in maintaining labour, necessarily wishes to employ it in such a manner as to produce as great a quantity of work as possible. He endeavours, therefore, both to make among his workmen the most proper distribution of employment, and to furnish them with the best machines which he can either invent or afford to purchase. His abilities, in both these respects, are generally in proportion to the extent of his stock, or to the number of people whom it can employ. The quantity of industry, therefore, not only increases in every country with the increase of the stock which employs it, but, in consequence of that increase, the same quantity of industry produces a much greater quantity of work.

Such are in general the effects of the increase of stock upon industry and its productive powers.

In the following book, I have endeavoured to explain the nature of stock, the effects of its accumulation into capital of different kinds, and the effects of the different employments of those capitals. This book is divided into five chapters. In the first chapter, I have endeavoured to show what are the different parts or branches into which the stock, either of an individual, or of a great society, naturally divides itself. In the second, I have endeavoured to explain the nature and operation of money, considered as a particular branch of the general stock of the society. The stock which is accumulated into a capital, may either be employed by the person to whom it belongs, or it may be lent to some other person. In the third and fourth chapters, I have endeavoured to examine the manner in which it operates in both these situations. The fifth and last chapter treats of the different effects which the different employments of capital immediately produce upon the quantity, both of national industry, and of the annual produce of land and labour.

Chapter I: Of the Division of Stock

When the stock which a man possesses is no more than sufficient to maintain him for a few days or a few weeks, he seldom thinks of deriving any revenue from it. He consumes it as sparingly as he can, and endeavours, by his labour, to acquire something which may supply its place before it be consumed altogether. His revenue is, in this case, derived from his labour only. This is the state of the greater part of the labouring poor in all countries.

But when he possesses stock sufficient to maintain him for months or years, he naturally endeavours to derive a revenue from the greater part of it, reserving only so much for his immediate consumption as may maintain him till this revenue begins to come in. His whole stock, therefore, is distinguished into two parts. That part which he expects is to afford him this revenue is called his capital. The other is that which supplies his immediate consumption, and which consists either, first, in that portion of his whole stock which was originally reserved for this purpose; or, secondly, in his revenue, from whatever source derived, as it gradually comes in; or, thirdly, in such things as had been purchased by either of these in former years, and which are not yet entirely consumed, such as a stock of clothes, household furniture, and the like. In one or other, or all of these three articles, consists the stock which men commonly reserve for their own immediate consumption.

There are two different ways in which a capital may be employed so as to yield a revenue or profit to its employer.

First, it may be employed in raising, manufacturing, or purchasing goods, and selling them again with a profit. The capital employed in this manner yields no revenue or profit to its employer, while it either remains in his possession, or continues in the same shape. The goods of the merchant yield him no revenue or profit till he sells them for money, and the money yields him as little till it is again exchanged for goods. His capital is continually going from him in one shape, and returning to him in another; and it is only by means of such circulation, or successive changes, that it can yield him any profit. Such capitals, therefore, may very properly be called circulating capitals.

Secondly, it may be employed in the improvement of land, in the purchase of useful machines and instruments of trade, or in such like things as yield a revenue or profit without changing masters, or circulating any further. Such capitals, therefore, may very properly be called fixed capitals.

Different occupations require very different proportions between the fixed and circulating capitals employed in them.

The capital of a merchant, for example, is altogether a circulating capital. He has occasion for no machines or instruments of trade, unless his shop or warehouse be considered as such.

Some part of the capital of every master artificer or manufacturer must be fixed in the instruments of his trade. This part, however, is very small in some, and very great in others. A master tailor requires no other instruments of trade but a parcel of needles. Those of the master shoemaker are a little, though but a very little, more expensive. Those of the weaver rise a good deal above those of the shoemaker. The far greater part of the capital of all such master artificers, however, is circulated either in the wages of their workmen, or in the price of their materials, and repaid with a profit by the price of the work.

In other works a much greater fixed capital is required. In a great iron-work, for example, the furnace for melting the ore, the forge, the slit-mill, are instruments of trade which cannot be erected without a very great expense. In coal works, and mines of every kind, the machinery necessary, both for drawing out the water, and for other purposes, is frequently still more expensive.

That part of the capital of the farmer which is employed in the instruments of agriculture is a fixed, that which is employed in the wages and maintenance of his labouring servants, is a circulating capital. He makes a profit of the one by keeping it in his own possession, and of the other by parting with it. The price or value of his labouring cattle is a fixed capital, in the same manner as that of the instruments of husbandry; their maintenance is a circulating capital, in the same manner as that of the labouring servants. The farmer makes his profit by keeping the labouring cattle, and by parting with their maintenance. Both the price and the maintenance of the cattle which are bought in and fattened, not for labour, but for sale, are a circulating capital. The farmer makes his profit by parting with them. A flock of sheep or a herd of cattle that, in a breeding country, is brought in neither for labour nor for sale, but in order to make a profit by their wool, by their milk, and by their increase, is a fixed capital. The profit is made by keeping them. Their maintenance is a circulating capital. The profit is made by parting with it; and it comes back with both its own profit and the profit upon the whole price of the cattle, in the price of the wool, the milk, and the increase. The whole value of the seed, too, is properly a fixed capital. Though it goes backwards and forwards between the ground and the granary, it never changes masters, and therefore does not properly circulate. The farmer makes his profit, not by its sale, but by its increase.

The general stock of any country or society is the same with that of all its inhabitants or members; and therefore naturally divides itself into the same three portions, each of which has a distinct function or office.

The first is that portion which is reserved for immediate consumption, and of which the characteristic is, that it affords no revenue or profit. It consists in the stock of food, clothes, household furniture, etc. which have been purchased by their proper consumers, but which are not yet entirely consumed. The whole stock of mere dwelling-houses, too, subsisting at any one time in the country, make a part of this first portion. The stock that is laid out in a house, if it is to be the dwelling-house of the proprietor, ceases from that moment to serve in the function of a capital, or to afford any revenue to its owner. A dwelling-house, as such, contributes nothing to the revenue of its inhabitant; and though it is, no doubt, extremely useful to him, it is as his clothes and household furniture are useful to him, which, however, make a part of his expense, and not of his revenue. If it is to be let to a tenant for rent, as the house itself can produce nothing, the tenant must always pay the rent out of some other revenue, which he derives, either from labour, or stock, or land. Though a house, therefore, may yield a revenue to its proprietor, and thereby serve in the function of a capital to him, it cannot yield any to the public, nor serve in the function of a capital to it, and the revenue of the whole body of the people can never be in the smallest degree increased by it. Clothes and household furniture, in the same manner, sometimes yield a revenue, and thereby serve in the function of a capital to particular persons. In countries where masquerades are common, it is a trade to let out masquerade dresses for a night. Upholsterers frequently let furniture by the month or by the year. Undertakers let the furniture of funerals by the day and by the week. Many people let furnished houses, and get a rent, not only for the use of the house, but for that of the furniture. The revenue, however, which is derived from such things, must always be ultimately drawn from some other source of revenue. Of all parts of the stock, either of an individual or of a society, reserved for immediate consumption, what is laid out in houses is most slowly consumed. A stock of clothes may last several years; a stock of furniture half a century or a century; but a stock of houses, well-built and properly taken care of, may last many centuries. Though the period of their total consumption, however, is more distant, they are still as really a stock reserved for immediate consumption as either clothes or household furniture.

The second of the three portions into which the general stock of the society divides itself, is the fixed capital; of which the characteristic is, that it affords a revenue or profit without circulating or changing masters. It consists chiefly of the four following articles:

First, of all useful machines and instruments of trade, which facilitate and abridge labour.

Secondly, of all those profitable buildings which are the means of procuring a revenue, not only to the proprietor who lets them for a rent, but to the person who possesses them, and pays that rent for them; such as shops, warehouses, workhouses, farmhouses, with all their necessary buildings, stables, granaries, etc. These are very different from mere dwelling-houses. They are a sort of instruments of trade, and may be considered in the same light.

Thirdly, of the improvements of land, of what has been profitably laid out in clearing, draining, enclosing, manuring, and reducing it into the condition most proper for tillage and culture. An improved farm may very justly be regarded in the same light as those useful machines which facilitate and abridge labour, and by means of which an equal circulating capital can afford a much greater revenue to its employer. An improved farm is equally advantageous and more durable than any of those machines, frequently requiring no other repairs than the most profitable application of the farmer's capital employed in cultivating it.

Fourthly, of the acquired and useful abilities of all the inhabitants and members of the society. The acquisition of such talents, by the maintenance of the acquirer during his education, study, or apprenticeship, always costs a real expense, which is a capital fixed and realized, as it were, in his person. Those talents, as they make a part of his fortune, so do they likewise that of the society to which he belongs. The improved dexterity of a workman may be considered in the same light as a machine or instrument of trade which facilitates and abridges labour, and which, though it costs a certain expense, repays that expense with a profit.

The third and last of the three portions into which the general stock of the society naturally divides itself, is the circulating capital; of which the characteristic is, that it affords a revenue only by circulating or changing masters. It is composed likewise of four parts:

First, of the money, by means of which all the other three are circulated and distributed to their proper consumers.

Secondly, of the stock of provisions which are in the possession of the butcher, the grazier, the farmer, the corn merchant, the brewer, etc. and from the sale of which they expect to derive a profit.

Thirdly, of the materials, whether altogether rude, or more or less manufactured, of clothes, furniture, and building which are not yet made up into any of those three shapes, but which remain in the hands of the growers, the manufacturers, the mercers, and drapers, the timber merchants, the carpenters and joiners, the brick makers, etc.

Fourthly, and lastly, of the work which is made up and completed, but which is still in the hands of the merchant and manufacturer, and not yet disposed of or distributed to the proper consumers; such as the finished work which we frequently find ready-made in the shops of the smith, the cabinet maker, the goldsmith, the jeweler, the china merchant, etc. The circulating capital consists, in this manner, of the provisions, materials, and finished work of all kinds that are in the hands of their respective dealers, and of the money that is necessary for circulating and distributing them to those who are finally to use or to consume them.

Of these four parts, three—provisions, materials, and finished work,—are either annually, or in a longer or shorter period, regularly withdrawn from it, and placed either in the fixed capital, or in the stock reserved for immediate consumption.

Every fixed capital is both originally derived from, and requires to be continually supported by, a circulating capital. All useful machines and instruments of trade are originally derived from a circulating capital, which furnishes the materials of which they are made, and the maintenance of the workmen who make them. They require, too, a capital of the same kind to keep them in constant repair.

No fixed capital can yield any revenue but by means of a circulating capital. The most useful machines and instruments of trade will produce nothing, without the circulating capital, which affords the materials they are employed upon, and the maintenance of the workmen who employ them. Land, however improved, will yield no revenue without a circulating capital, which maintains the labourers who cultivate and collect its produce.

To maintain and augment the stock which may be reserved for immediate consumption, is the sole end and purpose both of the fixed and circulating capitals. It is this stock which feeds, clothes, and lodges the people. Their riches or poverty depend upon the abundant or sparing supplies which those two capitals can afford to the stock reserved for immediate consumption.

So great a part of the circulating capital being continually withdrawn from it, in order to be placed in the other two branches of the general stock of the society, it must in its turn require continual supplies without which it would soon cease to exist. These supplies are principally drawn from three sources; the produce of land, of mines, and of fisheries. These afford continual supplies of provisions and materials, of which part is afterwards wrought up into finished work and by which are replaced the provisions, materials, and finished work, continually withdrawn from the circulating capital. From mines, too, is drawn what is necessary for maintaining and augmenting that part of it which consists in money. For though, in the ordinary course of business, this part is not, like the other three, necessarily withdrawn from it, in order to be placed in the other two branches of the general stock of the society, it must, however, like all other things, be wasted and worn out at last, and sometimes, too, be either lost or sent abroad, and must, therefore, require continual, though no doubt, much smaller supplies.

Lands, mines, and fisheries, require all both a fixed and circulating capital to cultivate them; and their produce replaces, with a profit not only those capitals, but all the others in the society. Thus, the farmer annually replaces to the manufacturer the provisions which he had consumed and the materials which he had wrought up the year before; and the manufacturer replaces to the farmer the finished work which he had wasted and worn out in the same time. This is the real exchange that is annually made between those two orders of people, though it seldom happens that the rude produce of the one and the manufactured produce of the other, are directly bartered for one another; because it seldom happens that the farmer sells his corn and his cattle, his flax and his wool, to the very same person of whom he chooses to purchase the clothes, furniture, and instruments of trade, which he wants. He sells, therefore, his rude produce for money, with which he can purchase, wherever it is to be had, the manufactured produce he has occasion for. Land even replaces, in part at least, the capitals with which fisheries and mines are cultivated. It is the produce of land which draws the fish from the waters; and it is the produce of the surface of the earth which extracts the minerals from its bowels.

The produce of land, mines, and fisheries, when their natural fertility is equal, is in proportion to the extent and proper application of the capitals employed about them. When the capitals are equal, and equally well applied, it is in proportion to their natural fertility.

In all countries where there is a tolerable security, every man of common understanding will endeavour to employ whatever stock he can command, in procuring either present enjoyment or future profit. If it is employed in procuring present enjoyment, it is a stock reserved for immediate consumption. If it is employed in procuring future profit, it must procure this profit either by staying with him, or by going from him. In the one case it is a fixed, in the other it is a circulating capital. A man must be perfectly crazy, who, where there is a tolerable security, does not employ all the stock which he commands, whether it be his own or borrowed of other people, in some one or other of those three ways.

In those unfortunate countries, indeed, where men are continually afraid of the violence of their superiors, they frequently bury or conceal a great part of their stock, in order to have it always at hand to carry with them to some place of safety, in case of their being threatened with any of those disasters to which they consider themselves at all times exposed. This is said to be a common practice in Turkey, in Indostan, and, I believe, in most other governments of Asia. It seems to have been a common practice among our ancestors during the violence of the feudal government. Treasure trove was, in these times, considered as no contemptible part of the revenue of the greatest sovereigns in Europe. It consisted in such treasure as was found concealed in the earth, and to which no particular person could prove any right. This was regarded in those times as so important an object, that it was always considered as belonging to the sovereign, and neither to the finder nor to the proprietor of the land, unless the right to it had been conveyed to the latter by an express clause in his charter. It was put upon the same footing with gold and silver mines, which, without a special clause in the charter, were never supposed to be comprehended in the general grant of the lands, though mines of lead, copper, tin, and coal were, as things of smaller consequence.

Chapter II: Of Money, Considered as a Particular Branch Of the General Stock of the Society, or of the Expense Of Maintaining the National Capital

It has been shown in the first book, that the price of the greater part of commodities resolves itself into three parts, of which one pays the wages of the labour, another the profits of the stock, and a third the rent of the land which had been employed in producing and bringing them to market; that there are, indeed, some commodities of which the price is made up of two of those parts only, the wages of labour, and the profits of stock; and a very few in which it consists altogether in one, the wages of labour; but that the price of every commodity necessarily resolves itself into some one or other, or all, of those three parts; every part of it which goes neither to rent nor to wages, being necessarily profit to some body.

Since this is the case, it has been observed, with regard to every particular commodity, taken separately, it must be so with regard to all the commodities which compose the whole annual produce of the land and labour of every country, taken complexly. The whole price or exchangeable value of that annual produce must resolve itself into the same three parts, and be parceled out among the different inhabitants of the country, either as the wages of their labour, the profits of their stock, or the rent of their land.

But though the whole value of the annual produce of the land and labour of every country is thus divided among, and constitutes a revenue to, its different inhabitants; yet, as in the rent of a private estate, we distinguish between the gross rent and the neat rent, so may we likewise in the revenue of all the inhabitants of a great country.

The gross rent of a private estate comprehends whatever is paid by the farmer; the neat rent, what remains free to the landlord, after deducting the expense of management, of repairs, and all other necessary charges; or what, without hurting his estate, he can afford to place in his stock reserved for immediate consumption, or to spend upon his table, equipage, the ornaments of his house and furniture, his private enjoyments and amusements. His real wealth is in proportion, not to his gross, but to his neat rent.

The gross revenue of all the inhabitants of a great country comprehends the whole annual produce of their land and labour; the neat revenue, what remains free to them after deducting the expense of maintaining first, their fixed, and, secondly, their circulating capital, or what, without encroaching upon their capital, they can place in their stock reserved for immediate consumption, or spend upon their subsistence, conveniences, and amusements. Their real wealth, too, is in proportion, not to their gross, but to their neat revenue.

The whole expense of maintaining the fixed capital must evidently be excluded from the neat revenue of the society. Neither the materials necessary for supporting their useful machines and instruments of trade, their profitable buildings, etc. nor the produce of the labour necessary for fashioning those materials into the proper form, can ever make any part of it. The price of that labour may indeed make a part of it; as the workmen so employed may place the whole value of their wages in their stock reserved for immediate consumption. But in other sorts of labour, both the price and the produce go to this stock; the price to that of the workmen, the produce to that of other people, whose subsistence, conveniences, and amusements, are augmented by the labour of those workmen.

The intention of the fixed capital is to increase the productive powers of labour, or to enable the same number of labourers to perform a much greater quantity of work. In a farm where all the necessary buildings, fences, drains, communications, etc. are in the most perfect good order, the same number of labourers and labouring cattle will raise a much greater produce, than in one of equal extent and equally good ground, but not furnished with equal conveniences. In manufactures, the same number of hands, assisted with the best machinery, will work up a much greater quantity of goods than with more imperfect instruments of trade. The expense which is properly laid out upon a fixed capital of any kind, is always repaid with great profit, and increases the annual produce by a much greater value than that of the support which such improvements require. This support, however, still requires a certain portion of that produce. A certain quantity of materials, and the labour of a certain number of workmen, both of which might have been immediately employed to augment the food, clothing, and lodging, the subsistence and conveniences of the society, are thus diverted to another employment, highly advantageous indeed, but still different from this one. It is upon this account that all such improvements in mechanics, as enable the same number of workmen to perform an equal quantity of work with cheaper and simpler machinery than had been usual before, are always regarded as advantageous to every society. A certain quantity of materials, and the labour of a certain number of workmen, which had before been employed in supporting a more complex and expensive machinery, can afterwards be applied to augment the quantity of work which that or any other machinery is useful only for performing. The undertaker of some great manufactory, who employs a thousand a year in the maintenance of his machinery, if he can reduce this expense to five hundred, will naturally employ the other five hundred in purchasing an additional quantity of materials, to be wrought up by an additional number of workmen. The quantity of that work, therefore, which his machinery was useful only for performing, will naturally be augmented, and with it all the advantage and convenience which the society can derive from that work.

The expense of maintaining the fixed capital in a great country may very properly be compared to that of repairs in a private estate. The expense of repairs may frequently be necessary for supporting the produce of the estate, and consequently both the gross and the neat rent of the landlord. When by a more proper direction, however, it can be diminished without occasioning any diminution of produce, the gross rent remains at least the same as before, and the neat rent is necessarily augmented.

But though the whole expense of maintaining the fixed capital is thus necessarily excluded from the neat revenue of the society, it is not the same case with that of maintaining the circulating capital. Of the four parts of which this latter capital is composed—money, provisions, materials, and finished work—the three last, it has already been observed, are regularly withdrawn from it, and placed either in the fixed capital of the society, or in their stock reserved for immediate consumption. Whatever portion of those consumable goods is not employed in maintaining the former, goes all to the latter, and makes a part of the neat revenue of the society. The maintenance of those three parts of the circulating capital, therefore, withdraws no portion of the annual produce from the neat revenue of the society, besides what is necessary for maintaining the fixed capital.

The circulating capital of a society is in this respect different from that of an individual. That of an individual is totally excluded from making any part of his neat revenue, which must consist altogether in his profits. But though the circulating capital of every individual makes a part of that of the society to which he belongs, it is not upon that account totally excluded from making a part likewise of their neat revenue. Though the whole goods in a merchant's shop must by no means be placed in his own stock reserved for immediate consumption, they may in that of other people, who, from a revenue derived from other funds, may regularly replace their value to him, together with its profits, without occasioning any diminution either of his capital or of theirs.

Money, therefore, is the only part of the circulating capital of a society, of which the maintenance can occasion any diminution in their neat revenue.

The fixed capital, and that part of the circulating capital which consists in money, so far as they affect the revenue of the society, bear a very great resemblance to one another.

First, as those machines and instruments of trade, etc. require a certain expense, first to erect them, and afterwards to support them, both which expenses, though they make a part of the gross, are deductions from the neat revenue of the society; so the stock of money which circulates in any country must require a certain expense, first to collect it, and afterwards to support it; both which expenses, though they make a part of the gross, are, in the same manner, deductions from the neat revenue of the society. A certain quantity of very valuable materials, gold and silver, and of very curious labour, instead of augmenting the stock reserved for immediate consumption, the subsistence, conveniences, and amusements of individuals, is employed in supporting that great but expensive instrument of commerce, by means of which every individual in the society has his subsistence, conveniences, and amusements, regularly distributed to him in their proper proportions.

Secondly, as the machines and instruments of trade, etc. which compose the fixed capital either of an individual or of a society, make no part either of the gross or of the neat revenue of either; so money, by means of which the whole revenue of the society is regularly distributed among all its different members, makes itself no part of that revenue. The great wheel of circulation is altogether different from the goods which are circulated by means of it. The revenue of the society consists altogether in those goods, and not in the wheel which circulates them. In computing either the gross or the neat revenue of any society, we must always, from the whole annual circulation of money and goods, deduct the whole value of the money, of which not a single farthing can ever make any part of either.

It is the ambiguity of language only which can make this proposition appear either doubtful or paradoxical. When properly explained and understood, it is almost self-evident.

When we talk of any particular sum of money, we sometimes mean nothing but the metal pieces of which it is composed, and sometimes we include in our meaning some obscure reference to the goods which can be had in exchange for it, or to the power of purchasing which the possession of it conveys. Thus, when we say that the circulating money of England has been computed at eighteen millions, we mean only to express the amount of the metal pieces, which some writers have computed, or rather have supposed, to circulate in that country. But when we say that a man is worth fifty or a hundred pounds a year, we mean commonly to express, not only the amount of the metal pieces which are annually paid to him, but the value of the goods which he can annually purchase or consume; we mean commonly to ascertain what is or ought to be his way of living, or the quantity and quality of the necessaries and conveniences of life in which he can with propriety indulge himself.

When, by any particular sum of money, we mean not only to express the amount of the metal pieces of which it is composed, but to include in its signification some obscure reference to the goods which can be had in exchange for them, the wealth or revenue which it in this case denotes, is equal only to one of the two values which are thus intimated somewhat ambiguously by the same word, and to the latter more properly than to the former, to the money's worth more properly than to the money.

Thus, if a guinea be the weekly pension of a particular person, he can in the course of the week purchase with it a certain quantity of subsistence, conveniences, and amusements. In proportion as this quantity is great or small, so are his real riches, his real weekly revenue. His weekly revenue is certainly not equal both to the guinea and to what can be purchased with it, but only to one or other of those two equal values, and to the latter more properly than to the former, to the guinea's worth rather than to the guinea.

If the pension of such a person was paid to him, not in gold, but in a weekly bill for a guinea, his revenue surely would not so properly consist in the piece of paper, as in what he could get for it. A guinea may be considered as a bill for a certain quantity of necessaries and conveniences upon all the tradesmen in the neighbourhood. The revenue of the person to whom it is paid, does not so properly consist in the piece of gold, as in what he can get for it, or in what he can exchange it for. If it could be exchanged for nothing, it would, like a bill upon a bankrupt, be of no more value than the most useless piece of paper.

Though the weekly or yearly revenue of all the different inhabitants of any country, in the same manner, may be, and in reality frequently is, paid to them in money, their real riches, however, the real weekly or yearly revenue of all of them taken together, must always be great or small, in proportion to the quantity of consumable goods which they can all of them purchase with this money. The whole revenue of all of them taken together is evidently not equal to both the money and the consumable goods, but only to one or other of those two values, and to the latter more properly than to the former.

Though we frequently, therefore, express a person's revenue by the metal pieces which are annually paid to him, it is because the amount of those pieces regulates the extent of his power of purchasing, or the value of the goods which he can annually afford to consume. We still consider his revenue as consisting in this power of purchasing or consuming, and not in the pieces which convey it.

But if this is sufficiently evident, even with regard to an individual, it is still more so with regard to a society. The amount of the metal pieces which are annually paid to an individual, is often precisely equal to his revenue, and is upon that account the shortest and best expression of its value. But the amount of the metal pieces which circulate in a society can never be equal to the revenue of all its members. As the same guinea which pays the weekly pension of one man today, may pay that of another tomorrow, and that of a third the day thereafter, the amount of the metal pieces which annually circulate in any country must always be of much less value than the whole money pensions annually paid with them. But the power of purchasing, or the goods which can successively be bought with the whole of those money pensions, as they are successively paid, must always be precisely of the same value with those pensions; as must likewise be the revenue of the different persons to whom they are paid. That revenue, therefore, cannot consist in those metal pieces, of which the amount is so much inferior to its value, but in the power of purchasing, in the goods which can successively be bought with them as they circulate from hand to hand.

Money, therefore, the great wheel of circulation, the great instrument of commerce, like all other instruments of trade, though it makes a part, and a very valuable part, of the capital, makes no part of the revenue of the society to which it belongs; and though the metal pieces of which it is composed, in the course of their annual circulation, distribute to every man the revenue which properly belongs to him, they make themselves no part of that revenue.

Thirdly, and lastly, the machines and instruments of trade, etc. which compose the fixed capital, bear this further resemblance to that part of the circulating capital which consists in money; that as every saving in the expense of erecting and supporting those machines, which does not diminish the introductive powers of labour, is an improvement of the neat revenue of the society; so every saving in the expense of collecting and supporting that part of the circulating capital which consists in money is an improvement of exactly the same kind.

It is sufficiently obvious, and it has partly, too, been explained already, in what manner every saving in the expense of supporting the fixed capital is an improvement of the neat revenue of the society. The whole capital of the undertaker of every work is necessarily divided between his fixed and his circulating capital. While his whole capital remains the same, the smaller the one part, the greater must necessarily be the other. It is the circulating capital which furnishes the materials and wages of labour, and puts industry into motion. Every saving, therefore, in the expense of maintaining the fixed capital, which does not diminish the productive powers of labour, must increase the fund which puts industry into motion, and consequently the annual produce of land and labour, the real revenue of every society.

The substitution of paper in the room of gold and silver money, replaces a very expensive instrument of commerce with one much less costly, and sometimes equally convenient. Circulation comes to be carried on by a new wheel, which it costs less both to erect and to maintain than the old one. But in what manner this operation is performed, and in what manner it tends to increase either the gross or the neat revenue of the society, is not altogether so obvious, and may therefore require some further explication.

There are several different sorts of paper money; but the circulating notes of banks and bankers are the species which is best known, and which seems best adapted for this purpose.

When the people of any particular country have such confidence in the fortune, probity, and prudence of a particular banker, as to believe that he is always ready to pay upon demand such of his promissory notes as are likely to be at any time presented to him, those notes come to have the same currency as gold and silver money, from the confidence that such money can at any time be had for them.

A particular banker lends among his customers his own promissory notes, to the extent, we shall suppose, of a hundred thousand pounds. As those notes serve all the purposes of money, his debtors pay him the same interest as if he had lent them so much money. This interest is the source of his gain. Though some of those notes are continually coming back upon him for payment, part of them continue to circulate for months and years together. Though he has generally in circulation, therefore, notes to the extent of a hundred thousand pounds, twenty thousand pounds in gold and silver may, frequently, be a sufficient provision for answering occasional demands. By this operation, therefore, twenty thousand pounds in gold and silver perform all the functions which a hundred thousand could otherwise have performed. The same exchanges may be made, the same quantity of consumable goods may be circulated and distributed to their proper consumers, by means of his promissory notes, to the value of a hundred thousand pounds, as by an equal value of gold and silver money. Eighty thousand pounds of gold and silver, therefore, can in this manner be spared from the circulation of the country; and if different operations of the same kind should, at the same time, be carried on by many different banks and bankers, the whole circulation may thus be conducted with a fifth part only of the gold and silver which would otherwise have been requisite.

Let us suppose, for example, that the whole circulating money of some particular country amounted, at a particular time, to one million sterling, that sum being then sufficient for circulating the whole annual produce of their land and labour. Let us suppose, too, that some time thereafter, different banks and bankers issued promissory notes payable to the bearer, to the extent of one million, reserving in their different coffers two hundred thousand pounds for answering occasional demands. There would remain, therefore, in circulation, eight hundred thousand pounds in gold and silver, and a million of bank notes, or eighteen hundred thousand pounds of paper and money together. But the annual produce of the land and labour of the country had before required only one million to circulate and distribute it to its proper consumers, and that annual produce cannot be immediately augmented by those operations of banking. One million, therefore, will be sufficient to circulate it after them. The goods to be bought and sold being precisely the same as before, the same quantity of money will be sufficient for buying and selling them. The channel of circulation, if I may be allowed such an expression, will remain precisely the same as before. One million we have supposed sufficient to fill that channel. Whatever, therefore, is poured into it beyond this sum cannot run into it, but must overflow. One million eight hundred thousand pounds are poured into it. Eight hundred thousand pounds, therefore, must overflow, that sum being over and above what can be employed in the circulation of the country. But though this sum cannot be employed at home, it is too valuable to be allowed to lie idle. It will, therefore, be sent abroad, in order to seek that profitable employment which it cannot find at home. But the paper cannot go abroad; because at a distance from the banks which issue it, and from the country in which payment of it can be exacted by law, it will not be received in common payments. Gold and silver, therefore, to the amount of eight hundred thousand pounds, will be sent abroad, and the channel of home circulation will remain filled with a million of paper instead of a million of those metals which filled it before.

But though so great a quantity of gold and silver is thus sent abroad, we must not imagine that it is sent abroad for nothing, or that its proprietors make a present of it to foreign nations. They will exchange it for foreign goods of some kind or another, in order to supply the consumption either of some other foreign country, or of their own.

If they employ it in purchasing goods in one foreign country, in order to supply the consumption of another, or in what is called the carrying trade, whatever profit they make will be in addition to the neat revenue of their own country. It is like a new fund, created for carrying on a new trade; domestic business being now transacted by paper, and the gold and silver being converted into a fund for this new trade.

If they employ it in purchasing foreign goods for home consumption, they may either, first, purchase such goods as are likely to be consumed by idle people who produce nothing, such as foreign wines, foreign silks, etc.; or, secondly, they may purchase an additional stock of materials, tools, and provisions, in order to maintain and employ an additional number of industrious people, who reproduce, with a profit, the value of their annual consumption.

So far as it is employed in the first way, it promotes prodigality, increases expense and consumption without increasing production, or establishing any permanent fund for supporting that expense, and is in every respect hurtful to the society.

So far as it is employed in the second way, it promotes industry; and though it increases the consumption of the society, it provides a permanent fund for supporting that consumption; the people who consume reproducing, with a profit, the whole value of their annual consumption. The gross revenue of the society, the annual produce of their land and labour, is increased by the whole value which the labour of those workmen adds to the materials upon which they are employed, and their neat revenue by what remains of this value, after deducting what is necessary for supporting the tools and instruments of their trade.

That the greater part of the gold and silver which being forced abroad by those operations of banking, is employed in purchasing foreign goods for home consumption, is, and must be, employed in purchasing those of this second kind, seems not only probable but almost unavoidable. Though some particular men may sometimes increase their expense very considerably, though their revenue does not increase at all, we may be assured that no class or order of men ever does so; because, though the principles of common prudence do not always govern the conduct of every individual, they always influence that of the majority of every class or order. But the revenue of idle people, considered as a class or order, cannot, in the smallest degree, be increased by those operations of banking. Their expense in general, therefore, cannot be much increased by them, though that of a few individuals among them may, and in reality sometimes is. The demand of idle people, therefore, for foreign goods being the same, or very nearly the same as before, a very small part of the money which, being forced abroad by those operations of banking, is employed in purchasing foreign goods for home consumption, is likely to be employed in purchasing those for their use. The greater part of it will naturally be destined for the employment of industry, and not for the maintenance of idleness.

When we compute the quantity of industry which the circulating capital of any society can employ, we must always have regard to those parts of it only which consist in provisions, materials, and finished work; the other, which consists in money, and which serves only to circulate those three, must always be deducted. In order to put industry into motion, three things are requisite; materials to work upon, tools to work with, and the wages or recompense for the sake of which the work is done. Money is neither a material to work upon, nor a tool to work with; and though the wages of the workman are commonly paid to him in money, his real revenue, like that of all other men, consists, not in the money, but in the money's worth; not in the metal pieces, but in what can be got for them.

The quantity of industry which any capital can employ must evidently be equal to the number of workmen whom it can supply with materials, tools, and a maintenance suitable to the nature of the work. Money may be requisite for purchasing the materials and tools of the work, as well as the maintenance of the workmen; but the quantity of industry which the whole capital can employ is certainly not equal both to the money which purchases, and to the materials, tools, and maintenance, which are purchased with it, but only to one or other of those two values, and to the latter more properly than to the former.

When paper is substituted in the room of gold and silver money, the quantity of the materials, tools, and maintenance, which the whole circulating capital can supply, may be increased by the whole value of gold and silver which used to be employed in purchasing them. The whole value of the great wheel of circulation and distribution is added to the goods which are circulated and distributed by means of it. The operation, in some measure, resembles that of the undertaker of some great work, who, in consequence of some improvement in mechanics, takes down his old machinery, and adds the difference between its price and that of the new to his circulating capital, to the fund from which he furnishes materials and wages to his workmen.

What is the proportion which the circulating money of any country bears to the whole value of the annual produce circulated by means of it, it is perhaps impossible to determine. It has been computed by different authors at a fifth, at a tenth, at a twentieth, and at a thirtieth, part of that value. But how small soever the proportion which the circulating money may bear to the whole value of the annual produce, as but a part, and frequently but a small part, of that produce, is ever destined for the maintenance of industry, it must always bear a very considerable proportion to that part. When, therefore, by the substitution of paper, the gold and silver necessary for circulation is reduced to, perhaps, a fifth part of the former quantity, if the value of only the greater part of the other four-fifths be added to the funds which are destined for the maintenance of industry, it must make a very considerable addition to the quantity of that industry, and consequently to the value of the annual produce of land and labour.

An operation of this kind has, within these five-and-twenty or thirty years, been performed in Scotland, by the erection of new banking companies in almost every considerable town, and even in some country villages. The effects of it have been precisely those above described. The business of the country is almost entirely carried on by means of the paper of those different banking companies, with which purchases and payments of all kinds are commonly made. Silver very seldom appears, except in the change of a twenty shilling bank note, and gold still seldomer. But though the conduct of all those different companies has not been unexceptionable, and has accordingly required an act of Parliament to regulate it, the country, notwithstanding, has evidently derived great benefit from their trade. I have heard it asserted, that the trade of the city of Glasgow doubled in about fifteen years after the first erection of the banks there; and that the trade of Scotland has more than quadrupled since the first erection of the two public banks at Edinburgh; of which the one, called the Bank of Scotland, was establish-ed by act of Parliament in 1695, and the other, called the Royal Bank, by royal charter in 1727. Whether the trade, either of Scotland in general, or of the city of Glasgow in particular, has really increased in so great a proportion, during so short a period, I do not pretend to know. If either of them has increased in this proportion, it seems to be an effect too great to be accounted for by the sole operation of this cause. That the trade and industry of Scotland, however, have increased very consid-erably during this period, and that the banks have contributed a good deal to this increase, cannot be doubted.

The value of the silver money which circulated in Scotland before the Union in 1707, and which, immediately after it, was brought into the Bank of Scotland in order to be re-coined, amounted to 411,117l. 10s. 9d. sterling. No account has been got of the gold coin; but it appears from the ancient accounts of the mint of Scotland, that the value of the gold annually coined somewhat exceeded that of the silver.[1] There were a good many people, too, upon this occasion, who, from a diffidence of repayment, did not bring their silver into the Bank of Scotland; and there was, besides, some English coin which was not called in. The whole value of the gold and silver, therefore, which circulated in Scot-land before the union, cannot be estimated at less than a million ster-ling. It seems to have constituted almost the whole circulation of that country; for though the circulation of the Bank of Scotland, which had then no rival, was considerable, it seems to have made but a very small part of the whole. In the present times, the whole circulation of Scot-land cannot be estimated at less than two millions, of which that part which consists in gold and silver most probably does not amount to half a million. But though the circulating gold and silver of Scotland have suffered so great a diminution during this period, its real riches and prosperity do not appear to have suffered any. Its agriculture, manufac-tures, and trade, on the contrary, the annual produce of its land and labour, have evidently been augmented.

It is chiefly by discounting bills of exchange, that is, by advancing money upon them before they are due, that the greater part of banks and bankers issue their promissory notes. They deduct always, upon whatever sum they advance, the legal interest till the bill shall become due. The payment of the bill, when it becomes due, replaces to the bank the value of what had been advanced, together with a clear profit of the interest. The banker who advances to the merchant whose bill he discounts, not gold and silver, but his own promissory notes, has the advantage of being able to discount to a greater amount by the whole value of his promissory notes, which he finds by experience are commonly in circulation. He is thereby enabled to make his clear gain of interest on so much a larger sum.

The commerce of Scotland, which at present is not very great, was still more inconsiderable when the two first banking companies were established; and those companies would have had but little trade, had they confined their business to the discounting of bills of exchange. They invented, therefore, another method of issuing their promissory notes; by granting what they call cash accounts, that is, by giving credit, to the extent of a certain sum (two or three thousand pounds for example), to any individual who could procure two persons of undoubted credit and good landed estate to become surety for him, that whatever money should be advanced to him, within the sum for which the credit had been given, should be repaid upon demand, together with the legal interest. Credits of this kind are, I believe, commonly granted by banks and bankers in all different parts of the world. But the easy terms upon which the Scotch banking companies accept of repayment are, so far as I know, peculiar to them, and have perhaps been the principal cause, both of the great trade of those companies and of the benefit which the country has received from it.

Whoever has a credit of this kind with one of those companies, and borrows a thousand pounds upon it, for example, may repay this sum piecemeal, by twenty and thirty pounds at a time, the company discounting a proportionable part of the interest of the great sum, from the day on which each of those small sums is paid in, till the whole be in this manner repaid. All merchants, therefore, and almost all men of business, find it convenient to keep such cash accounts with them, and are thereby interested to promote the trade of those companies, by readily receiving their notes in all payments, and by encouraging all those with whom they have any influence to do the same. The banks, when their customers apply to them for money, generally advance it to them in their own promissory notes. These the merchants pay away to the manufacturers for goods, the manufacturers to the farmers for materials and provisions, the farmers to their landlords for rent, the landlords repay them to the merchants for the conveniences and luxuries with which they supply them, and the merchants again return them to the banks in order to balance their cash accounts, or to replace what they may have borrowed of them; and thus almost the whole money business of the country is transacted by means of them. Hence the great trade of those companies.

By means of those cash accounts, every merchant can, without imprudence, carry on a greater trade than he otherwise could do. If there are two merchants, one in London and the other in Edinburgh, who employ equal stocks in the same branch of trade, the Edinburgh merchant can, without imprudence, carry on a greater trade and give employment to a greater number of people than the London merchant. The London merchant must always keep by him a considerable sum of money, either in his own coffers, or in those of his banker, who gives him no interest for it, in order to answer the demands continually coming upon him for payment of the goods which he purchases upon credit. Let the ordinary amount of this sum be supposed five hundred pounds; the value of the goods in his warehouse must always be less, by five hundred pounds, than it would have been, had he not been obliged to keep such a sum unemployed. Let us suppose that he generally disposes of his whole stock upon hand, or of goods to the value of his whole stock upon hand, once in the year. By being obliged to keep so great a sum unemployed, he must sell in a year five hundred pounds worth less goods than he might otherwise have done. His annual profits must be less by all that he could have made by the sale of five hundred pounds worth more goods; and the number of people employed in preparing his goods for the market must be less by all those that five hundred pounds more stock could have employed. The merchant in Edinburgh, on the other hand, keeps no money unemployed for answering such occasional demands. When they actually come upon him, he satisfies them from his cash account with the bank, and gradually replaces the sum borrowed with the money or paper which comes in from the occasional sales of his goods. With the same stock, therefore, he can, without imprudence, have at all times in his warehouse a larger quantity of goods than the London merchant; and can thereby both make a greater profit himself, and give constant employment to a greater number of industrious people who prepare those goods for the market. Hence the great benefit which the country has derived from this trade.

The facility of discounting bills of exchange, it may be thought indeed, gives the English merchants a convenience equivalent to the cash accounts of the Scotch merchants. But the Scotch merchants, it must be remembered, can discount their bills of exchange as easily as the English merchants; and have, besides, the additional convenience of their cash accounts.

The whole paper money of every kind which can easily circulate in any country never can exceed the value of the gold and silver, of which it supplies the place, or which (the commerce being supposed the same) would circulate there, if there was no paper money. If twenty shilling notes, for example, are the lowest paper money current in Scotland, the whole of that currency which can easily circulate there cannot exceed the sum of gold and silver which would be necessary for transacting the annual exchanges of twenty shillings value and upwards usually transacted within that country. Should the circulating paper at any time exceed that sum, as the excess could neither be sent abroad nor be employed in the circulation of the country, it must immediately return upon the banks to be exchanged for gold and silver. Many people would immediately perceive that they had more of this paper than was necessary for transacting their business at home; and as they could not send it abroad, they would immediately demand payment for it from the banks. When this superfluous paper was converted into gold and silver, they could easily find a use for it by sending it abroad; but they could find none while it remained in the shape of paper. There would immediately, therefore, be a run upon the banks to the whole extent of this superfluous paper, and if they showed any difficulty or backwardness in payment, to a much greater extent; the alarm which this would occasion necessarily increasing the run.

Over and above the expenses which are common to every branch of trade, such as the expense of house rent, the wages of servants, clerks, accountants, etc. the expenses peculiar to a bank consist chiefly in two articles; first, in the expense of keeping at all times in its coffers, for answering the occasional demands of the holders of its notes, a large sum of money, of which it loses the interest; and, secondly, in the expense of replenishing those coffers as fast as they are emptied by answering such occasional demands.

A banking company which issues more paper than can be employed in the circulation of the country, and of which the excess is continually returning upon them for payment, ought to increase the quantity of gold and silver which they keep at all times in their coffers, not only in proportion to this excessive increase of their circulation, but in a much greater proportion; their notes returning upon them much faster than in proportion to the excess of their quantity. Such a company, therefore, ought to increase the first article of their expense, not only in proportion to this forced increase of their business, but in a much greater proportion.

The coffers of such a company, too, though they ought to be filled much fuller, yet must empty themselves much faster than if their business was confined within more reasonable bounds, and must require not only a more violent, but a more constant and uninterrupted exertion of expense in order to replenish them. The coin, too, which is thus continually drawn in such large quantities from their coffers, cannot be employed in the circulation of the country. It comes in place of a paper which is over and above what can be employed in that circulation, and is, therefore, over and above what can be employed in it too. But as that coin will not be allowed to lie idle, it must, in one shape or another, be sent abroad, in order to find that profitable employment which it cannot find at home; and this continual exportation of gold and silver, by enhancing the difficulty, must necessarily enhance still farther the expense of the bank, in finding new gold and silver in order to replenish those coffers, which empty themselves so very rapidly. Such a company, therefore, must in proportion to this forced increase of their business, increase the second article of their expense still more than the first.

Let us suppose that all the paper of a particular bank, which the circulation of the country can easily absorb and employ, amounts exactly to forty thousand pounds, and that, for answering occasional demands, this bank is obliged to keep at all times in its coffers ten thousand pounds in gold and silver. Should this bank attempt to circulate forty-four thousand pounds, the four thousand pounds which are over and above what the circulation can easily absorb and employ, will return upon it almost as fast as they are issued. For answering occasional demands, therefore, this bank ought to keep at all times in its coffers, not eleven thousand pounds only, but fourteen thousand pounds. It will thus gain nothing by the interest of the four thousand pounds excessive circulation; and it will lose the whole expense of continually collecting four thousand pounds in gold and silver, which will be continually going out of its coffers as fast as they are brought into them.

Had every particular banking company always understood and attended to its own particular interest, the circulation never could have been overstocked with paper money. But every particular banking company has not always understood or attended to its own particular interest, and the circulation has frequently been overstocked with paper money.

By issuing too great a quantity of paper, of which the excess was continually returning, in order to be exchanged for gold and silver, the Bank of England was for many years together obliged to coin gold to the extent of between eight hundred thousand pounds and a million a year; or at an average, about eight hundred and fifty thousand pounds. For this great coinage, the bank (inconsequence of the worn and degraded state into which the gold coin had fallen a few years ago) was frequently obliged to purchase gold bullion at the high price of four pounds an ounce, which it soon after issued in coin at 3l. 17s. 10½d. an ounce, losing in this manner between two and a half and three per cent upon the coinage of so very large a sum. Though the bank, therefore, paid no seignorage, though the government was properly at the expense of this coinage, this liberality of government did not prevent altogether the expense of the bank.

The Scotch banks, in consequence of an excess of the same kind, were all obliged to employ constantly agents at London to collect money for them, at an expense which was seldom below one and a half or two per cent. This money was sent down by the waggon, and insured by the carriers at an additional expense of three quarters per cent or fifteen shillings on the hundred pounds. Those agents were not always able to replenish the coffers of their employers so fast as they were emptied. In this case, the resource of the banks was to draw upon their correspondents in London bills of exchange, to the extent of the sum which they wanted. When those correspondents afterwards drew upon them for the payment of this sum, together with the interest and commission, some of those banks, from the distress into which their excessive circulation had thrown them, had sometimes no other means of satisfying this draught, but by drawing a second set of bills, either upon the same, or upon some other correspondents in London; and the same sum, or rather bills for the same sum, would in this manner make sometimes more than two or three journeys; the debtor bank paying always the interest and commission upon the whole accumulated sum. Even those Scotch banks which never distinguished themselves by their extreme imprudence, were sometimes obliged to employ this ruinous resource.

The gold coin which was paid out, either by the Bank of England or by the Scotch banks, in exchange for that part of their paper which was over and above what could be employed in the circulation of the country, being likewise over and above what could be employed in that circulation, was sometimes sent abroad in the shape of coin, sometimes melted down and sent abroad in the shape of bullion, and sometimes melted down and sold to the Bank of England at the high price of four pounds an ounce. It was the newest, the heaviest, and the best pieces only, which were carefully picked out of the whole coin, and either sent abroad or melted down. At home, and while they remained in the shape of coin, those heavy pieces were of no more value than the light; but they were of more value abroad, or when melted down into bullion at home. The Bank of England, notwithstanding their great annual coinage, found to their astonishment that there was every year the same scarcity of coin as there had been the year before; and that, notwithstanding the great quantity of good and new coin which was every year issued from the bank, the state of the coin, instead of growing better and better, became every year worse and worse. Every year they found themselves under the necessity of coining nearly the same quantity of gold as they had coined the year before; and from the continual rise in the price of gold bullion, in consequence of the continual wearing and clipping of the coin, the expense of this great annual coinage became every year greater and greater. The Bank of England, it is to be observed, by supplying its own coffers with coin, is indirectly obliged to supply the whole kingdom, into which coin is continually flowing from those coffers in a great variety of ways. Whatever coin, therefore, was wanted to support this excessive circulation both of Scotch and English paper money, whatever vacuities this excessive circulation occasioned in the necessary coin of the kingdom, the Bank of England was obliged to supply them. The Scotch banks, no doubt, paid all of them very dearly for their own imprudence and inattention: But the Bank of England paid very dearly, not only for its own imprudence, but for the much greater imprudence of almost all the Scotch banks.

The overtrading of some bold projectors in both parts of the United Kingdom was the original cause of this excessive circulation of paper money.

What a bank can with propriety advance to a merchant or undertaker of any kind, is not either the whole capital with which he trades, or even any considerable part of that capital; but that part of it only which he would otherwise be obliged to keep by him unemployed and in ready money for answering occasional demands. If the paper money which the bank advances never exceeds this value, it can never exceed the value of the gold and silver which would necessarily circulate in the country if there was no paper money; it can never exceed the quantity which the circulation of the country can easily absorb and employ.

When a bank discounts to a merchant a real bill of exchange, drawn by a real creditor upon a real debtor, and which, as soon as it becomes due, is really paid by that debtor, it only advances to him a part of the value which he would otherwise be obliged to keep by him unemployed and in ready money for answering occasional demands. The payment of the bill, when it becomes due, replaces to the bank the value of what it had advanced, together with the interest. The coffers of the bank, so far as its dealings are confined to such customers, resemble a water pond, from which, though a stream is continually running out, yet another is continually running in, fully equal to that which runs out; so that, without any further care or attention, the pond keeps always equally, or very near equally full. Little or no expense can ever be necessary for replenishing the coffers of such a bank.

A merchant, without overtrading, may frequently have occasion for a sum of ready money, even when he has no bills to discount. When a bank, besides discounting his bills, advances him likewise upon such occasions, such sums upon his cash account, and accepts of a piecemeal repayment as the money comes in from the occasional sale of his goods, upon the easy terms of the banking companies of Scotland; it dispenses him entirely from the necessity of keeping any part of his stock by him unemployed and in ready money for answering occasional demands. When such demands actually come upon him, he can answer them sufficiently from his cash account. The bank, however, in dealing with such customers, ought to observe with great attention, whether in the course of some short period (of four, five, six, or eight months for example), the sum of the repayments which it commonly receives from them is, or is not, fully equal to that of the advances which it commonly makes to them. If, within the course of such short periods, the sum of the repayments from certain customers is, upon most occasions, fully equal to that of the advances, it may safely continue to deal with such customers. Though the stream which is in this case continually running out from its coffers may be very large, that which is continually running into them must be at least equally large, so that without any further care or attention those coffers are likely to be always equally or very near equally full, and scarce ever to require any extraordinary expense to replenish them. If, on the contrary, the sum of the repayments from certain other customers falls commonly very much short of the advances which it makes to them, it cannot with any safety continue to deal with such customers, at least if they continue to deal with it in this manner. The stream which is in this case continually running out from its coffers is necessarily much larger than that which is continually running in; so that, unless they are replenished by some great and continual effort of expense, those coffers must soon be exhausted altogether.

The banking companies of Scotland, accordingly, were for a long time very careful to require frequent and regular repayments from all their customers, and did not care to deal with any person, whatever might be his fortune or credit, who did not make, what they called, frequent and regular operations with them. By this attention, besides saving almost entirely the extraordinary expense of replenishing their coffers, they gained two other very considerable advantages.

First, by this attention they were enabled to make some tolerable judgment concerning the thriving or declining circumstances of their debtors, without being obliged to look out for any other evidence besides what their own books afforded them; men being, for the most part, either regular or irregular in their repayments, according as their circumstances are either thriving or declining. A private man who lends out his money to perhaps half a dozen or a dozen debtors, may, either by himself or his agents, observe and inquire both constantly and carefully into the conduct and situation of each of them. But a banking company, which lends money to perhaps five hundred different people, and of which the attention is continually occupied by objects of a very different kind, can have no regular information concerning the conduct and circumstances of the greater part of its debtors, beyond what its own books afford it. In requiring frequent and regular repayments from all their customers, the banking companies of Scotland had probably this advantage in view.

Secondly, by this attention they secured themselves from the possibility of issuing more paper money than what the circulation of the country could easily absorb and employ. When they observed that within moderate periods of time the repayments of a particular customer were, upon most occasions, fully equal to the advances which they had made to him, they might be assured that the paper money which they had advanced to him had not, at any time, exceeded the quantity of gold and silver which he would otherwise have been obliged to keep by him for answering occasional demands; and that, consequently, the paper money, which they had circulated by his means, had not at any time exceeded the quantity of gold and silver which would have circulated in the country had there been no paper money. The frequency, regularity, and amount of his repayments would sufficiently demonstrate that the amount of their advances had at no time exceeded that part of his capital which he would otherwise have been obliged to keep by him un-employed, and in ready money, for answering occasional demands; that is, for the purpose of keeping the rest of his capital in constant employment. It is this part of his capital only which, within moderate periods of time, is continually returning to every dealer in the shape of money, whether paper or coin, and continually going from him in the same shape. If the advances of the bank had commonly exceeded this part of his capital, the ordinary amount of his repayments could not, within moderate periods of time, have equaled the ordinary amount of its advances. The stream which, by means of his dealings, was continually running into the coffers of the bank, could not have been equal to the stream which, by means of the same dealings, was continually running out. The advances of the bank paper, by exceeding the quantity of gold and silver which, had there been no such advances, he would have been obliged to keep by him for answering occasional demands, might soon come to exceed the whole quantity of gold and silver which (the commerce being supposed the same) would have circulated in the country, had there been no paper money; and consequently to exceed the quantity which the circulation of the country could easily absorb and employ; and the excess of this paper money would immediately have returned upon the bank in order to be exchanged for gold and silver. This second advantage, though equally real, was not perhaps so well understood by all the different banking companies in Scotland as the first.

When, partly by the convenience of discounting bills, and partly by that of cash accounts, the creditable traders of any country can be dispensed from the necessity of keeping any part of their stock by them unemployed and in ready money for answering occasional demands, they can reasonably expect no farther assistance from banks and bankers, who, when they have gone thus far, cannot consistently with their own interest and safety, go farther. A bank cannot, consistently with its own interest, advance to a trader the whole, or even the greater part of the circulating capital with which he trades; because, though that capital is continually returning to him in the shape of money, and going from him in the same shape, yet the whole of the returns is too distant from the whole of the outgoings, and the sum of his repayments could not equal the sum of his advances within such moderate periods of time as suit the convenience of a bank. Still less could a bank afford to advance him any considerable part of his fixed capital; of the capital which the undertaker of an iron forge, for example, employs in erecting his forge and smelting-house, his workhouses, and warehouses, the dwelling-houses of his workmen, etc.; of the capital which the under-taker of a mine employs in sinking his shafts, in erecting engines for drawing out the water, in making roads and waggon-ways, etc.; of the capital which the person who undertakes to improve land employs in clearing, draining, enclosing, manuring, and ploughing waste and uncul-tivated fields; in building farmhouses, with all their necessary append-ages of stables, granaries, etc. The returns of the fixed capital are, in almost all cases, much slower than those of the circulating capital; and such expenses, even when laid out with the greatest prudence and judg-ment, very seldom return to the undertaker till after a period of many years, a period by far too distant to suit the convenience of a bank. Traders and other undertakers may, no doubt with great propriety, car-ry on a very considerable part of their projects with borrowed money. In justice to their creditors, however, their own capital ought in this case to be sufficient to insure, if I may say so, the capital of those creditors; or to render it extremely improbable that those creditors should incur any loss, even though the success of the project should fall very much short of the expectation of the projectors. Even with this precaution too, the money which is borrowed, and which it is meant should not be repaid till after a period of several years, ought not to be borrowed of a bank, but ought to be borrowed upon bond or mortgage of such private people as propose to live upon the interest of their money, without taking the trouble themselves to employ the capital, and who are upon that account willing to lend that capital to such people of good credit as are likely to keep it for several years. A bank, indeed, which lends its money without the expense of stamped paper, or of attorneys' fees for drawing bonds and mortgages, and which accepts of repayment upon the easy terms of the banking companies of Scotland, would, no doubt, be a very convenient creditor to such traders and undertakers. But such traders and undertakers would surely be most inconvenient debtors to such a bank.

It is now more than five-and-twenty years since the paper money issued by the different banking companies of Scotland was fully equal, or rather was somewhat more than fully equal, to what the circulation of the country could easily absorb and employ. Those companies, there-fore, had so long ago given all the assistance to the traders and other undertakers of Scotland which it is possible for banks and bankers, consistently with their own interest, to give. They had even done somewhat more. They had overtraded a little, and had brought upon themselves that loss, or at least that diminution of profit, which in this particular business never fails to attend the smallest degree of overtrading. Those traders and other undertakers, having got so much assistance from banks and bankers, wished to get still more. The banks, they seem to have thought, could extend their credits to whatever sum might be wanted, without incurring any other expense besides that of a few reams of paper. They complained of the contracted views and dastardly spirit of the directors of those banks, which did not, they said, extend their credits in proportion to the extension of the trade of the country; meaning, no doubt, by the extension of that trade, the extension of their own projects beyond what they could carry on either with their own capital, or with what they had credit to borrow of private people in the usual way of bond or mortgage. The banks, they seem to have thought, were in honour bound to supply the deficiency, and to provide them with all the capital which they wanted to trade with. The banks, however, were of a different opinion; and upon their refusing to extend their credits, some of those traders had recourse to an expedient which, for a time, served their purpose, though at a much greater expense, yet as effectually as the utmost extension of bank credits could have done. This expedient was no other than the well-known shift of drawing and redrawing; the shift to which unfortunate traders have sometimes recourse when they are upon the brink of bankruptcy. The practice of raising money in this manner had been long known in England, and during the course of the late war, when the high profits of trade afforded a great temptation to overtrading, is said to have been carried on to a very great extent. From England it was brought into Scotland, where, in proportion to the very limited commerce, and to the very moderate capital of the country, it was soon carried on to a much greater extent than it ever had been in England.

The practice of drawing and redrawing is so well-known to all men of business that it may perhaps be thought unnecessary to give any account of it. But as this book may come into the hands of many people who are not men of business, and as the effects of this practice upon the banking trade are not perhaps generally understood even by men of business themselves, I shall endeavour to explain it as distinctly as I can.

The customs of merchants, which were established when the barbarous laws of Europe did not enforce the performance of their contracts, and which during the course of the two last centuries have been adopted into the laws of all European nations, have given such extra-ordinary privileges to bills of exchange, that money is more readily advanced upon them than upon any other species of obligation, especially when they are made payable within so short a period as two or three months after their date. If, when the bill becomes due, the acceptor does not pay it as soon as it is presented, he becomes from that moment a bankrupt. The bill is protested, and returns upon the drawer, who, if he does not immediately pay it, becomes likewise a bankrupt. If, before it came to the person who presents it to the acceptor for payment, it had passed through the hands of several other persons, who had successively advanced to one another the contents of it either in money or goods, and who, to express that each of them had in his turn received those contents, had all of them in their order endorsed, that is, written their names upon the back of the bill; each endorser becomes in his turn liable to the owner of the bill for those contents, and, if he fails to pay, he becomes, too, from that moment a bankrupt. Though the drawer, acceptor, and endorsers of the bill should, all of them, be persons of doubtful credit; yet still the shortness of the date gives some security to the owner of the bill. Though all of them may be very likely to become bankrupts, it is a chance if they all become so in so short a time. The house is crazy, says a weary traveler to himself, and will not stand very long; but it is a chance if it falls tonight, and I will venture, therefore, to sleep in it tonight.

The trader A in Edinburgh, we shall suppose, draws a bill upon B in London, payable two months after date. In reality B in London owes nothing to A in Edinburgh; but he agrees to accept of A's bill, upon condition that before the term of payment he shall redraw upon A in Edinburgh for the same sum, together with the interest and a commission, another bill, payable likewise two months after date. B accordingly, before the expiration of the first two months, redraws this bill upon A in Edinburgh; who again, before the expiration of the second two months, draws a second bill upon B in London, payable likewise two months after date; and before the expiration of the third two months, B in London redraws upon A in Edinburgh another bill payable also two months after date. This practice has sometimes gone on, not only for several months, but for several years together, the bill always returning upon A in Edinburgh with the accumulated interest and commission of all the former bills. The interest was five per cent in the year, and the commission was never less than one half per cent on each draught. This commission being repeated more than six times in the year, whatever money A might raise by this expedient might necessarily have cost him something more than eight per cent in the year and sometimes a great deal more, when either the price of the commission happened to rise, or when he was obliged to pay compound interest upon the interest and commission of former bills. This practice was called raising money by circulation.

In a country where the ordinary profits of stock, in the greater part of mercantile projects, are supposed to run between six and ten per cent, it must have been a very fortunate speculation of which the returns could not only repay the enormous expense at which the money was thus borrowed for carrying it on; but afford, besides, a good surplus profit to the projector. Many vast and extensive projects, however, were undertaken, and for several years carried on, without any other fund to support them besides what was raised at this enormous expense. The projectors, no doubt, had in their golden dreams the most distinct vision of this great profit. Upon their awakening, however, either at the end of their projects, or when they were no longer able to carry them on, they very seldom, I believe, had the good fortune to find it.[2]

The bills which A in Edinburgh drew upon B in London, he regularly discounted two months before they were due, with some bank or banker in Edinburgh; and the bills which B in London redrew upon A in Edinburgh, he as regularly discounted, either with the Bank of England, or with some other banker in London. Whatever was advanced upon such circulating bills was in Edinburgh advanced in the paper of the Scotch banks; and in London, when they were discounted at the Bank of England in the paper of that bank. Though the bills upon which this paper had been advanced were all of them repaid in their turn as soon as they became due, yet the value which had been really advanced upon the first bill was never really returned to the banks which advanced it; because, before each bill became due, another bill was always drawn to somewhat a greater amount than the bill which was soon to be paid; and the discounting of this other bill was essentially necessary towards the payment of that which was soon to be due. This payment, therefore, was altogether fictitious. The stream which, by means of those circulating bills of exchange, had once been made to run out from the coffers of the banks, was never replaced by any stream which really ran into them.

The paper which was issued upon those circulating bills of exchange amounted, upon many occasions, to the whole fund destined for carrying on some vast and extensive project of agriculture, commerce, or manufactures; and not merely to that part of it which, had there been no paper money, the projector would have been obliged to keep by him unemployed, and in ready money, for answering occasional demands. The greater part of this paper was, consequently, over and above the value of the gold and silver which would have circulated in the country, had there been no paper money. It was over and above, therefore, what the circulation of the country could easily absorb and employ, and upon that account, immediately returned upon the banks, in order to be exchanged for gold and silver, which they were to find as they could. It was a capital which those projectors had very artfully contrived to draw from those banks, not only without their knowledge or deliberate consent, but for some time, perhaps, without their having the most distant suspicion that they had really advanced it.

When two people, who are continually drawing and redrawing upon one another, discount their bills always with the same banker, he must immediately discover what they are about, and see clearly that they are trading, not with any capital of their own, but with the capital which he advances to them. But this discovery is not altogether so easy when they discount their bills sometimes with one banker, and sometimes with another, and when the same two persons do not constantly draw and redraw upon one another, but occasionally run the round of a great circle of projectors, who find it for their interest to assist one another in this method of raising money, and to render it, upon that account, as difficult as possible to distinguish between a real and fictitious bill of exchange; between a bill drawn by a real creditor upon a real debtor, and a bill for which there was properly no real creditor but the bank which discounted it, nor any real debtor but the projector who made use of the money. When a banker had even made this discovery, he might sometimes make it too late, and might find that he had already discounted the bills of those projectors to so great an extent that, by refusing to discount any more, he would necessarily make them all bankrupts, and thus, by ruining them, might perhaps ruin himself. For his own interest and safety, therefore, he might find it necessary, in this very perilous situation, to go on for some time, endeavouring, however, to withdraw gradually, and upon that account making every day greater and greater difficulties about discounting, in order to force those projectors by degrees to have recourse, either to other bankers, or to other methods of raising money; so that he himself might, as soon as possible, get out of the circle. The difficulties, accordingly, which the Bank of England, which the principal bankers in London, and which even the more prudent Scotch banks began, after a certain time, and when all of them had already gone too far, to make about discounting, not only alarmed, but enraged in the highest degree those projectors. Their own distress, of which this prudent and necessary reserve of the banks was, no doubt, the immediate occasion, they called the distress of the country; and this distress of the country, they said, was altogether owing to the ignorance, pusillanimity, and bad conduct of the banks, which did not give a sufficiently liberal aid to the spirited undertakings of those who exerted themselves in order to beautify, improve, and enrich the country. It was the duty of the banks, they seemed to think, to lend for as long a time, and to as great an extent as they might wish to borrow. The banks, however, by refusing in this manner to give more credit to those to whom they had already given a great deal too much, took the only method by which it was now possible to save either their own credit or the public credit of the country.

In the midst of this clamour and distress, a new bank was established in Scotland for the express purpose of relieving the distress of the country. The design was generous; but the execution was imprudent, and the nature and causes of the distress which it meant to relieve were not, perhaps, well understood. This bank was more liberal than any other had ever been, both in granting cash accounts, and in discounting bills of exchange. With regard to the latter, it seems to have made scarce any distinction between real and circulating bills, but to have discounted all equally. It was the avowed principle of this bank to advance, upon any reasonable security, the whole capital which was to be employed in those improvements of which the returns are the most slow and distant, such as the improvements of land. To promote such improvements was even said to be the chief of the public-spirited purposes for which it was instituted. By its liberality in granting cash accounts, and in discounting bills of exchange, it, no doubt, issued great quantities of its bank notes. But those bank notes being, the greater part of them, over and above what the circulation of the country could easily absorb and employ, returned upon it, in order to be exchanged for gold and silver as fast as they were issued. Its coffers were never well filled. The capital which had been subscribed to this bank at two different subscriptions, amounted to a hundred and sixty thousand pounds, of which eighty per cent only was paid up. This sum ought to have been paid in at several different installments. A great part of the proprietors, when they paid in their first installment, opened a cash account with the bank; and the directors, thinking themselves obliged to treat their own proprietors with the same liberality with which they treated all other men, allowed many of them to borrow upon this cash account what they paid in upon all their subsequent installments. Such payments, therefore, only put into one coffer what had the moment before been taken out of another. But had the coffers of this bank been filled ever so well, its excessive circulation must have emptied them faster than they could have been replenished by any other expedient but the ruinous one of drawing upon London, and when the bill became due, paying it, together with interest and commission, by another draft upon the same place. Its coffers having been filled so very ill, it is said to have been driven to this resource within a very few months after it began to do business. The estates of the proprietors of this bank were worth several millions, and by their subscription to the original bond or contract of the bank, were really pledged for answering all its engagements. By means of the great credit which so great a pledge necessarily gave it, it was, notwithstanding its too liberal conduct, enabled to carry on business for more than two years. When it was obliged to stop, it had in the circulation about two hundred thousand pounds in bank notes. In order to support the circulation of those notes which were continually returning upon it as fast they were issued, it had been constantly in the practice of drawing bills of exchange upon London, of which the number and value were continually increasing, and, when it stopped, amounted to upwards of six hundred thousand pounds. This bank, therefore, had, in little more than the course of two years, advanced to different people upwards of eight hundred thousand pounds at five per cent. Upon the two hundred thousand pounds which it circulated in bank notes, this five per cent might, perhaps, be considered as clear gain, without any other deduction besides the expense of management. But upon upwards of six hundred thousand pounds, for which it was continually drawing bills of exchange upon London, it was paying, in the way of interest and commission, upwards of eight per cent, and was consequently losing more than three per cent upon more than three-fourths of all its dealings.

The operations of this bank seem to have produced effects quite opposite to those which were intended by the particular persons who planned and directed it. They seem to have intended to support the spirited undertakings, for as such they considered them, which were at that time carrying on in different parts of the country; and at the same time, by drawing the whole banking business to themselves, to supplant all the other Scotch banks, particularly those established in Edinburgh, whose backwardness in discounting bills of exchange had given some offense. This bank, no doubt, gave some temporary relief to those projectors, and enabled them to carry on their projects for about two years longer than they could otherwise have done. But it thereby only enabled them to get so much deeper into debt, so that, when ruin came, it fell so much the heavier both upon them and upon their creditors. The operations of this bank, therefore, instead of relieving, in reality aggravated in the long run the distress which those projectors had brought both upon themselves and upon their country. It would have been much better for themselves, their creditors, and their country, had the greater part of them been obliged to stop two years sooner than they actually did. The temporary relief, however, which this bank afforded to those projectors, proved a real and permanent relief to the other Scotch banks. All the dealers in circulating bills of exchange, which those other banks had become so backward in discounting, had recourse to this new bank, where they were received with open arms. Those other banks, therefore, were enabled to get very easily out of that fatal circle, from which they could not otherwise have disengaged themselves without incurring a considerable loss, and perhaps too even some degree of discredit.

In the long run, therefore, the operations of this bank increased the real distress of the country which it meant to relieve; and effectually relieved, from a very great distress, those rivals whom it meant to supplant.

At the first setting out of this bank, it was the opinion of some people that how fast soever its coffers might be emptied, it might easily replenish them by raising money upon the securities of those to whom it had advanced its paper. Experience, I believe, soon convinced them that this method of raising money was by much too slow to answer their purpose; and that coffers which originally were so ill filled, and which emptied themselves so very fast, could be replenished by no other expedient but the ruinous one of drawing bills upon London, and when they became due, paying them by other drafts upon the same place with accumulated interest and commission. But though they had been able by this method to raise money as fast as they wanted it, yet, instead of making a profit, they must have suffered a loss by every such operation; so that in the long run they must have ruined themselves as a mercantile company, though, perhaps, not so soon as by the more expensive practice of drawing and redrawing. They could still have made nothing by the interest of the paper, which, being over and above what the circulation of the country could absorb and employ, returned upon them, in order to be exchanged for gold and silver, as fast as they issued it; and for the payment of which they were themselves continually obliged to borrow money. On the contrary, the whole expense of this borrowing, of employing agents to look out for people who had money to lend, of negotiating with those people, and of drawing the proper bond or assignment, must have fallen upon them, and have been so much clear loss upon the balance of their accounts. The project of replenishing their coffers in this manner may be compared to that of a man who had a water pond from which a stream was continually running out, and into which no stream was continually running, but who proposed to keep it always equally full by employing a number of people to go continually with buckets to a well at some miles distance in order to bring water to replenish it.

But though this operation had proved not only practicable but profitable to the bank as a mercantile company, yet the country could have derived no benefit from it; but, on the contrary, must have suffered a very considerable loss by it. This operation could not augment in the smallest degree the quantity of money to be lent. It could only have erected this bank into a sort of general loan office for the whole country. Those who wanted to borrow must have applied to this bank instead of applying to the private persons who had lent it their money. But a bank which lends money perhaps to five hundred different people, the greater part of whom its directors can know very little about, is not likely to be more judicious in the choice of its debtors than a private person who lends out his money among a few people whom he knows, and in whose sober and frugal conduct he thinks he has good reason to confide. The debtors of such a bank as that whose conduct I have been giving some account of were likely, the greater part of them, to be chimerical projectors, the drawers and re-drawers of circulating bills of exchange, who would employ the money in extravagant undertakings, which, with all the assistance that could be given them, they would probably never be able to complete, and which, if they should be completed, would never repay the expense which they had really cost, would never afford a fund capable of maintaining a quantity of labour equal to that which had been employed about them. The sober and frugal debtors of private persons, on the contrary, would be more likely to employ the money borrowed in sober undertakings which were proportioned to their capitals, and which, though they might have less of the grand and the marvelous, would have more of the solid and the profit-able, which would repay with a large profit whatever had been laid out upon them, and which would thus afford a fund capable of maintaining a much greater quantity of labour than that which had been employed about them. The success of this operation, therefore, without increasing in the smallest degree the capital of the country, would only have trans-ferred a great part of it from prudent and profitable to imprudent and unprofitable undertakings.

That the industry of Scotland languished for want of money to em-ploy it was the opinion of the famous Mr. Law. By establishing a bank of a particular kind, which he seems to have imagined might issue paper to the amount of the whole value of all the lands in the country, he pro-posed to remedy this want of money. The Parliament of Scotland, when he first proposed his project, did not think proper to adopt it. It was af-terwards adopted, with some variations, by the Duke of Orleans, at that time Regent of France. The idea of the possibility of multiplying paper to almost any extent was the real foundation of what is called the Missis-sippi scheme, the most extravagant project both of banking and stock-jobbing that, perhaps, the world ever saw. The different operations of this scheme are explained so fully, so clearly, and with so much order and distinctness, by Mr. du Verney, in his *Examination of the Political Reflections upon Commerce and Finances of Mr. du Tot*, that I shall not give any account of them. The principles upon which it was founded are explained by Mr. Law himself, in a discourse concerning money and trade, which he published in Scotland when he first proposed his pro-ject. The splendid but visionary ideas which are set forth in that and some other works upon the same principles still continue to make an impression upon many people, and have, perhaps, in part, contributed to that excess of banking which has of late been complained of both in Scotland and in other places.

The Bank of England is the greatest bank of circulation in Europe. It was incorporated, in pursuance of an act of Parliament, by a charter un-der the Great Seal, dated the 27th of July, 1694. It at that time advanced to government the sum of one million two hundred thousand pounds, for an annuity of one hundred thousand pounds; or for ninety-six thou-sand pounds a year interest, at the rate of eight per cent, and four thou-sand pounds a year for the expense of management. The credit of the new government, established by the Revolution, we may believe, must have been very low, when it was obliged to borrow at so high an inter-est.

In 1697, the bank was allowed to enlarge its capital stock by an engraftment of 1,001,171l. 10s. Its whole capital stock, therefore, amounted at this time to 2,201,171l. 10s. This engraftment is said to have been for the support of public credit. In 1696, tallies had been at forty, and fifty, and sixty per cent discount, and bank notes at twenty per cent.[3] During the great re-coinage of the silver, which was going on at this time, the bank had thought proper to discontinue the payment of its notes, which necessarily occasioned their discredit.

In pursuance of the 7th Anne, c. vii the bank advanced and paid into the exchequer the sum of four hundred thousand pounds; making in all the sum of one million six hundred thousand pounds, which it had advanced upon its original annuity of ninety-six thousand pounds interest and four thousand pounds for expense of management. In 1708, therefore, the credit of government was as good as that of private persons, since it could borrow at six per cent interest, the common legal and market rate of those times. In pursuance of the same act, the bank cancelled exchequer bills to the amount of 1,775,027l. 17s. 10½d. at six per cent interest, and was at the same time allowed to take in subscriptions for doubling its capital. In 1708, therefore, the capital of the bank amounted to 4,402,343l.; and it had advanced to government the sum of 3,375,027l. 17s. 10½d.

By a call of fifteen per cent in 1709, there was paid in, and made stock, 656,204l. 1s. 9d.; and by another of ten per cent in 1710, 501,448l. 12s. 11d. In consequence of those two calls, therefore, the bank capital amounted to 5,559,995l. 14s. 8d.

In pursuance of the 3rd George I., c. 8, the bank delivered up two millions of exchequer bills to be cancelled. It had at this time, therefore, advanced to government 17s. 10d. In pursuance of the 8th George I., c. 21, the bank purchased of the South Sea Company stock to the amount of fourteen million pounds; and in 1722, in consequence of the subscriptions which it had taken in for enabling it to make this purchase, its capital stock was increased by three million and four hundred thousand pounds. At this time, therefore, the bank had advanced to the public 9,375,027l. 17s. 10½d.; and its capital stock amounted only to 8,959,995l. 14s. 8d. It was upon this occasion that the sum which the bank had advanced to the public, and for which it received interest, began first to exceed its capital stock, or the sum for which it paid a dividend to the proprietors of bank stock; or, in other words, that the bank began to have an undivided capital, over and above its divided one. It has continued to have an undivided capital of the same kind ever since.

In 1746, the bank had, upon different occasions, advanced to the public 11,686,800l. and its divided capital had been raised by different calls and subscriptions to 10,780,000l. The state of those two sums has continued to be the same ever since. In pursuance of the 4th George III., c. 25, the bank agreed to pay to government for the renewal of its charter 110,000l. without interest or repayment. This sum, therefore, did not increase either of those two other sums.

The dividend of the bank has varied according to the variations in the rate of the interest which it has, at different times, received for the money it had advanced to the public, as well as according to other circumstances. This rate of interest has gradually been reduced from eight to three per cent. For some years past the bank dividend has been at five and a half per cent.

The stability of the Bank of England is equal to that of the British government. All that it has advanced to the public must be lost before its creditors can sustain any loss. No other banking company in England can be established by act of Parliament, or can consist of more than six members. It acts, not only as an ordinary bank, but as a great engine of state. It receives and pays the greater part of the annuities which are due to the creditors of the public, it circulates exchequer bills, and it advances to government the annual amount of the land and malt taxes, which are frequently not paid up till some years thereafter. In those different operations, its duty to the public may sometimes have obliged it, without any fault of its directors, to overstock the circulation with paper money. It likewise discounts merchants' bills, and has, upon several different occasions, supported the credit of the principal houses, not only of England, but of Hamburgh and Holland. Upon one occasion, in 1763, it is said to have advanced for this purpose, in one week, about one million six hundred thousand pounds, a great part of it in bullion. I do not, however, pretend to warrant either the greatness of the sum, or the shortness of the time. Upon other occasions, this great company has been reduced to the necessity of paying in sixpences.

It is not by augmenting the capital of the country, but by rendering a greater part of that capital active and productive than would otherwise be so, that the most judicious operations of banking can increase the industry of the country. That part of his capital which a dealer is obliged to keep by him unemployed, and in ready money, for answering occasional demands, is so much dead stock, which, so long as it remains in this situation, produces nothing either to him or to his country. The judicious operations of banking enable him to convert this dead stock into active and productive stock; into materials to work upon, into tools to work with, and into provisions and subsistence to work for; into stock which produces something both to himself and to his country. The gold and silver money which circulates in any country, and by means of which the produce of its land and labour is annually circulated and distributed to the proper consumers, is, in the same manner as the ready money of the dealer, all dead stock. It is a very valuable part of the capital of the country, which produces nothing to the country. The judicious operations of banking, by substituting paper in the room of a great part of this gold and silver, enables the country to convert a great part of this dead stock into active and productive stock; into stock which produces something to the country. The gold and silver money which circulates in any country may very properly be compared to a highway, which, while it circulates and carries to market all the grass and corn of the country, produces itself not a single pile of either. The judicious operations of banking, by providing, if I may be allowed so violent a metaphor, a sort of waggon-way through the air, enable the country to convert, as it were, a great part of its highways into good pastures and corn fields, and thereby to increase very considerably the annual produce of its land and labour. The commerce and industry of the country, however, it must be acknowledged, though they may be somewhat augmented, cannot be altogether so secure when they are thus, as it were, suspended upon the Daedalian wings of paper money as when they travel about upon the solid ground of gold and silver. Over and above the accidents to which they are exposed from the unskillfulness of the conductors of this paper money, they are liable to several others, from which no prudence or skill of those conductors can guard them.

An unsuccessful war, for example, in which the enemy got possession of the capital, and consequently of that treasure which supported the credit of the paper money, would occasion a much greater confusion in a country where the whole circulation was carried on by paper, than in one where the greater part of it was carried on by gold and silver. The usual instrument of commerce having lost its value, no exchanges could be made but either by barter or upon credit. All taxes having been usually paid in paper money, the prince would not have wherewithal either to pay his troops, or to furnish his magazines; and the state of the country would be much more irretrievable than if the greater part of its circulation had consisted in gold and silver. A prince, anxious to maintain his dominions at all times in the state in which he can most easily defend them, ought, upon this account, to guard, not only against that excessive multiplication of paper money which ruins the very banks which issue it; but even against that multiplication of it which enables them to fill the greater part of the circulation of the country with it.

The circulation of every country may be considered as divided into two different branches; the circulation of the dealers with one another, and the circulation between the dealers and the consumers. Though the same pieces of money, whether paper or metal, may be employed sometimes in the one circulation and sometimes in the other, yet as both are constantly going on at the same time, each requires a certain stock of money of one kind or another to carry it on. The value of the goods circulated between the different dealers, never can exceed the value of those circulated between the dealers and the consumers; whatever is bought by the dealers, being ultimately destined to be sold to the consumers. The circulation between the dealers, as it is carried on by wholesale, requires generally a pretty large sum for every particular transaction. That between the dealers and the consumers, on the contrary, as it is generally carried on by retail, frequently requires but very small ones, a shilling, or even a halfpenny, being often sufficient. But small sums circulate much faster than large ones. A shilling changes masters more frequently than a guinea, and a halfpenny more frequently than a shilling. Though the annual purchases of all the consumers, therefore, are at least equal in value to those of all the dealers, they can generally be transacted with a much smaller quantity of money; the same pieces, by a more rapid circulation, serving as the instrument of many more purchases of the one kind than of the other.

Paper money may be so regulated as either to confine itself very much to the circulation between the different dealers, or to extend itself likewise to a great part of that between the dealers and the consumers. Where no bank notes are circulated under ten pounds value, as in London, paper money confines itself very much to the circulation between the dealers. When a ten pound bank note comes into the hands of a consumer, he is generally obliged to change it at the first shop where he has occasion to purchase five shillings' worth of goods, so that it often returns into the hands of a dealer before the consumer has spent the fortieth part of the money. Where bank notes are issued for so small sums as twenty shillings, as in Scotland, paper money extends itself to a considerable part of the circulation between dealers and consumers. Before the act of Parliament, which put a stop to the circulation of ten and five shilling notes, it filled a still greater part of that circulation. In the currencies of North America, paper was commonly issued for so small a sum as a shilling, and filled almost the whole of that circulation. In some paper currencies of Yorkshire, it was issued even for so small a sum as a sixpence.

Where the issuing of bank notes for such very small sums is allowed and commonly practiced, many mean people are both enabled and encouraged to become bankers. A person whose promissory note for five pounds, or even for twenty shillings, would be rejected by everybody, will get it to be received without scruple when it is issued for so small a sum as a sixpence. But the frequent bankruptcies to which such beggarly bankers must be liable may occasion a very considerable inconvenience, and sometimes even a very great calamity to many poor people who had received their notes in payment.

It were better, perhaps, that no bank notes were issued in any part of the kingdom for a smaller sum than five pounds. Paper money would then, probably, confine itself, in every part of the kingdom, to the circulation between the different dealers, as much as it does at present in London, where no bank notes are issued under ten pounds value; five pounds being, in most parts of the kingdom, a sum which, though it will purchase, perhaps, little more than half the quantity of goods, is as much considered, and is as seldom spent all at once, as ten pounds are amidst the profuse expense of London.

Where paper money, it is to be observed, is pretty much confined to the circulation between dealers and dealers, as at London, there is always plenty of gold and silver. Where it extends itself to a considerable part of the circulation between dealers and consumers, as in Scotland, and still more in North America, it banishes gold and silver almost entirely from the country; almost all the ordinary transactions of its interior commerce being thus carried on by paper. The suppression of ten and five shilling bank notes somewhat relieved the scarcity of gold and silver in Scotland; and the suppression of twenty shilling notes would probably relieve it still more. Those metals are said to have become more abundant in America since the suppression of some of their paper currencies. They are said, likewise, to have been more abundant before the institution of those currencies.

Though paper money should be pretty much confined to the circulation between dealers and dealers, yet banks and bankers might still be able to give nearly the same assistance to the industry and commerce of the country as they had done when paper money filled almost the whole circulation. The ready money which a dealer is obliged to keep by him, for answering occasional demands, is destined altogether for the circulation between himself and other dealers of whom he buys goods. He has no occasion to keep any by him for the circulation between himself and the consumers, who are his customers, and who bring ready money to him, instead of taking any from him. Though no paper money, therefore, was allowed to be issued but for such sums as would confine it pretty much to the circulation between dealers and dealers, yet, partly by discounting real bills of exchange, and partly by lending upon cash accounts, banks and bankers might still be able to relieve the greater part of those dealers from the necessity of keeping any considerable part of their stock by them, unemployed and in ready money, for answering occasional demands. They might still be able to give the utmost assistance which banks and bankers can, with propriety, give to traders of every kind.

To restrain private people, it may be said, from receiving in payment the promissory notes of a banker, for any sum whether great or small, when they themselves are willing to receive them, or to restrain a banker from issuing such notes, when all his neighbours are willing to accept of them, is a manifest violation of that natural liberty which it is the proper business of law not to infringe, but to support. Such regulations may, no doubt, be considered as in some respects a violation of natural liberty. But those exertions of the natural liberty of a few individuals, which might endanger the security of the whole society, are, and ought to be, restrained by the laws of all governments, of the most free as well as of the most despotical. The obligation of building party walls, in order to prevent the communication of fire, is a violation of natural liberty exactly of the same kind with the regulations of the banking trade which are here proposed.

A paper money consisting in bank notes, issued by people of undoubted credit, payable upon demand without any condition, and in fact always readily paid as soon as presented, is, in every respect, equal in value to gold and silver money; since gold and silver money can at any time be had for it. Whatever is either bought or sold for such paper must necessarily be bought or sold as cheap as it could have been for gold and silver.

The increase of paper money, it has been said, by augmenting the quantity, and consequently diminishing the value of the whole currency, necessarily augments the money price of commodities. But as the quantity of gold and silver, which is taken from the currency, is always equal to the quantity of paper which is added to it, paper money does not necessarily increase the quantity of the whole currency. From the beginning of the last century to the present time, provisions never were cheaper in Scotland than in 1759, though, from the circulation of ten and five shilling bank notes, there was then more paper money in the country than at present. The proportion between the price of provisions in Scotland and that in England is the same now as before the great multiplication of banking companies in Scotland. Corn is, upon most occasions, fully as cheap in England as in France; though there is a great deal of paper money in England, and scarce any in France. In 1751 and in 1752, when Mr. Hume published his *Political Discourses*, and soon after the great multiplication of paper money in Scotland, there was a very sensible rise in the price of provisions, owing, probably, to the badness of the seasons, and not to the multiplication of paper money.

It would be otherwise, indeed, with a paper money consisting in promissory notes, of which the immediate payment depended, in any respect, either upon the good will of those who issued them, or upon a condition which the holder of the notes might not always have it in his power to fulfil; or of which the payment was not exigible till after a certain number of years, and which in the meantime bore no interest. Such a paper money would, no doubt, fall more or less below the value of gold and silver, according as the difficulty or uncertainty of obtaining immediate payment was supposed to be greater or less; or according to the greater or less distance of time at which payment was exigible.

Some years ago the different banking companies of Scotland were in the practice of inserting into their bank notes, what they called an *optional clause*, by which they promised payment to the bearer, either as soon as the note should be presented, or, in the option of the directors, six months after such presentment, together with the legal interest for the said six months. The directors of some of those banks sometimes took advantage of this optional clause, and sometimes threatened those who demanded gold and silver in exchange for a considerable number of their notes that they would take advantage of it, unless such demanders would content themselves with a part of what they demanded. The promissory notes of those banking companies constituted at that time the far greater part of the currency of Scotland, which this uncertainty of payment necessarily degraded below the value of gold and silver money. During the continuance of this abuse (which prevailed chiefly in 1762, 1763, and 1764), while the exchange between London and Carlisle was at par, that between London and Dumfries would sometimes be four per cent against Dumfries, though this town is not thirty miles distant from Carlisle. But at Carlisle, bills were paid in gold and silver; whereas at Dumfries they were paid in Scotch bank notes, and the uncertainty of getting those bank notes exchanged for gold and silver coin had thus degraded them four per cent below the value of that coin. The same act of Parliament which suppressed ten and five shilling bank notes suppressed likewise this optional clause, and thereby restored the exchange between England and Scotland to its natural rate, or to what the course of trade and remittances might happen to make it.

In the paper currencies of Yorkshire, the payment of so small a sum as a sixpence sometimes depended upon the condition that the holder of the note should bring the change of a guinea to the person who issued it; a condition which the holders of such notes might frequently find it very difficult to fulfill, and which must have degraded this currency below the value of gold and silver money. An act of Parliament accordingly declared all such clauses unlawful, and suppressed, in the same manner as in Scotland, all promissory notes, payable to the bearer, under twenty shillings value.

The paper currencies of North America consisted, not in bank notes payable to the bearer on demand, but in government paper, of which the payment was not exigible till several years after it was issued; and though the colony governments paid no interest to the holders of this paper, they declared it to be, and in fact rendered it, a legal tender of payment for the full value for which it was issued. But allowing the colony security to be perfectly good, a hundred pounds payable fifteen years hence, for example, in a country where interest at six per cent, is worth little more than forty pounds ready money. To oblige a creditor, therefore, to accept of this as full payment for a debt of a hundred pounds actually paid down in ready money was an act of such violent injustice as has scarce, perhaps, been attempted by the government of any other country which pretended to be free. It bears the evident marks of having originally been, what the honest and downright Doctor Douglas assures us it was, a scheme of fraudulent debtors to cheat their creditors. The government of Pennsylvania, indeed, pretended, upon their first emission of paper money, in 1722, to render their paper of equal value with gold and silver by enacting penalties against all those who made any difference in the price of their goods when they sold them for a colony paper, and when they sold them for gold and silver; a regulation equally tyrannical, but much less effectual than that which it was meant to support. A positive law may render a shilling a legal tender for guinea, because it may direct the courts of justice to discharge the debtor who has made that tender. But no positive law can oblige a person who sells goods, and who is at liberty to sell or not to sell as he pleases, to accept of a shilling as equivalent to a guinea in the price of them. Notwithstanding any regulation of this kind, it appeared by the course of exchange with Great Britain, that a hundred pounds sterling was occasionally considered as equivalent, in some of the colonies, to a hundred and thirty pounds, and in others to so great a sum as eleven hundred pounds currency; this difference in the value arising from the difference in the quantity of paper emitted in the different colonies, and in the distance and probability of the term of its final discharge and redemption.

No law, therefore, could be more equitable than the act of Parliament, so unjustly complained of in the colonies, which declared that no paper currency to be emitted there in time coming should be a legal tender of payment.

Pennsylvania was always more moderate in its emissions of paper money than any other of our colonies. Its paper currency, accordingly, is said never to have sunk below the value of the gold and silver which was current in the colony before the first emission of its paper money. Before that emission, the colony had raised the denomination of its coin, and had, by act of assembly, ordered five shillings sterling to pass in the colony for six and threepence, and afterwards for six and eightpence. A pound colony currency, therefore, even when that currency was gold and silver, was more than thirty per cent below the value of a pound sterling, and when that currency was turned into paper it was seldom much more than thirty per cent below that value. The pretense for raising the denomination of the coin, was to prevent the exportation of gold and silver, by making equal quantities of those metals pass for greater sums in the colony than they did in the mother country. It was found, however, that the price of all goods from the mother country rose exactly in proportion as they raised the denomination of their coin, so that their gold and silver were exported as fast as ever.

The paper of each colony being received in the payment of the provincial taxes, for the full value for which it had been issued, it necessarily derived from this use some additional value over and above what it would have had from the real or supposed distance of the term of its final discharge and redemption. This additional value was greater or less, according as the quantity of paper issued was more or less above what could be employed in the payment of the taxes of the particular colony which issued it. It was in all the colonies very much above what could be employed in this manner.

A prince, who should enact that a certain proportion of his taxes should be paid in a paper money of a certain kind might thereby give a certain value to this paper money, even though the term of its final discharge and redemption should depend altogether upon the will of the prince. If the bank which issued this paper was careful to keep the quantity of it always somewhat below what could easily be employed in this manner, the demand for it might be such as to make it even bear a premium, or sell for somewhat more in the market than the quantity of gold or silver currency for which it was issued. Some people account in this manner for what is called the agio of the bank of Amsterdam, or for the superiority of bank money over current money; though this bank money, as they pretend, cannot be taken out of the bank at the will of the owner. The greater part of foreign bills of exchange must be paid in bank money, that is, by a transfer in the books of the bank; and the directors of the bank, they allege, are careful to keep the whole quantity of bank money always below what this use occasions a demand for. It is upon this account, they say, that bank money sells for a premium, or bears an agio of four or five per cent above the same nominal sum of the gold and silver currency of the country. This account of the bank of Amsterdam, however, it will appear hereafter, is in a great measure chimerical.

A paper currency which falls below the value of gold and silver coin does not thereby sink the value of those metals, or occasion equal quantities of them to exchange for a smaller quantity of goods of any other kind. The proportion between the value of gold and silver and that of goods of any other kind depends in all cases not upon the nature or quantity of any particular paper money, which may be current in any particular country, but upon the richness or poverty of the mines, which happen at any particular time to supply the great market of the commercial world with those metals. It depends upon the proportion between the quantity of labour which is necessary in order to bring a certain quantity of gold and silver to market, and that which is necessary in order to bring thither a certain quantity of any other sort of goods.

If bankers are restrained from issuing any circulating bank notes, or notes payable to the bearer, for less than a certain sum, and if they are subjected to the obligation of an immediate and unconditional payment of such bank notes as soon as presented, their trade may, with safety to the public, be rendered in all other respects perfectly free. The late multiplication of banking companies in both parts of the United Kingdom, an event by which many people have been much alarmed, instead of diminishing, increases the security of the public. It obliges all of them to be more circumspect in their conduct, and, by not extending their currency beyond its due proportion to their cash, to guard themselves against those malicious runs which the rivalship of so many competitors is always ready to bring upon them. It restrains the circulation of each particular company within a narrower circle, and reduces their circulating notes to a smaller number. By dividing the whole circulation into a greater number of parts, the failure of any one company, an accident which, in the course of things, must sometimes happen, becomes of less consequence to the public. This free competition, too, obliges all bankers to be more liberal in their dealings with their customers, lest their rivals should carry them away. In general, if any branch of trade, or any division of labour, be advantageous to the public, the freer and more general the competition, it will always be the more so.

Chapter III: Of the Accumulation of Capital, or of Productive and Unproductive Labour

There is one sort of labour which adds to the value of the subject upon which it is bestowed; there is another which has no such effect. The former, as it produces a value, may be called productive; the latter, unproductive[4] labour. Thus the labour of a manufacturer adds, generally, to the value of the materials which he works upon, that of his own maintenance, and of his master's profit. The labour of a menial servant, on the contrary, adds to the value of nothing. Though the manufacturer has his wages advanced to him by his master, he, in reality, costs him no expense, the value of those wages being generally restored, together with a profit, in the improved value of the subject upon which his labour is bestowed. But the maintenance of a menial servant never is restored. A man grows rich by employing a multitude of manufacturers; he grows poor by maintaining a multitude of menial servants. The labour of the latter, however, has its value, and deserves its reward as well as that of the former. But the labour of the manufacturer fixes and realizes itself in some particular subject or vendible commodity, which lasts for some time at least after that labour is past. It is, as it were, a certain quantity of labour stocked and stored up to be employed, if necessary, upon some other occasion. That subject, or what is the same thing, the price of that subject, can afterwards, if necessary, put into motion a quantity of labour equal to that which had originally produced it. The labour of the menial servant, on the contrary, does not fix or realize itself in any particular subject or vendible commodity. His services generally perish in the very instant of their performance, and seldom leave any trace or value behind them for which an equal quantity of service could afterwards be procured.

The labour of some of the most respectable orders in the society is, like that of menial servants, unproductive of any value, and does not fix or realize itself in any permanent subject, or vendible commodity, which endures after that labour is past, and for which an equal quantity of labour could afterwards be procured. The sovereign, for example, with all the officers both of justice and war who serve under him, the whole Army and Navy, are unproductive labourers. They are the servants of the public, and are maintained by a part of the annual produce of the industry of other people. Their service, how honourable, how useful, or how necessary soever, produces nothing for which an equal quantity of service can afterwards be procured. The protection, security, and defense of the commonwealth, the effect of their labour this year will not purchase its protection, security, and defense for the year to come. In the same class must be ranked, some both of the gravest and most important, and some of the most frivolous professions: churchmen, lawyers, physicians, men of letters of all kinds, players, buffoons, musicians, opera-singers, opera-dancers, etc. The labour of the meanest of these has a certain value, regulated by the very same principles which regulate that of every other sort of labour; and that of the noblest and most useful, produces nothing which could afterwards purchase or procure an equal quantity of labour. Like the declamation of the actor, the harangue of the orator, or the tune of the musician, the work of all of them perishes in the very instant of its production.

Both productive and unproductive labourers, and those who do not labour at all, are all equally maintained by the annual produce of the land and labour of the country. This produce, how great soever, can never be infinite, but must have certain limits. According, therefore, as a smaller or greater proportion of it is in any one year employed in maintaining unproductive hands, the more in the one case and the less in the other will remain for the productive, and the next year's produce will be greater or smaller accordingly; the whole annual produce, if we except the spontaneous productions of the earth, being the effect of productive labour.

Though the whole annual produce of the land and labour of every country is, no doubt, ultimately destined for supplying the consumption of its inhabitants, and for procuring a revenue to them, yet when it first comes either from the ground, or from the hands of the productive labourers, it naturally divides itself into two parts. One of them, and frequently the largest, is, in the first place, destined for replacing a capital, or for renewing the provisions, materials, and finished work, which had been withdrawn from a capital; the other for constituting a revenue either to the owner of this capital, as the profit of his stock, or to some other person, as the rent of his land. Thus, of the produce of land, one part replaces the capital of the farmer; the other pays his profit and the rent of the landlord; and thus constitutes a revenue both to the owner of this capital, as the profits of his stock; and to some other person, as the rent of his land. Of the produce of a great manufactory, in the same manner, one part, and that always the largest, replaces the capital of the undertaker of the work; the other pays his profit, and thus constitutes a revenue to the owner of this capital.

That part of the annual produce of the land and labour of any country which replaces a capital never is immediately employed to maintain any but productive hands. It pays the wages of productive labour only. That which is immediately destined for constituting a revenue, either as profit or as rent, may maintain indifferently either productive or unproductive hands.

Whatever part of his stock a man employs as a capital, he always expects is to be replaced to him with a profit. He employs it, therefore, in maintaining productive hands only; and after having served in the function of a capital to him, it constitutes a revenue to them. Whenever he employs any part of it in maintaining unproductive hands of any kind, that part is, from that moment, withdrawn from his capital, and placed in his stock reserved for immediate consumption.

Unproductive labourers, and those who do not labour at all, are all maintained by revenue; either, first, by that part of the annual produce which is originally destined for constituting a revenue to some particular persons, either as the rent of land or as the profits of stock; or, secondly, by that part which, though originally destined for replacing a capital and for maintaining productive labourers only, yet when it comes into their hands whatever part of it is over and above their necessary subsistence may be employed in maintaining indifferently either productive or unproductive hands. Thus, not only the great landlord or the rich merchant, but even the common workman, if his wages are considerable, may maintain a menial servant; or he may sometimes go to a play or a puppet show, and so contribute his share towards maintaining one set of unproductive labourers; or he may pay some taxes, and thus help to maintain another set, more honourable and useful indeed, but equally unproductive. No part of the annual produce, however, which had been originally destined to replace a capital, is ever directed towards maintaining unproductive hands till after it has put into motion its full complement of productive labour, or all that it could put into motion in the way in which it was employed. The workman must have earned his wages by work done before he can employ any part of them in this manner. That part, too, is generally but a small one. It is his spare revenue only, of which productive labourers have seldom a great deal. They generally have some, however; and in the payment of taxes the greatness of their number may compensate, in some measure, the smallness of their contribution. The rent of land and the profits of stock are everywhere, therefore, the principal sources from which unproductive hands derive their subsistence. These are the two sorts of revenue of which the owners have generally most to spare. They might both maintain indifferently either productive or unproductive hands. They seem, however, to have some predilection for the latter. The expense of a great lord feeds generally more idle than industrious people. The rich merchant, though with his capital he maintains industrious people only, yet by his expense, that is, by the employment of his revenue, he feeds commonly the very same sort as the great lord.

The proportion, therefore, between the productive and unproductive hands, depends very much in every country upon the proportion between that part of the annual produce, which, as soon as it comes either from the ground or from the hands of the productive labourers, is destined for replacing a capital, and that which is destined for constituting a revenue, either as rent or as profit. This proportion is very different in rich from what it is in poor countries.

Thus, at present, in the opulent countries of Europe, a very large, frequently the largest, portion of the produce of the land is destined for replacing the capital of the rich and independent farmer; the other for paying his profits and the rent of the landlord. But anciently, during the prevalence of the feudal government, a very small portion of the produce was sufficient to replace the capital employed in cultivation. It consisted commonly in a few wretched cattle, maintained altogether by the spontaneous produce of uncultivated land, and which might, therefore, be considered as a part of that spontaneous produce. It generally, too, belonged to the landlord, and was by him advanced to the occupiers of the land. All the rest of the produce properly belonged to him too, either as rent for his land, or as profit upon this paltry capital. The occupiers of land were generally bondmen, whose persons and effects were equally his property. Those who were not bondmen were tenants at will, and though the rent which they paid was often nominally little more than a quit-rent, it really amounted to the whole produce of the land. Their lord could at all times command their labour in peace and their service in war. Though they lived at a distance from his house, they were equally dependent upon him as his retainers who lived in it. But the whole produce of the land undoubtedly belongs to him who can dispose of the labour and service of all those whom it maintains. In the present state of Europe, the share of the landlord seldom exceeds a third, sometimes not a fourth part of the whole produce of the land. The rent of land, however, in all the improved parts of the country, has been tripled and quadrupled since those ancient times; and this third or fourth part of the annual produce is, it seems, three or four times greater than the whole had been before. In the progress of improvement, rent, though it increases in proportion to the extent, diminishes in proportion to the produce of the land.

In the opulent countries of Europe, great capitals are at present employed in trade and manufactures. In the ancient state, the little trade that was stirring, and the few homely and coarse manufactures that were carried on, required but very small capitals. These, however, must have yielded very large profits. The rate of interest was nowhere less than ten per cent, and their profits must have been sufficient to afford this great interest. At present the rate of interest, in the improved parts of Europe, is nowhere higher than six per cent, and in some of the most improved it is so low as four, three, and two per cent. Though that part of the revenue of the inhabitants which is derived from the profits of stock is always much greater in rich than in poor countries, it is because the stock is much greater; in proportion to the stock the profits are generally much less.

That part of the annual produce, therefore, which, as soon as it comes either from the ground or from the hands of the productive labourers, is destined for replacing a capital, is not only much greater in rich than in poor countries, but bears a much greater proportion to that which is immediately destined for constituting a revenue either as rent or as profit. The funds destined for the maintenance of productive labour are not only much greater in the former than in the latter, but bear a much greater proportion to those which, though they may be employed to maintain either productive or unproductive hands, have generally a predilection for the latter.

The proportion between those different funds necessarily determines in every country the general character of the inhabitants as to industry or idleness. We are more industrious than our forefathers; because in the present times the funds destined for the maintenance of industry are much greater in proportion to those which are likely to be employed in the maintenance of idleness than they were two or three centuries ago. Our ancestors were idle for want of a sufficient encouragement to industry. It is better, says the proverb, to play for nothing than to work for nothing. In mercantile and manufacturing towns, where the inferior ranks of people are chiefly maintained by the employment of capital, they are, in general, industrious, sober, and thriving; as in many English, and in most Dutch towns. In those towns which are principally supported by the constant or occasional residence of a court, and in which the inferior ranks of people are chiefly maintained by the spending of revenue, they are, in general, idle, dissolute, and poor; as at Rome, Versailles, Compiegne, and Fontainebleu. If you except Rouen and Bordeaux, there is little trade or industry in any of the Parliament towns of France; and the inferior ranks of people, being elderly maintained by the expense of the members of the courts of justice, and of those who come to plead before them, are in general idle and poor. The great trade of Rouen and Bordeaux seems to be altogether the effect of their situation. Rouen is necessarily the entrepôt of almost all the goods which are brought either from foreign countries, or from the maritime provinces of France, for the consumption of the great city of Paris. Bordeaux is in the same manner the entrepôt of the wines which grow upon the banks of the Garonne, and of the rivers which run into it, one of the richest wine countries in the world, and which seems to produce the wine fittest for exportation, or best suited to the taste of foreign nations. Such advantageous situations necessarily attract a great capital by the great employment which they afford it; and the employment of this capital is the cause of the industry of those two cities. In the other Parliament towns of France, very little more capital seems to be employed than what is necessary for supplying their own consumption; that is, little more than the smallest capital which can be employed in them. The same thing may be said of Paris, Madrid, and Vienna. Of those three cities, Paris is by far the most industrious; but Paris itself is the principal market of all the manufactures established at Paris, and its own consumption is the principal object of all the trade which it carries on. London, Lisbon, and Copenhagen, are, perhaps, the only three cities in Europe which are both the constant residence of a court, and can at the same time be considered as trading cities, or as cities which trade not only for their own consumption, but for that of other cities and countries. The situation of all the three is extremely advantageous, and naturally fits them to be the entrepôts of a great part of the goods destined for the consumption of distant places. In a city where a great revenue is spent, to employ, with advantage, a capital for any other pur-pose than for supplying the consumption of that city is probably more difficult than in one in which the inferior ranks of people have no other maintenance but what they derive from the employment of such a capital. The idleness of the greater part of the people who are main-tained by the expense of revenue corrupts, it is probable, the industry of those who ought to be maintained by the employment of capital, and renders it less advantageous to employ a capital there than in other places. There was little trade or industry in Edinburgh before the union. When the Scotch Parliament was no longer to be assembled in it, when it ceased to be the necessary residence of the principal nobility and gentry of Scotland, it became a city of some trade and industry. It still continues, however, to be the residence of the principal courts of justice in Scotland, of the Boards of Customs and Excise, etc. A considerable revenue, therefore, still continues to be spent in it. In trade and industry it is much inferior to Glasgow, of which the inhabitants are chiefly main-tained by the employment of capital. The inhabitants of a large village, it has sometimes been observed, after having made considerable progress in manufactures, have become idle and poor in consequence of a great lord having taken up his residence in their neighbourhood.

The proportion between capital and revenue, therefore, seems everywhere to regulate the proportion between industry and idleness. Wherever capital predominates, industry prevails; wherever revenue, idleness. Every increase or diminution of capital, therefore, naturally tends to increase or diminish the real quantity of industry, the number of productive hands, and consequently the exchangeable value of the annual produce of the land and labour of the country, the real wealth and revenue of all its inhabitants.

Capitals are increased by parsimony, and diminished by prodigality and misconduct.

Whatever a person saves from his revenue he adds to his capital, and either employs it himself in maintaining an additional number of productive hands, or enables some other person to do so, by lending it to him for an interest, that is, for a share of the profits. As the capital of an individual can be increased only by what he saves from his annual revenue or his annual gains, so the capital of a society, which is the same with that of all the individuals who compose it, can be increased only in the same manner.

Parsimony, and not industry, is the immediate cause of the increase of capital. Industry, indeed, provides the subject which parsimony accumulates. But whatever industry might acquire, if parsimony did not save and store up, the capital would never be the greater.

Parsimony, by increasing the fund which is destined for the maintenance of productive hands, tends to increase the number of those hands whose labour adds to the value of the subject upon which it is bestowed. It tends, therefore, to increase the exchangeable value of the annual produce of the land and labour of the country. It puts into motion an additional quantity of industry, which gives an additional value to the annual produce.

What is annually saved is as regularly consumed as what is annually spent, and nearly in the same time too; but it is consumed by a different set of people. That portion of his revenue which a rich man annually spends is, in most cases, consumed by idle guests and menial servants, who leave nothing behind them in return for their consumption. That portion which he annually saves, as, for the sake of the profit, it is immediately employed as a capital, is consumed in the same manner, and nearly in the same time too, but by a different set of people; by labourers, manufacturers, and artificers, who reproduce with a profit the value of their annual consumption. His revenue, we shall suppose, is paid him in money. Had he spent the whole, the food, clothing, and lodging, which the whole could have purchased, would have been distributed among the former set of people. By saving a part of it, as that part is for the sake of the profit immediately employed as a capital either by himself or by some other person, the food, clothing, and lodging, which may be purchased with it, are necessarily reserved for the latter. The consumption is the same, but the consumers are different.

By what a frugal man annually saves, he not only affords maintenance to an additional number of productive hands, for that of the ensuing year, but, like the founder of a public workhouse, he establishes as it were a perpetual fund for the maintenance of an equal number in all times to come. The perpetual allotment and destination of this fund, indeed, is not always guarded by any positive law, by any trust-right or deed of mortmain. It is always guarded, however, by a very powerful principle, the plain and evident interest of every individual to whom any share of it shall ever belong. No part of it can ever afterwards be employed to maintain any but productive hands without an evident loss to the person who thus perverts it from its proper destination.

The prodigal perverts it in this manner. By not confining his expense within his income, he encroaches upon his capital. Like him who perverts the revenues of some pious foundation to profane purposes, he pays the wages of idleness with those funds which the frugality of his forefathers had, as it were, consecrated to the maintenance of industry. By diminishing the funds destined for the employment of productive labour, he necessarily diminishes, so far as it depends upon him, the quantity of that labour which adds a value to the subject upon which it is bestowed, and, consequently, the value of the annual produce of the land and labour of the whole country, the real wealth and revenue of its inhabitants. If the prodigality of some was not compensated by the frugality of others, the conduct of every prodigal, by feeding the idle with the bread of the industrious, tends not only to beggar himself, but to impoverish his country.

Though the expense of the prodigal should be altogether in home-made, and no part of it in foreign commodities, its effect upon the productive funds of the society would still be the same. Every year there would still be a certain quantity of food and clothing, which ought to have maintained productive, employed in maintaining unproductive hands. Every year, therefore, there would still be some diminution in what would otherwise have been the value of the annual produce of the land and labour of the country.

This expense, it may be said, indeed, not being in foreign goods, and not occasioning any exportation of gold and silver, the same quantity of money would remain in the country as before. But if the quantity of food and clothing, which were thus consumed by unproductive, had been distributed among productive hands, they would have reproduced, together with a profit, the full value of their consumption. The same quantity of money would in this case equally have remained in the country, and there would besides have been a reproduction of an equal value of consumable goods. There would have been two values instead of one.

The same quantity of money, besides, cannot long remain in any country in which the value of the annual produce diminishes. The sole use of money is to circulate consumable goods. By means of it, provisions, materials, and finished work, are bought and sold, and distributed to their proper consumers. The quantity of money, therefore, which can be annually employed in any country must be determined by the value of the consumable goods annually circulated within it. These must consist either in the immediate produce of the land and labour of the country itself, or in something which had been purchased with some part of that produce. Their value, therefore, must diminish as the value of that produce diminishes, and along with it the quantity of money which can be employed in circulating them. But the money, which by this annual diminution of produce is annually thrown out of domestic circulation, will not be allowed to lie idle. The interest of whoever possesses it requires that it should be employed. But having no employment at home, it will, in spite of all laws and prohibitions, be sent abroad, and employed in purchasing consumable goods which may be of some use at home. Its annual exportation will in this manner continue for some time to add something to the annual consumption of the country beyond the value of its own annual produce. What in the days of its prosperity had been saved from that annual produce, and employed in purchasing gold and silver, will contribute for some little time to support its consumption in adversity. The exportation of gold and silver is, in this case, not the cause, but the effect of its declension, and may even, for some little time, alleviate the misery of that declension.

The quantity of money, on the contrary, must in every country naturally increase as the value of the annual produce increases. The value of the consumable goods annually circulated within the society being greater will require a greater quantity of money to circulate them. A part of the increased produce, therefore, will naturally be employed in purchasing, wherever it is to be had, the additional quantity of gold and silver necessary for circulating the rest. The increase of those metals will, in this case, be the effect, not the cause, of the public prosperity. Gold and silver are purchased everywhere in the same manner. The food, clothing, and lodging, the revenue and maintenance of all those whose labour or stock is employed in bringing them from the mine to the market, is the price paid for them in Peru as well as in England. The country which has this price to pay will never be long without the quantity of those metals which it has occasion for; and no country will ever long retain a quantity which it has no occasion for.

Whatever, therefore, we may imagine the real wealth and revenue of a country to consist in, whether in the value of the annual produce of its land and labour, as plain reason seems to dictate; or in the quantity of the precious metals which circulate within it, as vulgar prejudices suppose; in either view of the matter, every prodigal appears to be a public enemy, and every frugal man a public benefactor.

The effects of misconduct are often the same as those of prodigality. Every injudicious and unsuccessful project in agriculture, mines, fisheries, trade, or manufactures, tends in the same manner to diminish the funds destined for the maintenance of productive labour. In every such project, though the capital is consumed by productive hands only, yet, as by the injudicious manner in which they are employed they do not reproduce the full value of their consumption, there must always be some diminution in what would otherwise have been the productive funds of the society.

It can seldom happen, indeed, that the circumstances of a great nation can be much affected either by the prodigality or misconduct of individuals; the profusion or imprudence of some being always more than compensated by the frugality and good conduct of others.

With regard to profusion, the principle which prompts to expense is the passion for present enjoyment; which, though sometimes violent and very difficult to be restrained, is in general only momentary and occasional. But the principle which prompts to save is the desire of bettering our condition, a desire which, though generally calm and dispassionate, comes with us from the womb, and never leaves us till we go into the grave. In the whole interval which separates those two moments, there is scarce, perhaps a single instant, in which any man is so perfectly and completely satisfied with his situation as to be without any wish of alteration, or improvement of any kind. An augmentation of fortune is the means by which the greater part of men propose and wish to better their condition. It is the means the most vulgar and the most obvious; and the most likely way of augmenting their fortune is to save and accumulate some part of what they acquire, either regularly and annually, or upon some extraordinary occasions. Though the principle of expense, therefore, prevails in almost all men upon some occasions, and in some men upon almost all occasions, yet in the greater part of men, taking the whole course of their life at an average, the principle of frugality seems not only to predominate, but to predominate very greatly.

With regard to misconduct, the number of prudent and successful undertakings is everywhere much greater than that of injudicious and unsuccessful ones. After all our complaints of the frequency of bankruptcies, the unhappy men who fall into this misfortune make but a very small part of the whole number engaged in trade, and all other sorts of business; not much more, perhaps, than one in a thousand. Bankruptcy is perhaps the greatest and most humiliating calamity which can befall an innocent man. The greater part of men, therefore, are sufficiently careful to avoid it. Some, indeed, do not avoid it; as some do not avoid the gallows.

Great nations are never impoverished by private, though they sometimes are by public, prodigality and misconduct. The whole, or almost the whole public revenue, is in most countries employed in maintaining unproductive hands. Such are the people who compose a numerous and splendid court, a great ecclesiastical establishment, great fleets and armies, who in time of peace produce nothing, and in time of war acquire nothing which can compensate the expense of maintaining them, even while the war lasts. Such people, as they themselves produce nothing, are all maintained by the produce of other men's labour. When multiplied, therefore, to an unnecessary number, they may in a particular year consume so great a share of this produce, as not to leave a sufficiency for maintaining the productive labourers, who should reproduce it next year. The next year's produce, therefore, will be less than that of the foregoing, and if the same disorder should continue, that of the third year will be still less than that of the second. Those unproductive hands, who should be maintained by a part only of the spare revenue of the people, may consume so great a share of their whole revenue, and thereby oblige so great a number to encroach upon their capitals, upon the funds destined for the maintenance of productive labour, that all the frugality and good conduct of individuals may not be able to compensate the waste and degradation of produce occasioned by this violent and forced encroachment.

This frugality and good conduct, however, is upon most occasions, it appears from experience, sufficient to compensate not only the private prodigality and misconduct of individuals, but the public extravagance of government. The uniform, constant, and uninterrupted effort of every man to better his condition, the principle from which public and national, as well as private opulence is originally derived, is frequently powerful enough to maintain the natural progress of things towards improvement, in spite both of the extravagance of government and of the greatest errors of administration. Like the unknown principle of animal life, it frequently restores health and vigour to the constitution, in spite, not only of the disease, but of the absurd prescriptions of the doctor.

The annual produce of the land and labour of any nation can be increased in its value by no other means but by increasing either the number of its productive labourers, or the productive powers of those labourers who had before been employed. The number of its productive labourers, it is evident, can never be much increased, but in consequence of an increase of capital, or of the funds destined for maintaining them. The productive powers of the same number of labourers cannot be increased, but in consequence either of some addition and improvement to those machines and instruments which facilitate and abridge labour; or of a more proper division and distribution of employment. In either case an additional capital is almost always required. It is by means of an additional capital only that the undertaker of any work can either provide his workmen with better machinery or make a more proper distribution of employment among them. When the work to be done consists of a number of parts, to keep every man constantly employed in one way requires a much greater capital than where every man is occasionally employed in every different part of the work. When we compare, therefore, the state of a nation at two different periods, and find that the annual produce of its land and labour is evidently greater at the latter than at the former, that its lands are better cultivated, its manufactures more numerous and more flourishing, and its trade more extensive, we may be assured that its capital must have increased during the interval between those two periods, and that more must have been added to it by the good conduct of some than had been taken from it either by the private misconduct of others or by the public extravagance of government. But we shall find this to have been the case of almost all nations, in all tolerably quiet and peaceable times, even of those who have not enjoyed the most prudent and parsimonious governments. To form a right judgment of it, indeed, we must compare the state of the country at periods somewhat distant from one another. The progress is frequently so gradual that, at near periods, the improvement is not only not sensible, but from the declension either of certain branches of industry, or of certain districts of the country, things which sometimes happen though the country in general be in great prosperity, there frequently arises a suspicion that the riches and industry of the whole are decaying.

The annual produce of the land and labour of England, for example, is certainly much greater than it was, a little more than a century ago, at the restoration of Charles II. Though, at present, few people, I believe, doubt of this, yet during this period, five years have seldom passed away in which some book or pamphlet has not been published, written, too, with such abilities as to gain some authority with the public, and pretending to demonstrate that the wealth of the nation was fast declining, that the country was depopulated, agriculture neglected, manufactures decaying, and trade undone. Nor have these publications been all party pamphlets, the wretched offspring of falsehood and venality. Many of them have been written by very candid, and very intelligent people, who wrote nothing but what they believed, and for no other reason but because they believed it.

The annual produce of the land and labour of England, again, was certainly much greater at the Restoration, than we can suppose it to have been about an hundred years before, at the accession of Elizabeth. At this period, too, we have all reason to believe, the country was much more advanced in improvement than it had been about a century before, towards the close of the dissensions between the houses of York and Lancaster. Even then it was, probably, in a better condition than it had been at the Norman Conquest, and at the Norman Conquest than during the confusion of the Saxon Heptarchy. Even at this early period, it was certainly a more improved country than at the invasion of Julius Caesar, when its inhabitants were nearly in the same state with the savages in North America.

In each of those periods, however, there was not only much private and public profusion, many expensive and unnecessary wars, great perversion of the annual produce from maintaining productive to maintain unproductive hands; but sometimes, in the confusion of civil discord, such absolute waste and destruction of stock, as might be supposed, not only to retard, as it certainly did, the natural accumulation of riches, but to have left the country, at the end of the period, poorer than at the beginning. Thus, in the happiest and most fortunate period of them all, that which has passed since the Restoration, how many disorders and misfortunes have occurred, which, could they have been foreseen, not only the impoverishment, but the total ruin of the country would have been expected from them? The fire and the plague of London, the two Dutch wars, the disorders of the Revolution, the war in Ireland, the four expensive French wars of 1688, 1702, 1742, and 1756, together with the two rebellions of 1715 and 1745. In the course of the four French wars, the nation has contracted more than a hundred and forty-five millions of debt, over and above all the other extraordinary annual expense which they occasioned, so that the whole cannot be computed at less than two hundred millions. So great a share of the annual produce of the land and labour of the country has, since the Revolution, been employed upon different occasions in maintaining an extraordinary number of unproductive hands. But had not those wars given this particular direction to so large a capital, the greater part of it would naturally have been employed in maintaining productive hands, whose labour would have replaced, with a profit, the whole value of their consumption. The value of the annual produce of the land and labour of the country would have been considerably increased by it every year, and every year's increase would have augmented still more that of the following year. More houses would have been built, more lands would have been improved, and those which had been improved before would have been better cultivated, more manufactures would have been established, and those which had been established before would have been more extended; and to what height the real wealth and revenue of the country might, by this time, have been raised, it is not perhaps very easy even to imagine.

But though the profusion of government must, undoubtedly, have retarded the natural progress of England towards wealth and improvement, it has not been able to stop it. The annual produce of its land and labour is, undoubtedly, much greater at present than it was either at the Restoration or at the Revolution. The capital, therefore, annually employed in cultivating this land, and in maintaining this labour, must likewise be much greater. In the midst of all the exactions of government, this capital has been silently and gradually accumulated by the private frugality and good conduct of individuals, by their universal, continual, and uninterrupted effort to better their own condition. It is this effort, protected by law and allowed by liberty to exert itself in the manner that is most advantageous, which has maintained the progress of England towards opulence and improvement in almost all former times, and which, it is to be hoped, will do so in all future times. England, however, as it has never been blessed with a very parsimonious government, so parsimony has at no time been the characteristical virtue of its inhabitants. It is the highest impertinence and presumption, therefore, in kings and ministers, to pretend to watch over the economy of private people, and to restrain their expense, either by sumptuary laws, or by prohibiting the importation of foreign luxuries. They are themselves always, and without any exception, the greatest spendthrifts in the society. Let them look well after their own expense, and they may safely trust private people with theirs. If their own extravagance does not ruin the state, that of their subjects never will.

As frugality increases and prodigality diminishes the public capital, so the conduct of those whose expense just equals their revenue, without either accumulating or encroaching, neither increases nor diminishes it. Some modes of expense, however, seem to contribute more to the growth of public opulence than others.

The revenue of an individual may be spent either in things which are consumed immediately, and in which one day's expense can neither alleviate nor support that of another, or it may be spent in things more durable, which can therefore be accumulated, and in which every day's expense may, as he chooses, either alleviate or support and heighten the effect of that of the following day. A man of fortune, for example, may either spend his revenue in a profuse and sumptuous table, and in maintaining a great number of menial servants, and a multitude of dogs and horses; or contenting himself with a frugal table and few attendants, he may lay out the greater part of it in adorning his house or his country villa, in useful or ornamental buildings, in useful or ornamental furniture, in collecting books, statues, pictures; or in things more frivolous, jewels, baubles, ingenious trinkets of different kinds; or, what is most trifling of all, in amassing a great wardrobe of fine clothes, like the favourite and minister of a great prince who died a few years ago. Were two men of equal fortune to spend their revenue, the one chiefly in the one way, the other in the other, the magnificence of the person whose expense had been chiefly in durable commodities, would be continually increasing, every day's expense contributing something to support and heighten the effect of that of the following day; that of the other, on the contrary, would be no greater at the end of the period than at the beginning. The former, too, would, at the end of the period, be the richer man of the two. He would have a stock of goods of some kind or other, which, though it might not be worth all that it cost, would always be worth something. No trace or vestige of the expense of the latter would remain, and the effects of ten or twenty years profusion would be as completely annihilated as if they had never existed.

As the one mode of expense is more favourable than the other to the opulence of an individual, so is it likewise to that of a nation. The houses, the furniture, the clothing of the rich, in a little time, become useful to the inferior and middling ranks of people. They are able to

66

purchase them when their superiors grow weary of them, and the general accommodation of the whole people is thus gradually improved, when this mode of expense becomes universal among men of fortune. In countries which have long been rich, you will frequently find the inferior ranks of people in possession both of houses and furniture perfectly good and entire, but of which neither the one could have been built, nor the other have been made for their use. What was formerly a seat of the family of Seymour is now an inn upon the Bath road. The marriage bed of James the First of Great Britain, which his queen brought with her from Denmark as a present fit for a sovereign to make to a sovereign, was, a few years ago, the ornament of an ale-house at Dunfermline. In some ancient cities, which either have been long stationary, or have gone somewhat to decay, you will sometimes scarce find a single house which could have been built for its present inhabitants. If you go into those houses too, you will frequently find many excellent, though antiquated pieces of furniture, which are still very fit for use, and which could as little have been made for them. Noble palaces, magnificent villas, great collections of books, statues, pictures, and other curiosities, are frequently both an ornament and an honour, not only to the neighbourhood, but to the whole country to which they belong. Versailles is an ornament and an honour to France, Stowe and Wilton to England. Italy still continues to command some sort of veneration by the number of monuments of this kind which it possesses, though the wealth which produced them has decayed, and though the genius which planned them seems to be extinguished, perhaps from not having the same employment.

The expense too, which is laid out in durable commodities, is favourable, not only to accumulation, but to frugality. If a person should at any time exceed in it, he can easily reform without exposing himself to the censure of the public. To reduce very much the number of his servants, to reform his table from great profusion to great frugality, to lay down his equipage after he has once set it up, are changes which cannot escape the observation of his neighbours, and which are supposed to imply some acknowledgment of preceding bad conduct. Few, therefore, of those who have once been so unfortunate as to launch out too far into this sort of expense, have afterwards the courage to reform, till ruin and bankruptcy oblige them. But if a person has, at any time, been at too great an expense in building, in furniture, in books or pictures, no imprudence can be inferred from his changing his conduct. These are things in which further expense is frequently rendered unnecessary by former expense; and when a person stops short, he appears to do so, not because he has exceeded his fortune, but because he has satisfied his fancy.

The expense, besides, that is laid out in durable commodities gives maintenance, commonly, to a greater number of people than that which is employed in the most profuse hospitality. Of two or three hundred weight of provisions, which may sometimes be served up at a great festival, one half, perhaps, is thrown to the dunghill, and there is always a great deal wasted and abused. But if the expense of this entertainment had been employed in setting to work masons, carpenters, upholsterers, mechanics, etc., a quantity of provisions, of equal value, would have been distributed among a still greater number of people who would have bought them in pennyworths and pound weights, and not have lost or thrown away a single ounce of them. In the one way, besides, this expense maintains productive, in the other unproductive hands. In the one way, therefore, it increases, in the other, it does not increase the exchangeable value of the annual produce of the land and labour of the country.

I would not, however, by all this be understood to mean that the one species of expense always betokens a more liberal or generous spirit than the other. When a man of fortune spends his revenue chiefly in hospitality, he shares the greater part of it with his friends and companions; but when he employs it in purchasing such durable commodities, he often spends the whole upon his own person, and gives nothing to anybody without an equivalent. The latter species of expense, therefore, especially when directed towards frivolous objects, the little ornaments of dress and furniture, jewels, trinkets, gewgaws, frequently indicates, not only a trifling, but a base and selfish disposition. All that I mean is, that the one sort of expense, as it always occasions some accumulation of valuable commodities, as it is more favourable to private frugality, and, consequently, to the increase of the public capital, and as it maintains productive, rather than unproductive hands, conduces more than the other to the growth of public opulence.

Chapter IV: Of Stock Lent at Interest

The stock which is lent at interest is always considered as a capital by the lender. He expects that in due time it is to be restored to him, and that in the meantime the borrower is to pay him a certain annual rent for the use of it. The borrower may use it either as a capital, or as a stock reserved for immediate consumption. If he uses it as a capital, he employs it in the maintenance of productive labourers, who reproduce the value with a profit. He can, in this case, both restore the capital and pay the interest without alienating or encroaching upon any other source of revenue. If he uses it as a stock reserved for immediate consumption, he acts the part of a prodigal, and dissipates in the maintenance of the idle what was destined for the support of the industrious. He can, in this case, neither restore the capital nor pay the interest without either alienating or encroaching upon some other source of revenue, such as the property or the rent of land.

The stock which is lent at interest is, no doubt, occasionally employed in both these ways, but in the former much more frequently than in the latter. The man who borrows in order to spend will soon be ruined, and he who lends to him will generally have occasion to repent of his folly. To borrow or to lend for such a purpose, therefore, is in all cases, where gross usury is out of the question, contrary to the interest of both parties; and though it no doubt happens sometimes that people do both the one and the other; yet, from the regard that all men have for their own interest, we may be assured that it cannot happen so very frequently as we are sometimes apt to imagine. Ask any rich man of common prudence to which of the two sorts of people he has lent the greater part of his stock, to those who, he thinks, will employ it profitably, or to those who will spend it idly, and he will laugh at you for proposing the question. Even among borrowers, therefore, not the people in the world most famous for frugality, the number of the frugal and industrious surpasses considerably that of the prodigal and idle.

The only people to whom stock is commonly lent, without their being expected to make any very profitable use of it, are country gentlemen who borrow upon mortgage. Even they scarce ever borrow merely to spend. What they borrow, one may say, is commonly spent before they borrow it. They have generally consumed so great a quantity of goods, advanced to them upon credit by shopkeepers and tradesmen, that they find it necessary to borrow at interest in order to pay the debt.

The capital borrowed replaces the capitals of those shopkeepers and tradesmen, which the country gentlemen could not have replaced from the rents of their estates. It is not properly borrowed in order to be spent, but in order to replace a capital which had been spent before.

Almost all loans at interest are made in money, either of paper, or of gold and silver. But what the borrower really wants, and what the lender really supplies him with, is not the money, but the money's worth, or the goods which it can purchase. If he wants it as a stock for immediate consumption, it is those goods only which he can place in that stock. If he wants it as a capital for employing industry, it is from those goods only that the industrious can be furnished with the tools, materials, and maintenance necessary for carrying on their work. By means of the loan, the lender, as it were, assigns to the borrower his right to a certain portion of the annual produce of the land and labour of the country to be employed as the borrower pleases.

The quantity of stock, therefore, or, as it is commonly expressed, of money which can be lent at interest in any country, is not regulated by the value of the money, whether paper or coin, which serves as the instrument of the different loans made in that country, but by the value of that part of the annual produce which, as soon as it comes either from the ground, or from the hands of the productive labourers, is destined not only for replacing a capital, but such a capital as the owner does not care to be at the trouble of employing himself. As such capitals are commonly lent out and paid back in money, they constitute what is called the monied interest. It is distinct, not only from the landed, but from the trading and manufacturing interests, as in these last the owners themselves employ their own capitals. Even in the monied interest, however, the money is, as it were, but the deed of assignment, which conveys from one hand to another those capitals which the owners do not care to employ themselves. Those capitals may be greater in almost any proportion than the amount of the money which serves as the instrument of their conveyance; the same pieces of money successively serving for many different loans, as well as for many different purchases. A, for example, lends to W a thousand pounds, with which W immediately purchases of B a thousand pounds worth of goods. B having no occasion for the money himself, lends the identical pieces to X, with which X immediately purchases of C another thousand pounds worth of goods. C, in the same manner, and for the same reason, lends them to Y, who again purchases goods with them of D. In this manner the same pieces, either of coin or paper, may in the course of a few days, serve as the instrument of three different loans, and of three different purchases, each of which is, in value, equal to the whole amount of those pieces. What the three monied men A, B, and C assign to the three borrowers, W, X, Y, is the power of making those purchases. In this power consist both the value and the use of the loans. The stock lent by the three monied men is equal to the value of the goods which can be purchased with it, and is three times greater than that of the money with which the purchases are made. Those loans, however, may be all perfectly well secured, the goods purchased by the different debtors being so employed as, in due time, to bring back, with a profit, an equal value either of coin or of paper. And as the same pieces of money can thus serve as the instrument of different loans to three, or for the same reason, to thirty times their value, so they may likewise successively serve as the instrument of repayment.

A capital lent at interest may, in this manner, be considered as an assignment from the lender to the borrowers of a certain considerable portion of the annual produce; upon condition that the borrower in return shall, during the continuance of the loan, annually assign to the lender a smaller portion, called the interest; and at the end of it a portion equally considerable with that which had originally been assigned to him, called the repayment. Though money, either coin or paper, serves generally as the deed of assignment both to the smaller and to the more considerable portion, it is itself altogether different from what is assigned by it.

In proportion as that share of the annual produce which, as soon as it comes either from the ground or from the hands of the productive labourers, is destined for replacing a capital, increases in any country, what is called the monied interest naturally increases with it. The increase of those particular capitals from which the owners wish to derive a revenue, without being at the trouble of employing them themselves, naturally accompanies the general increase of capitals; or, in other words, as stock increases, the quantity of stock to be lent at interest grows gradually greater and greater.

As the quantity of stock to be lent at interest increases, the interest, or the price which must be paid for the use of that stock, necessarily diminishes, not only from those general causes which make the market price of things commonly diminish as their quantity increases, but from other causes which are peculiar to this particular case. As capitals increase in any country, the profits which can be made by employing them necessarily diminish. It becomes gradually more and more difficult to find within the country a profitable method of employing any new capital. There arises in consequence a competition between different capitals, the owner of one endeavouring to get possession of that employment which is occupied by another. But upon most occasions he can hope to jostle that other out of this employment by no other means but by dealing upon more reasonable terms. He must not only sell what he deals in somewhat cheaper, but in order to get it to sell, he must sometimes, too, buy it dearer. The demand for productive labour, by the increase of the funds which are destined for maintaining it, grows every day greater and greater. Labourers easily find employment, but the owners of capitals find it difficult to get labourers to employ. Their competition raises the wages of labour and sinks the profits of stock. But when the profits which can be made by the use of a capital are in this manner diminished, as it were, at both ends, the price which can be paid for the use of it, that is, the rate of interest, must necessarily be diminished with them.

Mr. Locke, Mr. Law, and Mr. Montesquieu, as well as many other writers, seem to have imagined that the increase of the quantity of gold and silver, in consequence of the discovery of the Spanish West Indies, was the real cause of the lowering of the rate of interest through the greater part of Europe. Those metals, they say, having become of less value themselves, the use of any particular portion of them necessarily became of less value too, and consequently the price which could be paid for it. This notion, which at first sight seems plausible, has been so fully exposed by Mr. Hume, that it is, perhaps, unnecessary to say anything more about it. The following very short and plain argument, however, may serve to explain more distinctly the fallacy which seems to have misled those gentlemen.

Before the discovery of the Spanish West Indies, ten per cent seems to have been the common rate of interest through the greater part of Europe. It has since that time in different countries sunk to six, five, four, and three per cent. Let us suppose that in every particular country the value of silver has sunk precisely in the same proportion as the rate of interest; and that in those countries, for example, where interest has been reduced from ten to five per cent, the same quantity of silver can now purchase just half the quantity of goods which it could have purchased before. This supposition will not, I believe, be found anywhere agreeable to the truth, but it is the most favourable to the opinion which we are going to examine; and even upon this supposition it is utterly impossible that the lowering of the value of silver could have the smallest tendency to lower the rate of interest. If a hundred pounds are in those countries now of no more value than fifty pounds were then, ten pounds must now be of no more value than five pounds were then. Whatever were the causes which lowered the value of the capital, the same must necessarily have lowered that of the interest, and exactly in the same proportion. The proportion between the value of the capital and that of the interest must have remained the same, though the rate had been altered. By altering the rate, on the contrary, the proportion between those two values is necessarily altered. If a hundred pounds now are worth no more than fifty were then, five pounds now can be worth no more than two pounds ten shillings were then. By reducing the rate of interest, therefore, from ten to five per cent, we give for the use of a capital, which is supposed to be equal to half of its former value, an interest which is equal to a fourth only of the value of the former interest.

Any increase in the quantity of silver, while that of the commodities circulated by means of it remained the same, could have no other effect than to diminish the value of that metal. The nominal value of all sorts of goods would be greater, but their real value would be precisely the same as before. They would be exchanged for a greater number of pieces of silver; but the quantity of labour which they could command, the number of people whom they could maintain and employ, would be precisely the same. The capital of the country would be the same, though a greater number of pieces might be requisite for conveying any equal portion of it from one hand to another. The deeds of assignment, like the conveyances of a verbose attorney, would be more cumbersome, but the thing assigned would be precisely the same as before, and could produce only the same effects. The funds for maintaining productive labour being the same, the demand for it would be the same. Its price or wages, therefore, though nominally greater, would really be the same. They would be paid in a greater number of pieces of silver; but they would purchase only the same quantity of goods. The profits of stock would be the same both nominally and really. The wages of labour are commonly computed by the quantity of silver which is paid to the labourer. When that is increased, therefore, his wages appear to be increased, though they may sometimes be no greater than before. But the profits of stock are not computed by the number of pieces of silver with which they are paid, but by the proportion which those pieces bear to the whole capital employed. Thus, in a particular country, five shillings a week are said to be the common wages of labour, and ten per cent the common profits of stock. But the whole capital of the country being the same as before, the competition between the different capitals of individuals into which it was divided would likewise be the same. They would all trade with the same advantages and disadvantages. The common proportion between capital and profit, therefore, would be the same, and consequently the common interest of money; what can commonly be given for the use of money being necessarily regulated by what can commonly be made by the use of it.

Any increase in the quantity of commodities annually circulated within the country, while that of the money which circulated them remained the same, would, on the contrary, produce many other important effects, besides that of raising the value of the money. The capital of the country, though it might nominally be the same, would really be augmented. It might continue to be expressed by the same quantity of money, but it would command a greater quantity of labour. The quantity of productive labour which it could maintain and employ would be increased, and consequently the demand for that labour. Its wages would naturally rise with the demand, and yet might appear to sink. They might be paid with a smaller quantity of money, but that smaller quantity might purchase a greater quantity of goods than a greater had done before. The profits of stock would be diminished both really and in appearance. The whole capital of the country being augmented, the competition between the different capitals of which it was composed would naturally be augmented along with it. The owners of those particular capitals would be obliged to content themselves with a smaller proportion of the produce of that labour which their respective capitals employed. The interest of money, keeping pace always with the profits of stock, might, in this manner, be greatly diminished, though the value of money, or the quantity of goods which any particular sum could purchase, was greatly augmented.

In some countries the interest of money has been prohibited by law. But as something can everywhere be made by the use of money, something ought everywhere to be paid for the use of it. This regulation, instead of preventing, has been found from experience to increase the evil of usury; the debtor being obliged to pay, not only for the use of the money, but for the risk which his creditor runs by accepting a compensation for that use. He is obliged, if one may say so, to insure his creditor from the penalties of usury

In countries where interest is permitted, the law, in order to prevent the extortion of usury, generally fixes the highest rate which can be taken without incurring a penalty. This rate ought always to be somewhat above the lowest market price, or the price which is commonly paid for the use of money by those who can give the most undoubted security. If this legal rate should be fixed below the lowest market rate, the effects of this fixation must be nearly the same as those of a total prohibition of interest. The creditor will not lend his money for less than the use of its worth, and the debtor must pay him for the risk which he runs by accepting the full value of that use. If it is fixed precisely at the lowest market price, it ruins, with honest people who respect the laws of their country, the credit of all those who cannot give the very best security, and obliges them to have recourse to exorbitant usurers. In a country, such as Great Britain, where money is lent to government at three per cent and to private people upon a good security at four and four-and-a-half, the present legal rate, five per cent, is perhaps as proper as any.

The legal rate, it is to be observed, though it ought to be somewhat above, ought not to be much above the lowest market rate. If the legal rate of interest in Great Britain, for example, was fixed so high as eight or ten per cent, the greater part of the money which was to be lent would be lent to prodigals and projectors, who alone would be willing to give this high interest. Sober people, who will give for the use of money no more than a part of what they are likely to make by the use of it, would not venture into the competition. A great part of the capital of the country would thus be kept out of the hands which were most likely to make a profitable and advantageous use of it, and thrown into those which were most likely to waste and destroy it. Where the legal rate of interest, on the contrary, is fixed but a very little above the lowest market rate, sober people are universally preferred, as borrowers, to prodigals and projectors. The person who lends money gets nearly as much interest from the former as he dares to take from the latter, and his money is much safer in the hands of the one set of people than in those of the other. A great part of the capital of the country is thus thrown into the hands in which it is most likely to be employed with advantage.

No law can reduce the common rate of interest below the lowest ordinary market rate at the time when that law is made. Notwithstanding the edict of 1766, by which the French king attempted to reduce the rate of interest from five to four per cent, money continued to be lent in France at five per cent, the law being evaded in several different ways.

The ordinary market price of land, it is to be observed, depends everywhere upon the ordinary market rate of interest. The person who has a capital from which he wishes to derive a revenue, without taking the trouble to employ it himself, deliberates whether he should buy land with it or lend it out at interest. The superior security of land, together with some other advantages which almost everywhere attend upon this species of property, will generally dispose him to content himself with a smaller revenue from land than what he might have by lending out his money at interest. These advantages are sufficient to compensate a certain difference of revenue; but they will compensate a certain difference only; and if the rent of land should fall short of the interest of money by a greater difference, nobody would buy land, which would soon reduce its ordinary price. On the contrary, if the advantages should much more than compensate the difference, everybody would buy land, which again would soon raise its ordinary price. When interest was at ten per cent, land was commonly sold for ten and twelve years purchase. As interest sunk to six, five, and four per cent, the price of land rose to twenty, twenty-five, and thirty years purchase. The market rate of interest is higher in France than in England; and the common price of land is lower. In England it commonly sells at thirty, in France at twenty years purchase.

Chapter V: Of the Different Employment of Capitals

Though all capitals are destined for the maintenance of productive labour only, yet the quantity of that labour which equal capitals are capable of putting into motion varies extremely, according to the diversity of their employment; as does likewise the value which that employment adds to the annual produce of the land and labour of the country.

A capital may be employed in four different ways: Either, first, in procuring the rude produce annually required for the use and consumption of the society; or, secondly, in manufacturing and preparing that rude produce for immediate use and consumption; or, thirdly, in transporting either the rude or manufactured produce from the places where they abound to those where they are wanted; or, lastly, in dividing particular portions of either into such small parcels as suit the occasional demands of those who want them. In the first way are employed the capitals of all those who undertake the improvement or cultivation of lands, mines, or fisheries; in the second, those of all master manufacturers; in the third, those of all wholesale merchants; and in the fourth, those of all retailers. It is difficult to conceive that a capital should be employed in any way which may not be classed under some one or other of those four.

Each of these four methods of employing a capital is essentially necessary either to the existence or extension of the other three, or to the general convenience of the society.

Unless a capital was employed in furnishing rude produce to a certain degree of abundance, neither manufactures nor trade of any kind could exist.

Unless a capital was employed in manufacturing that part of the rude produce which requires a good deal of preparation before it can be fit for use and consumption, it either would never be produced, because there could be no demand for it; or if it was produced spontaneously, it would be of no value in exchange, and could add nothing to the wealth of the society.

Unless a capital was employed in transporting either the rude or manufactured produce from the places where it abounds to those where it is wanted, no more of either could be produced than was necessary for the consumption of the neighbourhood. The capital of the merchant exchanges the surplus produce of one place for that of another, and thus encourages the industry and increases the enjoyments of both.

Unless a capital was employed in breaking and dividing certain portions either of the rude or manufactured produce into such small parcels as suit the occasional demands of those who want them, every man would be obliged to purchase a greater quantity of the goods he wanted than his immediate occasions required. If there was no such trade as a butcher, for example, every man would be obliged to purchase a whole ox or a whole sheep at a time. This would generally be inconvenient to the rich, and much more so to the poor. If a poor workman was obliged to purchase a month's or six months' provisions at a time, a great part of the stock which he employs as a capital in the instruments of his trade, or in the furniture of his shop, and which yields him a revenue, he would be forced to place in that part of his stock which is reserved for immediate consumption, and which yields him no revenue. Nothing can be more convenient for such a person than to be able to purchase his subsistence from day to day, or even from hour to hour, as he wants it. He is thereby enabled to employ almost his whole stock as a capital. He is thus enabled to furnish work to a greater value, and the profit, which he makes by it in this way, much more than compensates the additional price which the profit of the retailer imposes upon the goods. The prejudices of some political writers against shop-keepers and tradesmen are altogether without foundation. So far is it from being necessary either to tax them or to restrict their numbers that they can never be multiplied so as to hurt the public, though they may so as to hurt one another. The quantity of grocery goods, for example, which can be sold in a particular town is limited by the demand of that town and its neighbourhood. The capital, therefore, which can be employed in the grocery trade cannot exceed what is sufficient to purchase that quantity. If this capital is divided between two different grocers, their competition will tend to make both of them sell cheaper than if it were in the hands of one only; and if it were divided among twenty, their competition would be just so much the greater, and the chance of their combining together, in order to raise the price, just so much the less. Their competition might perhaps ruin some of themselves; but to take care of this is the business of the parties concerned, and it may safely be trusted to their discretion. It can never hurt either the consumer or the producer; on the contrary, it must tend to make the retailers both sell cheaper and buy dearer than if the whole trade was monopolized by one or two persons. Some of them, perhaps, may sometimes decoy a weak customer to buy what he has no occasion for. This evil, however, is of too little importance to deserve the public attention, nor would it necessarily be prevented by restricting their numbers. It is not the multitude of ale-houses, to give the most suspicious example, that occasions a general disposition to drunkenness among the common people; but that disposition arising from other causes necessarily gives employment to a multitude of ale-houses.

The persons whose capitals are employed in any of those four ways are themselves productive labourers. Their labour, when properly directed, fixes and realizes itself in the subject or vendible commodity upon which it is bestowed, and generally adds to its price the value at least of their own maintenance and consumption. The profits of the farmer, of the manufacturer, of the merchant, and retailer, are all drawn from the price of the goods which the two first produce, and the two last buy and sell. Equal capitals, however, employed in each of those four different ways, will immediately put into motion very different quantities of productive labour, and augment, too, in very different proportions the value of the annual produce of the land and labour of the society to which they belong.

The capital of the retailer replaces, together with its profits, that of the merchant of whom he purchases goods, and thereby enables him to continue his business. The retailer himself is the only productive labourer whom it immediately employs. In his profit consists the whole value which its employment adds to the annual produce of the land and labour of the society.

The capital of the wholesale merchant replaces, together with their profits, the capitals of the farmers and manufacturers of whom he purchases the rude and manufactured produce which he deals in, and thereby enables them to continue their respective trades. It is by this service chiefly that he contributes indirectly to support the productive labour of the society, and to increase the value of its annual produce. His capital employs, too, the sailors and carriers who transport his goods from one place to another, and it augments the price of those goods by the value, not only of his profits, but of their wages. This is all the productive labour which it immediately puts into motion, and all the value which it immediately adds to the annual produce. Its operation in both these respects is a good deal superior to that of the capital of the retailer.

Part of the capital of the master manufacturer is employed as a fixed capital in the instruments of his trade, and replaces, together with its profits, that of some other artificer of whom he purchases them. Part of his circulating capital is employed in purchasing materials, and replaces, with their profits, the capitals of the farmers and miners of whom he purchases them. But a great part of it is always, either annually, or in a much shorter period, distributed among the different workmen whom he employs. It augments the value of those materials by their wages, and by their matters' profits upon the whole stock of wages, materials, and instruments of trade employed in the business. It puts immediately into motion, therefore, a much greater quantity of productive labour, and adds a much greater value to the annual produce of the land and labour of the society than an equal capital in the hands of any wholesale merchant.

No equal capital puts into motion a greater quantity of productive labour than that of the farmer. Not only his labouring servants, but his labouring cattle, are productive labourers. In agriculture, too, nature labours along with man; and though her labour costs no expense, its produce has its value, as well as that of the most expensive workmen. The most important operations of agriculture seem intended not so much to increase, though they do that too, as to direct the fertility of nature towards the production of the plants most profitable to man. A field overgrown with briars and brambles may frequently produce as great a quantity of vegetables as the best cultivated vineyard or corn field. Planting and tillage frequently regulate more than they animate the active fertility of nature; and after all their labour, a great part of the work always remains to be done by her. The labourers and labouring cattle, therefore, employed in agriculture, not only occasion, like the workmen in manufactures, the reproduction of a value equal to their own consumption, or to the capital which employs them, together with its owners' profits; but of a much greater value. Over and above the capital of the farmer and all its profits, they regularly occasion the re-production of the rent of the landlord. This rent may be considered as the produce of those powers of nature, the use of which the landlord lends to the farmer. It is greater or smaller according to the supposed extent of those powers, or in other words, according to the supposed natural or improved fertility of the land. It is the work of nature which remains after deducting or compensating everything which can be re-garded as the work of man. It is seldom less than a fourth, and fre-quently more than a third of the whole produce. No equal quantity of productive labour employed in manufactures can ever occasion so great a reproduction. In them nature does nothing; man does all; and the reproduction must always be in proportion to the strength of the agents that occasion it. The capital employed in agriculture, therefore, not only puts into motion a greater quantity of productive labour than any equal capital employed in manufactures; but in proportion, too, to the quan-tity of productive labour which it employs, it adds a much greater value to the annual produce of the land and labour of the country, to the real wealth and revenue of its inhabitants. Of all the ways in which a capital can be employed, it is by far the most advantageous to the society.

The capitals employed in the agriculture and in the retail trade of any society must always reside within that society. Their employment is confined almost to a precise spot, to the farm and to the shop of the retailer. They must generally, too, though there are some exceptions to this, belong to resident members of the society.

The capital of a wholesale merchant, on the contrary, seems to have no fixed or necessary residence anywhere, but may wander about from place to place, according as it can either buy cheap or sell dear.

The capital of the manufacturer must no doubt reside where the manufacture is carried on; but where this shall be is not always neces-sarily determined. It may frequently be at a great distance both from the place where the materials grow, and from that where the complete manufacture is consumed. Lyons is very distant both from the places which afford the materials of its manufactures, and from those which consume them. The people of fashion in Sicily are clothed in silks made in other countries, from the materials which their own produces. Part of the wool of Spain is manufactured in Great Britain, and some part of that cloth is afterwards sent back to Spain.

Whether the merchant whose capital exports the surplus produce of any society, be a native or a foreigner, is of very little importance. If he is a foreigner, the number of their productive labourers is necessarily less than if he had been a native by one man only, and the value of their annual produce by the profits of that one man. The sailors or carriers whom he employs may still belong indifferently either to his country or to their country, or to some third country, in the same manner as if he had been a native. The capital of a foreigner gives a value to their surplus produce equally with that of a native by exchanging it for something for which there is a demand at home. It as effectually replaces the capital of the person who produces that surplus, and as effectually enables him to continue his business; the service by which the capital of a wholesale merchant chiefly contributes to support the productive labour, and to augment the value of the annual produce of the society to which he belongs.

It is of more consequence that the capital of the manufacturer should reside within the country. It necessarily puts into motion a greater quantity of productive labour, and adds a greater value to the annual produce of the land and labour of the society. It may, however, be very useful to the country, though it should not reside within it. The capitals of the British manufacturers who work up the flax and hemp annually imported from the coasts of the Baltic are surely very useful to the countries which produce them. Those materials are a part of the surplus produce of those countries which, unless it was annually exchanged for something which is in demand there, would be of no value, and would soon cease to be produced. The merchants who export it replace the capitals of the people who produce it, and thereby encourage them to continue the production; and the British manufacturers replace the capitals of those merchants.

A particular country, in the same manner as a particular person, may frequently not have capital sufficient both to improve and cultivate all its lands, to manufacture and prepare their whole rude produce for immediate use and consumption, and to transport the surplus part either of the rude or manufactured produce to those distant markets where it can be exchanged for something for which there is a demand at home. The inhabitants of many different parts of Great Britain have not capital sufficient to improve and cultivate all their lands. The wool of the southern counties of Scotland is, a great part of it, after a long land carriage through very bad roads, manufactured in Yorkshire, for want of capital to manufacture it at home. There are many little manufacturing towns in Great Britain, of which the inhabitants have not capital sufficient to transport the produce of their own industry to those distant markets where there is demand and consumption for it. If there are any merchants among them, they are properly only the agents of wealthier merchants who reside in some of the greater commercial cities.

When the capital of any country is not sufficient for all those three purposes, in proportion as a greater share of it is employed in agriculture, the greater will be the quantity of productive labour which it puts into motion within the country; as will likewise be the value which its employment adds to the annual produce of the land and labour of the society. After agriculture, the capital employed in manufactures puts into motion the greatest quantity of productive labour, and adds the greatest value to the annual produce. That which is employed in the trade of exportation has the least effect of any of the three.

The country, indeed, which has not capital sufficient for all those three purposes has not arrived at that degree of opulence for which it seems naturally destined. To attempt, however, prematurely and with an insufficient capital to do all the three, is certainly not the shortest way for a society, no more than it would be for an individual, to acquire a sufficient one. The capital of all the individuals of a nation has its limits in the same manner as that of a single individual, and is capable of executing only certain purposes. The capital of all the individuals of a nation is increased in the same manner as that of a single individual by their continually accumulating and adding to it whatever they save out of their revenue. It is likely to increase the fastest, therefore, when it is employed in the way that affords the greatest revenue to all the inhabitants of the country, as they will thus be enabled to make the greatest savings. But the revenue of all the inhabitants of the country is necessarily in proportion to the value of the annual produce of their land and labour.

It has been the principal cause of the rapid progress of our American colonies towards wealth and greatness that almost their whole capitals have hitherto been employed in agriculture. They have no manufactures, those household and courser manufactures excepted which necessarily accompany the progress of agriculture, and which are the work of the women and children in every private family. The greater part both of the exportation and coasting trade of America is carried on by the capitals of merchants who reside in Great Britain. Even the stores and warehouses from which goods are retailed in some provinces, particularly in Virginia and Maryland, belong many of them to merchants who reside in the mother country, and afford one of the few instances of the retail trade of a society being carried on by the capitals of those who are not resident members of it. Were the Americans, either by combination or by any other sort of violence, to stop the importation of European manufactures, and, by thus giving a monopoly to such of their own countrymen as could manufacture the like goods, divert any considerable part of their capital into this employment, they would retard instead of accelerating the further increase in the value of their annual produce, and would obstruct instead of promoting the progress of their country towards real wealth and greatness. This would be still more the case were they to attempt, in the same manner, to monopolize to themselves their whole exportation trade.

The course of human prosperity, indeed, seems scarce ever to have been of so long continuance as to enable any great country to acquire capital sufficient for all those three purposes; unless, perhaps, we give credit to the wonderful accounts of the wealth and cultivation of China, of those of ancient Egypt, and of the ancient state of Indostan. Even those three countries, the wealthiest, according to all accounts, that ever were in the world, are chiefly renowned for their superiority in agriculture and manufactures. They do not appear to have been eminent for foreign trade. The ancient Egyptians had a superstitious antipathy to the sea; a superstition nearly of the same kind prevails among the Indians; and the Chinese have never excelled in foreign commerce. The greater part of the surplus produce of all those three countries seems to have been always exported by foreigners, who gave in exchange for it something else for which they found a demand there, frequently gold and silver.

It is thus that the same capital will in any country put into motion a greater or smaller quantity of productive labour, and add a greater or smaller value to the annual produce of its land and labour, according to the different proportions in which it is employed in agriculture, manufactures, and wholesale trade. The difference, too, is very great, according to the different sorts of wholesale trade in which any part of it is employed.

All wholesale trade, all buying in order to sell again by wholesale, may be reduced to three different sorts. The home trade, the foreign trade of consumption, and the carrying trade. The home trade is employed in purchasing in one part of the same country, and selling in another, the produce of the industry of that country. It comprehends both the inland and the coasting trade. The foreign trade of consumption is employed in purchasing foreign goods for home consumption. The carrying trade is employed in transacting the commerce of foreign countries, or in carrying the surplus produce of one to another.

The capital which is employed in purchasing in one part of the country, in order to sell in another, the produce of the industry of that country, generally replaces by every such operation two distinct capitals that had both been employed in the agriculture or manufactures of that country, and thereby enables them to continue that employment. When it sends out from the residence of the merchant a certain value of commodities, it generally brings back in return at least an equal value of other commodities. When both are the produce of domestic industry, it necessarily replaces, by every such operation, two distinct capitals which had both been employed in supporting productive labour, and thereby enables them to continue that support. The capital which sends Scotch manufactures to London, and brings back English corn and manufactures to Edinburgh, necessarily replaces, by every such operation, two British capitals which had both been employed in the agriculture or manufactures of Great Britain.

The capital employed in purchasing foreign goods for home consumption, when this purchase is made with the produce of domestic industry, replaces, too, by every such operation, two distinct capitals; but one of them only is employed in supporting domestic industry. The capital which sends British goods to Portugal, and brings back Portuguese goods to Great Britain, replaces by every such operation only one British capital. The other is a Portuguese one. Though the returns, therefore, of the foreign trade of consumption should be as quick as those of the home trade, the capital employed in it will give but half the encouragement to the industry or productive labour of the country.

But the returns of the foreign trade of consumption are very seldom so quick as those of the home trade. The returns of the home trade generally come in before the end of the year, and sometimes three or four times in the year. The returns of the foreign trade of consumption seldom come in before the end of the year, and sometimes not till after two or three years. A capital, therefore, employed in the home trade will sometimes make twelve operations, or be sent out and returned twelve times, before a capital employed in the foreign trade of consumption has made one. If the capitals are equal, therefore, the one will give four-and-twenty times more encouragement and support to the industry of the country than the other.

The foreign goods for home consumption may sometimes be purchased, not with the produce of domestic industry, but with some other foreign goods. These last, however, must have been purchased either immediately with the produce of domestic industry, or with something else that had been purchased with it; for, the case of war and conquest excepted, foreign goods can ever be acquired but in exchange for something that had been produced at home, either immediately, or after two or more different exchanges. The effects, therefore, of a capital employed in such a roundabout foreign trade of consumption, are, in every respect, the same as those of one employed in the most direct trade of the same kind, except that the final returns are likely to be still more distant, as they must depend upon the returns of two or three distinct foreign trades. If the flax and hemp of Riga are purchased with the tobacco of Virginia, which had been purchased with British manufactures, the merchant must wait for the returns of two distinct foreign trades before he can employ the same capital in repurchasing a like quantity of British manufactures. If the tobacco of Virginia had been purchased, not with British manufactures, but with the sugar and rum of Jamaica which had been purchased with those manufactures, he must wait for the returns of three. If those two or three distinct foreign trades should happen to be carried on by two or three distinct merchants, of whom the second buys the goods imported by the first, and the third buys those imported by the second, in order to export them again, each merchant indeed will in this case receive the returns of his own capital more quickly; but the final returns of the whole capital employed in the trade will be just as slow as ever. Whether the whole capital employed in such a roundabout trade belong to one merchant or to three can make no difference with regard to the country, though it may with regard to the particular merchants. Three times a greater capital must, in both cases, be employed in order to exchange a certain value of British manufactures for a certain quantity of flax and hemp than would have been necessary had the manufactures, and the flax and hemp, been directly exchanged for one another. The whole capital employed, therefore, in such a roundabout foreign trade of consumption will generally give less encouragement and support to the productive labour of the country than an equal capital employed in a more direct trade of the same kind.

Whatever be the foreign commodity with which the foreign goods for home consumption are purchased, it can occasion no essential difference either in the nature of the trade, or in the encouragement and support which it can give to the productive labour of the country from which it is carried on. If they are purchased with the gold of Brazil, for example, or with the silver of Peru, this gold and silver, like the tobacco of Virginia, must have been purchased with something that either was the produce of the industry of the country, or that had been purchased with something else that was so. So far, therefore, as the productive labour of the country is concerned, the foreign trade of consumption which is carried on by means of gold and silver has all the advantages and all the inconveniences of any other equally roundabout foreign trade of consumption, and will replace just as fast or just as slow the capital which is immediately employed in supporting that productive labour. It seems even to have one advantage over any other equally roundabout foreign trade. The transportation of those metals from one place to another, on account of their small bulk and great value, is less expensive than that of almost any other foreign goods of equal value. Their freight is much less, and their insurance not greater; and no goods, besides, are less liable to suffer by the carriage. An equal quantity of foreign goods, therefore, may frequently be purchased with a smaller quantity of the produce of domestic industry, by the intervention of gold and silver, than by that of any other foreign goods. The demand of the country may frequently, in this manner, be supplied more completely, and at a smaller expense, than in any other. Whether, by the continual exportation of those metals, a trade of this kind is likely to impoverish the country from which it is carried on in any other way; I shall have occasion to examine at great length hereafter.

That part of the capital of any country which is employed in the carrying trade, is altogether withdrawn from supporting the productive labour of that particular country, to support that of some foreign countries. Though it may replace, by every operation, two distinct capitals, yet neither of them belongs to that particular country. The capital of the Dutch merchant, which carries the corn of Poland to Portugal, and brings back the fruits and wines of Portugal to Poland, replaces by every such operation two capitals, neither of which had been employed in supporting the productive labour of Holland; but one of them in supporting that of Poland, and the other that of Portugal. The profits only return regularly to Holland, and constitute the whole addition which this trade necessarily makes to the annual produce of the land and labour of that country. When, indeed, the carrying trade of any particular country is carried on with the ships and sailors of that country, that part of the capital employed in it which pays the freight is distributed among, and puts into motion, a certain number of productive labourers of that country. Almost all nations that have had any considerable share of the carrying trade have, in fact, carried it on in this manner. The trade itself has probably derived its name from it, the people of such countries being the carriers to other countries. It does not, however, seem essential to the nature of the trade that it should be so. A Dutch merchant may, for example, employ his capital in transacting the commerce of Poland and Portugal, by carrying part of the surplus produce of the one to the other, not in Dutch, but in British bottoms. It may be presumed that he actually does so upon some particular occasions. It is upon this account, however, that the carrying trade has been supposed peculiarly advantageous to such a country as Great Britain, of which the defense and security depend upon the number of its sailors and shiping. But the same capital may employ as many sailors and shipping, either in the foreign trade of consumption, or even in the home trade, when carried on by coasting vessels, as it could in the carrying trade. The number of sailors and shipping which any particular capital can employ does not depend upon the nature of the trade, but partly upon the bulk of the goods in proportion to their value, and partly upon the distance of the ports between which they are to be carried; chiefly upon the former of those two circumstances. The coal trade from Newcastle to London, for example, employs more shipping than all the carrying trade of England, though the ports are at no great distance. To force, therefore, by extraordinary encouragements, a larger share of the capital of any country into the carrying trade, than what would naturally go to it, will not always necessarily increase the shipping of that country.

The capital, therefore, employed in the home trade of any country will generally give encouragement and support to a greater quantity of productive labour in that country, and increase the value of its annual produce more than an equal capital employed in the foreign trade of consumption; and the capital employed in this latter trade has in both these respects a still greater advantage over an equal capital employed in the carrying trade. The riches, and so far as power depends upon riches, the power of every country must always be in proportion to the value of its annual produce, the fund from which all taxes must ultimately be paid. But the great object of the political economy of every country is to increase the riches and power of that country. It ought, therefore, to give no preference, nor superior encouragement, to the foreign trade of consumption above the home trade, nor to the carrying trade above either of the other two. It ought neither to force, nor to allure into either of those two channels, a greater share of the capital of the country than what would naturally flow into them of its own accord.

When the produce of any particular branch of industry exceeds what the demand of the country requires, the surplus must be sent abroad and exchanged for something for which there is a demand at home. Without such exportation, a part of the productive labour of the country must cease, and the value of its annual produce diminish. The land and labour of Great Britain produce generally more corn, woolens, and hardware than the demand of the home market requires. The surplus part of them, therefore, must be sent abroad, and exchanged for something for which there is a demand at home. It is only by means of such exportation that this surplus can acquire a value sufficient to compensate the labour and expense of producing it. The neighbourhood of the sea coast, and the banks of all navigable rivers, are advantageous situations for industry, only because they facilitate the exportation and exchange of such surplus produce for something else which is more in demand there.

When the foreign goods which are thus purchased with the surplus produce of domestic industry exceed the demand of the home market, the surplus part of them must be sent abroad again and exchanged for something more in demand at home. About ninety-six thousand hogsheads of tobacco are annually purchased in Virginia and Maryland, with a part of the surplus produce of British industry. But the demand of Great Britain does not require, perhaps, more than fourteen thousand. If the remaining eighty-two thousand, therefore, could not be sent abroad and exchanged for something more in demand at home, the importation of them must cease immediately, and with it the productive labour of all those inhabitants of Great Britain, who are at present employed in preparing the goods with which these eighty-two thousand hogsheads are annually purchased. Those goods, which are part of the produce of the land and labour of Great Britain, having no market at home, and being deprived of that which they had abroad, must cease to be produced. The most roundabout foreign trade of consumption, therefore, may, upon some occasions, be as necessary for supporting the productive labour of the country, and the value of its annual produce, as the most direct.

When the capital stock of any country is increased to such a degree that it cannot be all employed in supplying the consumption, and supporting the productive labour of that particular country, the surplus part of it naturally disgorges itself into the carrying trade, and is employed in performing the same offices to other countries. The carrying trade is the natural effect and symptom of great national wealth; but it does not seem to be the natural cause of it. Those statesmen who have been disposed to favour it with particular encouragements seem to have mistaken the effect and symptom for the cause. Holland, in proportion to the extent of the land and the number of its inhabitants, by far the richest country in Europe, has, accordingly, the greatest share of the carrying trade of Europe. England, perhaps the second richest country of Europe, is likewise supposed to have a considerable share of it; though what commonly passes for the carrying trade of England will frequently, perhaps, be found to be no more than a roundabout foreign trade of consumption. Such are, in a great measure, the trades which carry the goods of the East and West Indies, and of America, to different European markets. Those goods are generally purchased either immediately with the produce of British industry, or with something else which had been purchased with that produce, and the final returns of those trades are generally used or consumed in Great Britain. The trade which is carried on in British bottoms between the different ports of the Mediterranean, and some trade of the same kind carried on by British merchants between the different ports of India, make, perhaps, the principal branches of what is properly the carrying trade of Great Britain.

The extent of the home trade and of the capital which can be employed in it, is necessarily limited by the value of the surplus produce of all those distant places within the country which have occasion to exchange their respective productions with another; that of the foreign trade of consumption, by the value of the surplus produce of the whole country and of what can be purchased with it; that of the carrying trade, by the value of the surplus produce of all the different countries in the world. Its possible extent, therefore, is in a manner infinite in comparison of that of the other two, and is capable of absorbing the greatest capitals.

The consideration of his own private profit is the sole motive which determines the owner of any capital to employ it either in agriculture, in manufactures, or in some particular branch of the wholesale or retail trade. The different quantities of productive labour which it may put into motion, and the different values which it may add to the annual produce of the land and labour of the society, according as it is employed in one or other of those different ways, never enter into his thoughts. In countries, therefore, where agriculture is the most profitable of all employments, and farming and improving the most direct roads to a splendid fortune, the capitals of individuals will naturally be employed in the manner most advantageous to the whole society. The profits of agriculture, however, seem to have no superiority over those of other employments in any part of Europe. Projectors, indeed, in every corner of it, have within these few years amused the public with most magnificent accounts of the profits to be made by the cultivation and improvement of land. Without entering into any particular discussion of their calculations, a very simple observation may satisfy us that the result of them must be false. We see every day the most splendid fortunes that have been acquired in the course of a single life by trade and manufacturers, frequently from a very small capital, sometimes from no capital. A single instance of such a fortune acquired by agriculture in the same time, and from such a capital, has not, perhaps, occurred in Europe during the course of the present century. In all the great countries of Europe, however, much good land still remains uncultivated, and the greater part of what is cultivated is far from being improved to the degree of which it is capable. Agriculture, therefore, is almost everywhere capable of absorbing a much greater capital than has ever yet been employed in it. What circumstances in the policy of Europe have given the trades which are carried on in towns so great an advantage over that which is carried on in the country that private persons frequently find it more for their advantage to employ their capitals in the most distant carrying trades of Asia and America than in the improvement and cultivation of the most fertile fields in their own neighbourhood, I shall endeavour to explain at full length in the two following books.

❖ ❖ ❖

Notes

1. See Ruddiman's *Preface to Anderson's Diplomata, etc.* Scotiae.

2. The method described in the text was by no means either the most common or the most expensive one in which those adventurers sometimes raised money by circulation. It frequently happened that A in Edinburgh would enable B in London to pay the first bill of exchange by drawing, a few days before it became due, a second bill at three months date upon the same B in London. This bill, being payable to his own order, A sold in Edinburgh at par; and with its contents purchased bills upon London payable at sight to the order of B, to whom he sent them by the post. Towards the end of the late war, the exchange between Edinburgh and London was frequently three per cent against Edinburgh and those bills at sight must frequently have cost A that premium. This transaction, therefore being repeated at least four times in the year, and being loaded with a commission of at least one half per cent upon each repetition, must at that period have cost A at least fourteen per cent in the year. At other times A would enable B to discharge the first bill of exchange by drawing, a few days before it became due, a second bill at two months date; not upon B, but upon some third person, C, for example, in London. This other bill was made payable to the order of B, who, upon its being accepted by C, discounted it with some banker in London; and A enabled C to discharge it by drawing, a few days before it became due, a third bill, likewise at two months date, sometimes upon his first correspondent B and sometimes upon some fourth or fifth person, D or E, for example. This third bill was made payable to the order of C; who, as soon as it was accepted, discounted it in the same manner with some banker in London. Such operations being repeated at least six times in the year, and being loaded with a commission of at least one half per cent upon each repetition, together with the legal interest of five per cent, this method of raising money, in the same manner as that described in the text, must have cost A something more than eight per cent. By saving, however, the exchange between Edinburgh and London it was less expensive than that mentioned in the foregoing part of this note; but then it required an established credit with more houses than one in London, an advantage which many of these adventurers could not always find it easy to procure.

3. James Postlethwaite's *History of the Public Revenue*, p. 301.

4. Some French authors of great learning and ingenuity have used those words in a different sense. In the last chapter of the fourth book I shall endeavour to show that their sense is an improper one.

A Treatise on Political Economy
Book III: Of the Consumption of Wealth

Jean-Baptiste Say; 1803

Chapter I: Of the Different Kinds of Consumption

In the course of my work I have frequently been obliged to antici-
pate the explanation of terms and notions which in the natural order
should have been postponed to a later period of the investigation. Thus,
I was obliged in the first book to explain the sense in which I used the
term *consumption* because production cannot be effected without consumption.

My reader will have seen from the explanation there given that in
like manner as by production is meant the creation, not of substance
but of utility, so by consumption is meant the destruction of utility, and
not of substance or matter. When once the utility of a thing is destroyed, there is an end of the source and basis of its value;—an extinction of that which made it an object of desire and of demand. It thenceforward ceases to possess value, and is no longer an item of wealth.

Thus, the terms, to *consume,* to *destroy* the *utility,* to *annihilate* the
value of anything, are as strictly synonymous as the opposite terms to
produce, to *communicate utility,* to *create value,* and convey to the
mind precisely the same idea. Consumption, then, being the destruction
of value is commensurate not with the bulk, the weight, or the number
of the products consumed, but with their value. Large consumption is
the destruction of large value, whatever form that value may happen to
have assumed.

Every product is liable to be consumed; because the value, which
can be added to, can likewise be subtracted from any object. If it has
been added by human exertion or industry, it may be subtracted by
human use or a variety of accidents. But it cannot be more than once
consumed; value once destroyed cannot be destroyed a second time.
Consumption is sometimes rapid, sometimes gradual. A house, a ship,

an implement of iron, are equally consumable as a loaf, a joint of meat, or a coat. Consumption again may be but partial. A horse, an article of furniture, or a house when resold by the possessor, has been but partially consumed; there is still a residue of value for which an equivalent is received in exchange on the resale. Sometimes consumption is involuntary, and either accidental, as when a house is burnt, or a vessel ship wrecked, or contrary to the consumer's intention, as when a cargo is thrown overboard, or stores set on fire to prevent their falling into enemies' hands.

Value may be consumed either long after its production or at the very moment, and in the very act of production, as in the case of the pleasure afforded by a concert or theatrical exhibition. Time and labour may be consumed; for labour, applicable to an useful purpose, is an object of value, and when once consumed, can never be consumed again.

Whatever cannot possibly lose its value is not liable to consumption. A landed estate cannot be consumed; but its annual productive agency may; for when once that agency has been exerted, it cannot be exerted again. The improvements of an estate may be consumed, although their value may possibly exceed that of the estate itself; for these improvements are the effect of human exertion and industry; but the land itself is inconsumable.

So likewise it is with any industrious faculty. One may consume a labourer's day's work, but not his faculty of working; which, however, is liable to destruction by the death of the person possessing it.

All products are consumed sooner or later; indeed they are produced solely for the purpose of consumption, and whenever the consumption of a product is delayed after it has reached the point of absolute maturity, it is value inert and neutralized for the time. For as all value may be employed reproductively and made to yield a profit to the possessor, the withholding a product from consumption is a loss of the possible profit, in other words, of the interest its value would have yielded if usefully employed.

But, products being universally destined for consumption, and that too in the quickest way, how, it may be asked, can there be ever an accumulation of capital, that is to say, of values produced?

I answer—that value may be accumulated without being necessarily vested all the while in the same identical product, provided only it be perpetuated in same product or other. Now, values employed as capital are perpetuated by reproduction; the various products of which capital consists are consumed like all other products; but their value is no sooner destroyed by consumption than it reappears in another, or a similar substance. A manufactory cannot be kept up without a consumption of victuals and clothes for the workmen, as well as of the raw material of manufacture; but while value in those forms is undergoing consumption, new value is communicated to the object of manufacture. The items that composed the capital so expended are consumed and gone; but the capital, the accumulated value, still exists and reappears under a new form applicable to a second course of consumption. Whereas, if consumed unproductively, it never reappears at all.

The annual consumption of an individual is the aggregate of all the values consumed by that individual within the year. The annual consumption of a nation is the aggregate of values consumed within the year by all the individuals and communities whereof the nation consists.

In the estimate of individual or national consumption must be included every kind of consumption, whatever be its motive or consequence, whether productive of new value or not; in like manner, as the estimate of the annual production of a nation comprises the total value of its products raised within the year. Thus, a soap manufactory is said to consume such or such a quantity or value of alkali in a year, although this value be reproduced from the manufactory in the shape of soap; on the other hand, it is said to produce annually such and such a quantity or value of soap, although the production may have cost the destruction of a great variety of values which, if deducted, would vastly reduce the apparent product. By annual production, or consumption, national or individual, is therefore meant the gross and not the net amount.

Whence it naturally follows that all the commodities which a nation imports must be reckoned as a part of its annual product, and all its exports as part of its annual consumption. The trade of France consumes the total value of the silk it exports to the United States; and produces, on the other hand, the total value of cotton received in return. And, in like manner, the manufacture of France consumes the value of alkali employed by the soap-boiler and produces the value of soap derived from the concern.

The total annual consumption of a nation, or an individual, is a very different thing from the aggregate of capital. A capital may be wholly or partially consumed several times a year. When a shoemaker buys leather, and cuts and works it up into shoes, there is so much capital consumed and reproduced. Every time he repeats the operation there is so much more capital consumed. Suppose the leather purchased to amount to forty dollars, and the operation to be repeated twelve times in the year, there will have been an annual consumption of four hundred and eighty dollars upon a capital of forty dollars. On the other hand, there may be portions of his capital, implements of trade for instance, which it may take several years to consume. Of this part of his capital he may consume annually but a fourth or a tenth perhaps.

In each country the wants of the consumer determine the quality of the product. The product most wanted is most in demand; and that which is most in demand yields the largest profit to industry, capital, and land, which are therefore employed in raising this particular product in preference; and, vice versa, when a product becomes less in demand, there is a less profit to be got by its production; it is, therefore, no longer produced. All the stock on hand falls in price; the low price encourages the consumption, which soon absorbs the stock on hand.

The total national consumption may be divided into the heads of public consumption and private consumption; the former is effected by the public, or in its service; the latter by individuals or families. Either class may be productive or unproductive.

In every community each member is a consumer; for no one can subsist without the satisfaction of some necessary wants, however confined and limited; on the other hand, all who do not live on mere charity or gratuitous bounty contribute somehow to production by their industry, their capital, or their land; wherefore, the consumers may be said to be themselves the producers; and the great bulk of consumption takes place amongst the middling and poorer classes, whose numbers more than counterbalance the smallness of the share allotted to each.

Opulent, civilized, and industrious nations are greater consumers than poor ones because they are infinitely greater producers. They annually, and in some cases, several times in the course of the year, reconsume their productive capital, which is thus continually renovated; and consume unproductively, the greater part of their revenues, whether derived from industry, from capital, or from land.

It is not uncommon to find authors proposing, as the model for imitation, those nations whose wants are few; whereas, it is far preferable to have numerous wants along with the power to gratify them. This is the way at once to multiply the human species, and to give to each a more enlarged existence.

Stewart extols the Lacedaemonian policy, which consisted in practicing the art of self-denial in the extreme, without aiming at progressive advancement in the art of production. But herein the Spartans were rivalled by the rudest tribes of savages, which are commonly neither numerous nor amply provided. Upon this principle, it would be the very *acme* of perfection to produce nothing and to have no wants; that is to say, to annihilate human existence.

Chapter II: Of the Effect of Consumption in General

The immediate effect of consumption of every kind is the loss of value, consequently, of wealth, to the owner of the article consumed. This is the invariable and inevitable consequence, and should never be lost sight of in reasoning on this matter. A product consumed is a value lost to all the world and to all eternity; but the further consequence that may follow will depend upon the circumstances and nature of the consumption.

If the consumption be unproductive, there usually results the gratification of some want, but no reproduction of value whatever; if productive, there results the satisfaction of no want, but a creation of new value, equal, inferior, or superior in amount to that consumed, and profitable or unprofitable to the adventurer accordingly.

Thus, consumption may be regarded as an act of barter, wherein the owner of the value consumed gives up that value on the one hand, and receives in return, either the satisfaction of a personal want, or a fresh value, equivalent to the value consumed.

It may be proper here to remark that consumption, productive of nothing beyond a present gratification, requires no skill or talent in the consumer. It requires neither labour nor ingenuity to eat a good dinner, or dress in fine clothes. On the contrary, productive consumption, besides yielding no immediate or present gratification, requires an exertion of combined labour and skill, or, of what has all along been denominated, *industry*.

When the owner of a product ready for consumption has himself no industrious faculty and wishes, but knows not how to consume it productively, he lends it to someone more industrious than himself, who commences by destroying it, but in such a way as to reproduce another, and thereby enable himself to make a full restitution to the lender after retaining the profit of his own skill and labour. The value returned consists of different objects from that lent, it is true; indeed, the condition of a loan is in substance this; to replace the value lent, of whatever amount, say two thousand dollars, at a time specified, by other value equivalent to the same amount of silver coin of the like weight and quality at the time of repayment. An object, lent on condition of specific restitution, cannot be available for reproduction; because by the terms of the loan, it is not to be consumed.

Sometimes a producer is the consumer of his own product; as when the farmer eats his own poultry or vegetables, or the clothier wears his own cloth. But, the objects of human consumption being far more varied and numerous than the objects of each person's production, respectively, most operations of consumption are preceded by a process of barter. He first turns into money, or receives in that shape, the values composing his individual revenue; and then changes again that money for the articles he purposes to consume. Wherefore, in common parlance, to spend and to consume have become nearly synonymous. Yet, by the mere act of buying, the value expended is not lost; for the article purchased has likewise a value, which may be parted with again for what it cost, if it has not been bought over-dear. The loss of value does not happen till the actual consumption, after which the value is destroyed; it then ceases to exist, and is not the object of a second consumption. For this reason it is, that in domestic life, the bad management of the wife soon runs through a moderate fortune; for she in general regulates the daily consumption of the family, which is the chief source of expense, and one that is always recurring.

This will serve to expose the error of the notion that where there is no loss of money, there can be no loss of wealth. It is the commonest thing in the world to hear it roundly asserted that the money spent is not lost, but remains in the country, and, therefore, that the country cannot be impoverished by its internal expenditure. It is true, the value of the money remains as before; but the object, or the hundred objects, perhaps, that have been successively bought with the same money, have been consumed, and their value destroyed.

Wherefore, it is superfluous, I had almost said ridiculous, to confine at home the national money for the purpose of preserving national wealth. Money by no means prevents the consumption of value and the consequent diminution of wealth; on the contrary, it facilitates the arrival of consumable objects at their ultimate destination; which is a most beneficial act when the end is well chosen and the result satisfactory. Nor would it be correct even to maintain that the export of specie is at all events a loss, although its presence in the country may be no hindrance to consumption or to the diminution of wealth. For unless it be made without any view to a return, which is rarely the case, it is in fact the same thing as productive consumption; being merely a sacrifice of one value, for the purpose of obtaining another. Where no return whatever is in view, there indeed is so much loss of national capital; but the loss would be quite as great, were goods, and not money, so exported.

Chapter III: Of the Effect of Productive Consumption

The nature of productive consumption has been explained in Book I. The value absorbed by it is what has been called *capital*. The trader, manufacturer, and cultivator purchase the raw material and productive agency, which they consume in the preparation of new products; and the immediate effect is precisely the same as that of unproductive consumption, namely to create a demand for the objects of their consumption, which operates upon their price and upon their production; and to cause a destruction of value. But the ultimate effect is different; there is no satisfaction of a human want and no resulting gratification, except that accruing to the adventurer from the possession of the fresh product the value which replaces that of the products consumed, and commonly affords him a profit into the bargain.

To this position, that productive consumption does not immediately satisfy any human want, a cursory observer may possibly object that the wages of labour, though a productive outlay, go to satisfy the wants of the labourer in food, raiment, and amusement perhaps. But, in this operation there is a double consumption; 1. Of the capital consumed productively in the purchase of productive agency, wherefrom results no human gratification; 2. Of the daily or weekly revenue of the labourer, i.e. of his productive agency, the recompense for which is consumed unproductively by himself and his family, in like manner as the rent of the manufactory which forms the revenue of the landlord, is by him consumed unproductively. And this does not imply the consumption of the same value twice over, first productively and afterwards unproductively; for the values consumed are two distinct values resting on bases altogether different. The first, the productive agency of the labourer, is the effect of his muscular power and skill, which is itself a positive product bearing value like any other. The second is a portion of capital given by the adventurer in exchange for that productive agency. After the act of exchange is once completed, the consumption of the value given on either side is contemporaneous, but with a different object in view; the one being intended to create a new product, the other to satisfy the wants of the productive agent and his family. Thus, the object expended and consumed by the adventurer is the equivalent he receives for his capital; and that, consumed unproductively by the labourer, is the equivalent for his revenue. The interchange of these two values by no means makes them one and the same.

So, likewise, the intellectual industry of superintendence is reproductively consumed in the concern; and the profits accruing to the adventurer as its recompense are consumed unproductively by himself and his family.

In short, this double consumption is precisely analogous to that of the raw material used in the concern. The clothier presents himself to the wool-dealer, with one thousand crowns in his hand; there are, at this moment, two values in existence, on the one side, that of the one thousand crowns which is the result of previous production and now forms a part of the capital of the clothier; on the other, the wool constituting a part of the annual product of a grazing farm. These products are interchanged, and each is separately consumed; the capital converted into wool in a way to produce cloth; the product of the farm converted into crown-pieces, in the satisfaction of the wants of the farmer or his landlord.

Since everything consumed is so much lost, the gain of reproductive consumption is equal, whether proceeding from reduced consumption or from enlarged production. In China, they make a great saving in the consumption of seed-corn by following the drilling in lieu of the broad-cast method. The effect of this saving is precisely the same as if the land were, in China, proportionately more productive than in Europe.

In manufacture, when the raw material used is of no value whatever, it is not to be reckoned as forming any part of the requisite consumption of the concern; thus, the stone used by the lime-burner and the sand employed by the glass-blower are no part of their respective consumption whenever they have cost them nothing.

A saving of productive agency, whether of industry, of land, or of capital, is equally real and effectual as a saving of raw material; and it is practicable in two ways; either by making the same productive means yield more agency, or by obtaining the same result from a smaller quantity of productive means.

Such savings generally operate in a very short time to the benefit of the community at large; they reduce the charges of production, and in proportion as the economical process becomes better understood, and more generally practiced, the competition of producers brings the price of the product gradually to a level with the charges of production. But for this very reason, all who do not learn to economize like their neighbours must necessarily lose while others are gaining. Manufacturers have been ruined by hundreds because they would go to work in a grand style with too costly and complex an apparatus, provided of course at an excessive expense of capital.

Fortunately, in the great majority of cases, self-interest is most sensibly and immediately affected by a loss of this kind; and in the concerns of business, like pain in the human frame, gives timely warning of injuries that require care and reparation. If the rash or ignorant adventurer in production were not the first to suffer the punishment of his own errors or misconduct, we should find it far more common than it is to dash into improvident speculation; which is quite as fatal to public prosperity as profusion and extravagance. A merchant that spends ten thousand dollars in the acquisition of six thousand dollars stands in respect to his private concerns and to the general wealth of the community, upon exactly the same footing, as a man of fashion who spends four thousand dollars in horses, mistresses, gluttony, or ostentation; except, perhaps, that the latter has more pleasure and personal gratification for his money.

What has been said on this subject in Book I of this work makes it needless to enlarge here on the head of productive consumption. I shall, therefore, henceforward direct my reader's attention to the subject of unproductive consumption, its motives, and consequences; premising that in what I am about to say, the word *consumption,* used alone, will import unproductive consumption, as it does in common conversation.

Chapter IV: Of the Effect of Unproductive Consumption in General

Having just considered the nature and effect of consumption in general, as well as the general effect of productive consumption in particular, it remains only to consider, in this and the following chapters, such consumption as is effected with no other end or object in view than the mere satisfaction of a want, or the enjoyment of some pleasurable sensation.

Whoever has thoroughly comprehended the nature of consumption and production, as displayed in the preceding pages, will have arrived at the conviction that no consumption of the class denominated unproductive has any ulterior effect beyond the satisfaction of a want by the destruction of existing value. It is a mere exchange of a portion of existing wealth on the one side for human gratification on the other, and nothing more. Beyond this, what can be expected?—reproduction? How can the same identical utility be afforded a second time? Wine cannot be both drunk and distilled into brandy, too. Neither can the object consumed serve to establish a fresh demand, and thus indirectly to stimulate future productive exertion; for it has already been explained that the only effectual demand is created by the possession of wherewithal to purchase,—of something to give in exchange; and what can that be except a product, which, before the act of exchange and consumption, must have been an item either of revenue or of capital? The existence and intensity of the demand must invariably depend upon the amount of revenue and of capital: The bare existence of revenue and of capital is all that is necessary for the stimulus of production, which nothing else can stimulate. The choice of one object of consumption necessarily precludes that of another; what is consumed in the shape of silks cannot be consumed in the shape of linens or woolens; nor can what has once been devoted to pleasure or amusement be made productive also of more positive or substantial utility.

Wherefore, the sole object of inquiry, with regard to unproductive consumption, is the degree of gratification resulting from the act of consumption itself; and this inquiry will, in the remainder of this chapter, be pursued in respect of unproductive consumption in general, after which we shall give in the following chapters a separate consideration to that of individuals, and that of the public or community at large. The sole point is to weigh the loss occasioned to the consumer by his consumption against the satisfaction it affords him. The degree of correctness, with which the balance of loss and gain is struck, will determine whether the consumption be judicious or otherwise; which is a point that next to the actual production of wealth has the most powerful influence upon the well or ill-being of families and of nations.

In this point of view, the most judicious kinds of consumption seem to be:

1. Such as conduce to the satisfaction of positive wants; by which term I mean those, upon the satisfaction of which depends the existence, the health, and the contentment of the generality of mankind,

being the very reverse of such as are generated by refined sensuality, pride, and caprice. Thus, the national consumption will, on the whole, be judicious if it absorb the articles rather of convenience than of display: The more linen and the less lace; the more plain and wholesome dishes and the fewer dainties; the more warm clothing, and the less embroidery, the better. In a nation whose consumption is so directed, the public establishments will be remarkable rather for utility than splendor; its hospitals will be less magnificent than salutary and extensive; its roads well-furnished with inns rather than unnecessarily wide and spacious, and its towns well paved, though with few palaces to attract the gaze of strangers.

The luxury of ostentation affords a much less substantial and solid gratification than the luxury of comfort, if I may be allowed the expression. Besides, the latter is less costly, that is to say, involves the necessity of a smaller consumption; whereas the former is insatiable; it spreads from one to another, from the mere proneness to imitation; and the extent to which it may reach is as absolutely unlimited. "Pride," says Franklin, "is a beggar quite as clamorous as want, but infinitely more insatiable."

Taking society in the aggregate, it will be found that, one with another, the gratification of real wants is more important to the community than the gratification of artificial ones. The wants of the rich man occasion the production and consumption of an exquisite perfume, perhaps those of the poor man, the production and consumption of a good warm winter cloak; supposing the value to be equal, the diminution of the general wealth is the same in both cases, but the resulting gratification will, in the one case, be trifling, transient, and scarcely perceptible; in the other, solid, ample, and of long duration.

2. Such as are the most gradual, and absorb products of the best quality. A nation or an individual will do wisely to direct consumption chiefly to those articles that are the longest time in wearing out, and the most frequently in use. Good houses and furniture are, therefore, objects of judicious preference; for there are few products that take longer time to consume than a house, or that are of more frequent utility; in fact, the best part of one's life is passed in it. Frequent changes of fashion are unwise; for fashion takes upon itself to throw things away long before they have lost their utility, and sometimes before they have lost even the freshness of novelty, thus multiplying consumption exceedingly, and rejecting as good for nothing what is perhaps still useful, convenient, or even elegant. So that a rapid succession of fashions impoverish-

es a state, as well by the consumption it occasions, as by that which it arrests.

There is an advantage in consuming articles of superior quality, although somewhat dearer, and for this reason: In every kind of manufacture there are some charges that are always the same, whether the product be of good or bad quality. Coarse linen will have cost in weaving, packing, storing, retailing, and carriage, before it comes to the ultimate consumer, quite as much trouble and labour, as linen of the finest quality, therefore in purchasing an inferior quality, the only saving is the cost of the raw material; the labour and trouble must always be paid in full and at the same rate, yet the product of that labour and trouble are much quicker consumed, when the linen is of inferior, than when it is of superior quality.

This reasoning is applicable indifferently to every class of product; for in every one there are some kinds of productive agency that are paid equally without reference to quality, and that agency is more profitably bestowed in the raising of products of good than of bad quality; therefore, it is generally more advantageous for a nation to consume the former. But this cannot be done unless the nation can discern between good and bad, and have acquired taste for the former; wherein again appears the necessity of knowledge to the furtherance of national prosperity; and unless, besides, the bulk of the population be so far removed above penury as not to be obliged to buy whatever is the cheapest in the first instance, although it be in the long run the dearest to the consumer.

It is evident that the interference of public authority in regulating the details of the manufacture, supposing it to succeed in making the manufacturer produce goods of the best quality, which is very problematical, must be quite ineffectual in promoting their consumption; for it can give the consumer, neither the taste of what is of the better quality, nor the ability to purchase. The difficulty lies not in finding a producer, but in finding a consumer. It will be no hard matter to supply good and elegant commodities, if there be consumers both willing and able to purchase them. But such a demand can exist only in nations enjoying comparative affluence; it is affluence that both furnishes the means of buying articles of good quality, and gives a taste for them. Now, the interference of authority is not the road to affluence, which results from activity of production, seconded by the spirit of frugality; from habits of industry pervading every channel of occupation, and of frugality tending to accumulation of capital. In a country where these qualities are prevalent, and in no other, can individuals be at all nice or fastidious in what they consume. On the contrary, profusion and embarrassment are inseparable companions; there is no choice when necessity drives.

The pleasures of the table, of play, of pyrotechnic exhibitions, and the like, are to be reckoned amongst those of shortest duration. I have seen villages that, although in want of good water, do not hesitate to spend in a wake or festival that lasts but one day as much money as would suffice to construct a conduit for the supply of that necessary of life, and a fountain or public cistern on the village green; the inhabitants preferring to get once drunk in honour of the squire or saint, and to go day after day with the greatest inconvenience, and bring muddy water from half a league distance. The filth and discomfort prevalent in rustic habitations are attributable partly to poverty, and partly to injudicious consumption.

In most countries, if a part of what is squandered in frivolous and hazardous amusements, whether in town or country, were spent in the embellishment and convenience of the habitations, in suitable clothing, in neat and useful furniture, or in the instruction of the population, the whole community would soon assume an appearance of improvement, civilization, and affluence, infinitely more attractive to strangers, as well as more gratifying to the people themselves.

3. The collective consumption of numbers. There are some kinds of agency that need not be multiplied in proportion to the increased consumption. One cook can dress dinner for ten as easily as for one; the same grate will roast a dozen joints as well as one; and this is the reason why there is so much economy in the mess-table of a college, a monastery, a regiment, or a large manufactory, in the supply of great numbers from a common kettle or kitchen, and in the dispensaries of cheap soups.

4. And lastly, on grounds entirely different, those kinds of consumption are judicious, which are consistent with moral rectitude; and, on the contrary, those which infringe its laws generally end in public, as well as private calamity. But it would be too wide a digression from my subject to attempt the illustration of this position.

It is observable that great inequality of private fortune is hostile to those kinds of consumption that must be regarded as most judicious. In proportion as that inequality is more marked, the artificial wants of the population are more numerous, the real ones more scantily supplied, and the rapid consumption more common and destructive. The patrician spendthrifts and imperial gluttons of ancient Rome thought they never could squander enough. Besides, immoral kinds of consumption are infinitely more general, where the extremes of wealth and poverty are found blended together. In such a state of society there are few who can indulge in the refinement of luxury, but a vast number who look on their enjoyments with envy, and are ever impatient to imitate them. To get into the privileged class is the grand object, be the means ever so questionable; and those who are little scrupulous in the acquirement are seldom more so in the employment of wealth.

The government has, in all countries, a vast influence in determining the character of the national consumption; not only because it absolutely directs the consumption of the state itself, but because a great proportion of the consumption of individuals is gained by its will and example. If the government indulge a taste for splendor and ostentation, splendor and ostentation will be the order of the day, with the whole host of imitators; and even those of better judgment and discretion must, in some measure, yield to the torrent. For how seldom are they independent of that consideration and good opinion, which, under such circumstances, are to be earned not by personal qualities, but by a course of extravagance they cannot approve?

First and foremost in the list of injudicious kinds of consumption stand those which yield disgust and displeasure in lieu of the gratification anticipated. Under this class may be ranged, excess and intemperance in private individuals; and, in the state, wars undertaken with the motive of pure vengeance, like that of Louis XIV in revenge for the attacks of a Dutch newspaper, or with that of empty glory which leads commonly to disgrace and odium. Yet such wars are even less to be deplored for the waste of national wealth and resources than for the irremediable loss of personal virtue and talent sacrificed in the struggle; a loss which involves families in distress enough when exacted by the public good, and by the pressure of inexorable necessity; but must be doubly shocking and afflicting when it originates in the caprice, the wickedness, the folly, or the ungovernable passions of national rulers.

Chapter V: Of Individual Consumption—Its Motives and Its Effects

The consumption of individuals, as contrasted with that of the public or community at large, is such as is made with the object of satisfying the wants of families and individuals. These wants chiefly consist in those of food, raiment, lodging, and amusement. They are supplied with the necessary articles of consumption in each department, out of the respective revenue of each family or individual, whether derived from personal industry, from capital, or from land. The wealth of a family advances, declines, or remains stationary according as its consumption equals, exceeds, or falls short of its revenue. The aggregate of the consumption of all the individuals, added to that of the government for public purposes, forms the grand total of national consumption.

A family, or indeed a community or nation, may certainly consume the whole of its revenue without being thereby impoverished; but it by no means follows that it either must, or would act wisely, in so doing. Common prudence would counsel to provide against casualties. Who can say with certainty that his income will not fall off, or that his fortune is exempt from the injustice, the fraud, or the violence of mankind? Lands may be confiscated, ships may be wrecked, litigation may involve him in its expenses and uncertainties. The richest merchant is liable to be ruined by one unlucky speculation or by the failure of others. Were he to spend his whole income, his capital might, and in all probability would, be continually on the decline.

But, supposing it to remain stationary, should one be content with keeping it so? A fortune, however large, will seem little enough when it comes to be divided amongst a number of children. And even if there be no occasion to divide it, what harm is there in enlarging it; so it be done by honourable means? What else is it, but the desire of each individual to better his situation, that suggests the frugality that accumulates capital, and thereby assists the progress of industry, and leads to national opulence and civilization? Had not previous generations been actuated by this stimulus, the present one would now be in the savage state; and it is impossible to say how much farther it may yet be possible to carry civilization. It has never been proved to my satisfaction that nine-tenths of the population must inevitably remain in that degree of misery and semi-barbarism which they are found in at present in most countries of Europe.

The observance of the rules of private economy keeps the consumption of a family within reasonable bounds; that is to say, the bounds prescribed in each instance by a judicious comparison of the value sacrificed in consumption, with the satisfaction it affords. None but the individual himself can fairly and correctly estimate the loss and gain resulting to himself or family from each particular act of consumption; for the balance will depend upon the fortune, the rank, and the wants of himself and family; and, in some degree, perhaps, upon personal taste and feelings. To restrain consumption within too narrow limits would involve the privation of gratification that fortune has placed within reach; and, on the other hand, a too profuse consumption might trench upon resources that it might be but common prudence to husband.

Individual consumption has constant reference to the character and passions of the consumer. It is influenced alternately by the noblest and the vilest propensities of our nature; at one time it is stimulated by sensuality; at another by vanity, by generosity, by revenge, or even by covetousness. It is checked by prudence or foresight, by groundless apprehension, by distrust, or by selfishness. As these various qualities happen in turn to predominate, they direct mankind in the use they make of their wealth. In this, as in every other action of life, the line of true wisdom is the most difficult to observe. Human infirmity is perpetually deviating to the one side or the other, and seldom steers altogether clear of excess.

In respect to consumption, prodigality and avarice are the two faults to be avoided; both of them neutralize the benefits that wealth is calculated to confer on its possessor; prodigality by exhausting, avarice by not using, the means of enjoyment. Prodigality is, indeed, the more amiable of the two because it is allied to many amiable and social qualities. It is regarded with more indulgence because it imparts its pleasures to others; yet it is of the two the more mischievous to society, for it squanders and makes away with the capital that should be the support of industry; it destroys industry, the grand agent of production, by the destruction of the other agent, capital. If, by expense and consumption, are meant those kinds only which minister to our pleasures and luxuries, it is a great mistake to say that money is good for nothing but to be spent, and that products are only raised to be consumed. Money may be employed in the work of reproduction; when so employed, it must be productive of great benefit, and every time that a fixed capital is squandered, a corresponding quantity of industry must be extinguished in some quarter or other. The spendthrift, in running through his fortune, is at the same time exhausting, *pro tanto,* the source of the profits upon industry.

The miser, who in the dread of losing his money hesitates to turn it to account, does, indeed, nothing to promote the progress of industry; but at least he cannot be said to reduce the means of production. His hoard is scraped together by the abridgment of his personal gratifications, not at the expense of the public, according to the vulgar notion; it has been withdrawn from no productive occupation and will at any rate reappear at his death, and be available for the purpose of extending the operations of industry, if it be not squandered by his heirs, or so effectually concealed as to evade all search or recovery.

It is absurd in spendthrifts to boast of their prodigality which is quite as unworthy the nobleness of our nature as the sordid meanness of the opposite character. There is no merit in consuming all one can lay hands upon, and desisting only when one can get no more to consume; every animal can do as much; nay, there are some animals that set a better example of provident management. It is more becoming the character of a being gifted with reason and foresight, never to consume, in any instance, without some reasonable object in view. At least, this is the course that economy would prescribe.

In short, economy is nothing more than the direction of human consumption with judgment and discretion,—the knowledge of our means, and the best mode of employing them. There is no fixed rule of economy; it must be guided by a reference to the fortune, condition, and wants of the consumer. An expense that may be authorized by the strictest economy in a person of moderate fortune would, perhaps, be pitiful in a rich man, and absolute extravagance in a poor one. In a state of sickness, a man must allow himself indulgences that he would not think of in health. An act of beneficence that trenches on the personal enjoyments of the benefactor is deserving of the highest praise; but it would be highly blamable if done at the expense of his children's subsistence.

Economy is equally distant from avarice and profusion. Avarice hoards, not for the purpose of consuming or reproducing, but for the mere sake of hoarding; it is a kind of instinct or mechanical impulse, much to the discredit of those in whom it is detected; whereas true economy is the offspring of prudence and sound reason, and does not sacrifice necessaries to superfluities, like the miser when he denies himself present comforts in the view of luxury, ever prospective and never to be enjoyed. The most sumptuous entertainment may be conducted with economy, without diminishing, but rather adding to its splendor which the slightest appearance of avarice would tarnish and deface. The economical man balances his means against his present or future wants, and those of his family and friends, not forgetting the calls of humanity. The miser regards neither family nor friends, scarcely attends to his own personal wants, and is an utter stranger to those of mankind at large. Economy never consumes without an object; avarice never willingly consumes at all; the one is a sober and rational study, the only one that supplies the means of fulfilling our duties and being at the same time just and generous; the other, a vile propensity to sacrifice everything to the sordid consideration of self.

Economy has not unreasonably been ranked among the virtues of mankind; for like the other virtues, it implies self-command and control, and is productive of the happiest consequences; the good education of children, physical and moral; the careful attendance of old age; the calmness of mind, so necessary to the good conduct of middle life; and that independence of circumstances which alone can secure against mercenary motives, are all referable to this quality. Without it there can be no liberality, none at least of a permanent and wholesome kind; for when it degenerates into prodigality, it is an indiscriminate largess alike to deserving and undeserving; stinting those who have claims in favour of those who have none. It is common to see the spendthrift reduced to beg a favour from people that he has loaded with his bounty; for what he gives now, one expects a return will some day be called for; whereas, the gifts of the economical man are purely gratuitous; for he never gives except from his superfluities. The latter is rich with a moderate fortune; but the miser and the prodigal are poor, though in possession of the largest resources.

Economy is inconsistent with disorder, which stumbles blindfold over wealth, sometimes missing what it most desires, although close within its reach, and sometimes seizing and devouring what it is most interested in preserving; ever impelled by the occurrences of the moment which it either cannot foresee, or cannot emancipate itself from; and always unconscious of its own position, and utterly incapable of choosing the proper course for the future. A household, conducted without order, is preyed upon by all the world; neither the fidelity of the servants, nor even the parsimony of the master, can save it from ultimate ruin. For it is exposed to the perpetual recurrence of a variety of little outgoings, on every occasion, however trivial.

Among the motives that operate to determine the consumption of individuals, the most prominent is luxury, that frequent theme of declamation, which, however, I should probably not have dwelt upon, could I expect that everybody would take the trouble of applying the principles I have been labouring to establish; and were it not always useful to substitute reason for declamation.

Luxury has been defined to be the use of superfluities. For my own part, I am at a loss to draw the line between superfluities and necessaries; the shades of difference are as indistinct and completely blended as the colours of the rainbow.

Taste, education, temperament, bodily health, make the degrees of utility and necessity infinitely variable, and render it impossible to employ in an absolute sense, terms, which always of necessity convey an idea of relation and comparison.

The line of demarcation between necessaries and superfluities shifts with the fluctuating condition of society. Strictly speaking, mankind might exist upon roots and herbs, with a sheepskin for clothing, and a wigwam for lodging; yet, in the present state of European society, we cannot look upon bread or butcher's meat, woolen-clothes or houses of masonry, as luxuries. For the same reason, the line varies also according to the varying circumstances of individual fortune; what is a necessary in a large town, or in a particular line of life, may, in another line of life, or in the country, be a mere superfluity. Wherefore, it is impossible exactly to define the boundary between the one and the other. Smith has fixed it a little in advance of Stewart; including in the rank of necessaries, besides natural wants, such as the established rules of decency and propriety have made necessary in the lower classes of society. But Smith was wrong in attempting to fix at all what must, in the nature of things, be ever varying.

Luxury may be said, in a general way, to be the use or consumption of dear articles; for the term dear is one of relation, and therefore may be properly enough applied in the definition of another term, whose sense is likewise relative. Luxury with us in France conveys the idea rather of ostentation than of sensuality; applied to dress, it denotes rather the superior beauty and impression upon the beholder, than superior convenience and comfort to the wearer; applied to the table, it means rather the splendor of a sumptuous banquet, than the exquisite farce of the solitary epicure. The grand aim of luxury in this sense is to attract admiration by the rarity, the costliness, and the magnificence of the objects displayed, recommended probably neither by utility, nor convenience, nor pleasurable qualities, but merely by their dazzling exterior and effect upon the opinions of mankind at large. Luxury conveys the idea of ostentation; but ostentation has itself a far more extensive meaning, and comprehends every quality assumed for the purpose of display. A man may be ostentatiously virtuous, but is never luxuriously so; for luxury implies expense. Thus, luxury of with or genius is a metaphorical expression, implying a profuse display or expenditure, if it may be so called, of those qualities of the intellect which it is the characteristic of good taste to deal out with a sparing hand.

Although, with us in France, what we term luxury is chiefly directed to ostentatious indulgence, the excess and refinement of sensuality are equally unjustifiable, and of precisely similar effect; that is to say, of a frivolous and inconsiderable enjoyment or satisfaction, obtained by a large consumption, calculated to satisfy more urgent and extensive wants. But I should not stigmatize as luxury that degree of variety or abundance, which a prudent and well-informed person in a civilized community would like to see upon his table upon domestic and common occasions, or aim at in his dress and abode, when under no compulsion to keep up an appearance. I should call this degree of indulgence judicious and suitable to his condition, but not an instance of luxury.

Having thus defined the term luxury, we may go on to investigate its effect upon the well-ordering or economy of nations.

Under the head of unproductive consumption is comprised the satisfaction of many actual and urgent wants, which is a purpose of sufficient consequence to outweigh the mischief that must ensue from the destruction of values. But what is there to compensate that mischief, where such consumption has not for its object the satisfaction of such wants? Where money is spent for the mere sake of spending, and the value destroyed without any object beyond its destruction?

It is supposed to be beneficial, at all events, to the producers of the articles consumed. But it is to be considered that the same expenditure must take place, though not, perhaps, upon objects quite so frivolous; for the money withheld from luxurious indulgences is not absolutely thrown into the sea; it is sure to be spent either upon more judicious gratifications or upon reproduction. In one way or other, all the revenue not absolutely sunk or buried is consumed by the receiver of it, or by someone in his stead; and in all cases whatever, the encouragement held out by consumption to the producer is coextensive with the total amount of revenue to be expended. Whence it follows:

1. That the encouragement which ostentatious extravagance affords to one class of production is necessarily withdrawn from another.

2. That the encouragement resulting from this kind of consumption cannot increase, except in the event of an increase in the revenue of the consumers; which revenue, as we cannot but know by this time, is not to be increased by luxurious, but solely by reproductive consumption.

How great then must be the mistake of those, who on observing the obvious fact that the production always equals the consumption, as it must necessarily do since a thing cannot be consumed before it is produced, have confounded the cause with the effect, and laid it down as a maxim that consumption originates production; therefore that frugality is directly adverse to public prosperity, and that the most useful citizen is the one who spends the most.

The partisans of the two opposite systems above adverted to, the economists and the advocates of exclusive commerce or the balance of trade, have made this maxim a fundamental article of their creed. The merchants and manufacturers, who seldom look beyond the actual sale of their products or inquire into the causes which may operate to extend their sale, have warmly supported a position, apparently so consistent with their interests; the poets, who are ever apt to be seduced by appearances, and do not consider themselves bound to be wiser than politicians and men of business, have been loud in the praise of luxury; and the rich have not been backward in adopting principles that exalt their ostentation into a virtue, and their self-gratification into benevolence.

This prejudice, however, must vanish as the increasing knowledge of political economy begins to reveal the real sources of wealth, the means of production, and the effect of consumption. Vanity may take pride in idle expense, but will ever be held in no less contempt by the wise, on account of its pernicious effects, than it has been all along for the motives by which it is actuated.

These conclusions of theory have been confirmed by experience. Misery is the inseparable companion of luxury. The man of wealth and ostentation squanders upon costly trinkets, sumptuous repasts, magnificent mansions, dogs, horses, and mistresses, a portion of value which, vested in productive occupation, would enable a multitude of willing labourers, whom his extravagance now consigns to idleness and misery, to provide themselves with warm clothing, nourishing food, and household conveniences. The gold buckles of the rich man leave the poor one without shoes to his feet; and the labourer will want a shirt to his back, while his rich neighbour glitters in velvet and embroidery.

It is vain to resist the nature of things. Magnificence may do what it will to keep poverty out of sight, yet it will cross it at every turn, still haunting, as if to reproach it for its excesses. This contrast was to be met with at Versailles, at Rome, at Madrid, and in every seat of royal residence. In a recent instance it occurred in France in an afflicting degree after a long series of extravagant and ostentatious administration; yet the principle is so undeniable that one would not suppose it had required so terrible an illustration.

Those who are little in the habit of looking through the appearance to the reality of things are apt to be seduced by the glitter and the bustle of ostentatious luxury. They take the display of consumption as conclusive evidence of national prosperity. If they could open their eyes, they would see that a nation verging towards decline will for some time continue to preserve a show of opulence; like the establishment of a spendthrift on the high road to ruin. But this false glare cannot last long; the effort dries up the sources of reproduction, and therefore must infallibly be followed by a state of apathy and exhaustion of the political frame, which is only to be remedied by slow degrees, and by the adoption of a regimen the very reverse of that by which it has thus been reduced.

It is distressing to see the fatal habits and customs of the nation one is attached to by birth, fortune, and social affection, extending their influence over the wisest individuals, and those best able to appreciate this danger and foresee its disastrous consequences. The number of persons who have sufficient spirit and independence of fortune to act up to their principles, and set themselves forward as an example, is extremely small. Most men yield to the torrent, and rush on ruin with their eyes open, in search of happiness; although it requires a very small share of philosophy to see the madness of this course, and to perceive that when once the common wants of nature are satisfied, happiness is to be found not in the frivolous enjoyments of luxurious vanity, but in the moderate exercise of our physical and moral faculties.

Wherefore, those who abuse great power or talent by exerting it in diffusing a taste for luxury are the worst enemies of social happiness. If there is one habit that deserves more encouragement than another, in monarchies as well as republics, in great as well as small, it is this of economy. Yet, after all, no encouragement is wanted; it is quite enough to withdraw favour and honour from habits of profusion; to afford in-

violable security to all savings and acquirements; to give perfect freedom to their investment and occupation in every branch of industry that
is not absolutely criminal.

It is alleged that to excite mankind to spend or consume, is to excite them to produce, inasmuch as they can only spend what they may
acquire. This fallacy is grounded on the assumption that production is
equally within the ability of mankind as consumption; that it is as easy
to augment as to expend one's revenue. But, supposing it were so, nay
further, that the desire to spend begets a liking for labour, although
experience by no means warrants such a conclusion, yet there can be no
enlargement of production without an augmentation of capital, which is
one of the necessary elements of production; but it is clear that capital
can only be accumulated by frugality; and how can that be expected
from those whose only stimulus to production is the desire of enjoyment?

Moreover, when the desire of acquirement is stimulated by the
love of display, how can the slow and limited progress of real production keep pace with the ardour of that motive? Will it not find a shorter
road to its object, in the rapid and disreputable profits of jobbing and
intrigue, classes of industry most fatal to national welfare, because they
produce nothing themselves but only aim at appropriating a share of
the produce of other people? It is this motive that sets in motion the de-
spicable art and cunning of the knave, leads the pettifogger to speculate
on the obscurity of the laws, and the man of authority to sell to folly and
wickedness that patronage which it is his duty to dispense gratuitously
to merit and to right. Pliny mentions having seen Paulina at a supper,
dressed in a network of pearls and emeralds that cost forty millions of
sestertii, as she was ready to prove by her jeweler's bills. It was bought
with the fruit of her ancestor's speculations. "Thus," says the Roman
writer, "it was to dress out his granddaughter in jewels at an entertainment, that Lollius forgot himself so far, as to lay waste whole provinces,
to become the object of detestation to the Asiatics he governed, to for-
feit the favour of Caesar, and end his life by poison."

This is the kind of industry generated by love of display.

If it be pretended that a system which encourages profusion operates only upon the wealthy, and thus tends to a beneficial end inasmuch
as it reduces the evil of the inequality of fortune, there can be little difficulty in showing that profusion in the higher begets a similar spirit in the
middling and lower classes of society, which last must, of course, the
soonest arrive at the limits of their income; so that, in fact, the universal

profusion has the effect of increasing, instead of reducing, that inequality. Besides, the profusion of the wealthier class is always preceded or followed by that of the government, which must be fed and supplied by taxation, that is always sure to fall more heavily upon small incomes than on large ones.

The apologists of luxury have sometimes gone so far as to cry up the advantages of misery and indigence; on the ground that without the stimulus of want, the lower classes of mankind could never be impelled to labour, so that neither the upper classes, nor society at large, could have the benefit of their exertions.

Happily, this position is as false in principle as it would be cruel in practice. Were nakedness a sufficient motive of exertion, the savage would be the most diligent and laborious, for he is the nearest to nakedness of his species. Yet his indolence is equally notorious and incurable. Savages will often fret themselves to death if compelled to work. It is observable throughout Europe, that the laziest nations are those nearest approaching to the savage state; a mechanic in good circumstances, at London or Paris, would execute twice as much work in a given time, as the rude mechanic of a poor district. Wants multiply as fast as they are satisfied; a man who has a jacket is for having a coat; and when he has his coat he must have a greatcoat too. The artisan that is lodged in an apartment by himself extends his views to a second; if he has two shirts, he soon wants a dozen, for the comforts of more frequent change of linen; whereas, if he has none at all, he never feels the want of it. No man feels any disinclination to make a further acquisition, in consequence of having made one already.

The comforts of the lower classes are, therefore, by no means incompatible with the existence of society, as too many have maintained. The shoemaker will make quite as good shoes in a warm room, with a good coat to his back and wholesome food for himself and his family, as when perishing with cold in an open stall; he is not less skilful or inclined to work because he has the reasonable conveniences of life. Linen is washed as well in England, where washing is carried on comfortably within doors, as where it is executed in the nearest stream in the neighbourhood.

It is time for the rich to abandon the puerile apprehension of losing the objects of their sensuality, if the poor man's comforts be promoted. On the contrary, reason and experience concur in teaching that the greatest variety, abundance, and refinement of enjoyment are to be found in those countries where wealth abounds most, and is the most widely diffused.

Chapter VI: On Public Consumption

Section I: Of the Nature and General Effect of Public Consumption

Besides the wants of individuals and of families which it is the object of private consumption to satisfy, the collection of many individuals into a community gives rise to a new class of wants; the wants of the society in its aggregate capacity, the satisfaction of which is the object of public consumption. The public buys and consumes the personal service of the minister that directs its affairs, the soldier that protects it from external violence, the civil or criminal judge that protects the rights and interests of each member against the aggression of the rest. All these different vocations have their use, although they may often be unnecessarily multiplied or overpaid; but that arises from a defective political organization, which it does not fall within the scope of this work to investigate.

We shall see presently whence it is, that the public derives all the values, wherewith it purchases the services of its agents, as well as the articles its wants require. All we have to consider in this chapter is the mode in which its consumption is effected and the consequences resulting from it.

If I have made myself understood in the commencement of this third book, my readers will have no difficulty in comprehending that public consumption, or that which takes place for the general utility of the whole community, is precisely analogous to that consumption which goes to satisfy the wants of individuals or families. In either case, there is a destruction of values and a loss of wealth; although, perhaps, not a shilling of specie goes out of the country.

By way of insuring conviction of the truth of this position, let us trace from first to last the passage of a product towards ultimate consumption on the public account.

The government exacts from a taxpayer the payment of a given tax in the shape of money. To meet this demand, the taxpayer exchanges part of the products at his disposal for coin, which he pays to the tax-gatherer; a second set of government agents is busied in buying with that coin, cloth, and other necessaries for the soldiery. Up to this point, there is no value lost or consumed; there has only been a gratuitous transfer of value, and a subsequent act of barter, but the value contributed by the subject still exists in the shape of stores and supplies in the military depot. In the end, however, this value is consumed; and then the portion of wealth which passes from the hands of the taxpayer into those of the tax-gatherer is destroyed and annihilated.

Yet it is not the sum of money that is destroyed; that has only passed from one hand to another, either without any return, as when it passed from the taxpayer to the tax-gatherer; or in exchange for an equivalent, as when it passed from the government agent to the contractor for clothing and supplies. The value of the money survives the whole operation, and goes through three, four, or a dozen hands without any sensible alteration; it is the value of the clothing and necessaries that disappears with precisely the same effect as if the taxpayer had, with the same money, purchased clothing and necessaries for his own private consumption. The sole difference is that the individual in the one case, and the state in the other, enjoys the satisfaction resulting from that consumption.

The same reasoning may be easily applied to all other kinds of public consumption. When the money of the taxpayer goes to pay the salary of a public officer, that officer sells his time, his talents, and his exertions to the public, all of which are consumed for public purposes. On the other hand, that officer consumes, instead of the taxpayer, the value he receives in lieu of his services; in the same manner as any clerk or person in the private employ of the taxpayer would do.

There has been long a prevalent notion that the values paid by the community for the public service return to it again in some shape or other; in the vulgar phrase, that what government and its agents receive is refunded again by their expenditure. This is a gross fallacy; but one that has been productive of infinite mischief, inasmuch as it has been the pretext for a great deal of shameless waste and dilapidation. The value paid to government by the taxpayer is given without equivalent or return: It is expended by the government in the purchase of personal service, of objects of consumption; in one word, of products of equivalent value, which are actually transferred. Purchase or exchange is a very different thing from restitution.

Turn it which way you will, this operation, though often very complex in the execution, must always be reducible by analysis to this plain statement. A product consumed must always be a product lost, be the consumer who he may; lost without return, whenever no value or advantage is received in return; but, to the taxpayer, the advantage derived from the services of the public functionary, or from the consumption effected in the prosecution of public objects, is a positive return.

If, then, public and private expenditure affect social wealth in the same manner, the principles of economy, by which it should be regulated, must be the same in both cases. There are not two kinds of economy any more than two kinds of honesty, or of morality. If a government or an individual consume in such a way as to give birth to a product larger than that consumed, a successful effort of productive industry will be made. If no product result from the act of consumption, there is a loss of value, whether to the state or to the individual; yet, probably, that loss of value may have been productive of all the good anticipated. Military stores and supplies, and the time and labour of civil and military functionaries, engaged in the effectual defense of the state, are well bestowed, though consumed and annihilated; it is the same with them as with the commodities and personal service that have been consumed in a private establishment. The sole benefit resulting in the latter case is the satisfaction of a want; if the want had no existence, the expense or consumption is a positive mischief incurred without an object. So likewise of the public consumption; consumption for the mere purpose of consumption, systematic profusion, the creation of an office for the sole purpose of giving a salary, the destruction of an article for the mere pleasure of paying for it, are acts of extravagance either in a government or an individual, in a small state or a large one, a republic or a monarchy. Nay, there is more criminality in public than in private extravagance and profusion; inasmuch as the individual squanders only what belongs to him; but the government has nothing of its own to squander, being, in fact, a mere trustee of the public treasure.

What, then, are we to think of the principles laid down by those writers who have laboured to draw an essential distinction between public and private wealth; to show that economy is the way to increase private fortune, but on the contrary, that public wealth increases with the increase of public consumption; inferring thence this false and dangerous conclusion, that the rules of conduct in the management of private fortune and of public treasure are not only different, but in direct opposition?

If such principles were to be found only in books, and had never crept into practice, one might suffer them without care or regret to swell the monstrous heap of printed absurdity; but it must excite our compassion and indignation to hear them professed by men of eminent rank, talents, and intelligence; and still more to see them reduced into practice by the agents of public authority who can enforce error and absurdity at the point of the bayonet or mouth of the cannon.

Madame de Maintenon mentions in a letter to the Cardinal de Noailles that when she one day urged Louis XIV to be more liberal in charitable donations, he replied that royalty dispenses charity by its profuse expenditure; a truly alarming dogma, and one that shows the ruin of France to have been reduced to principle. False principles are more fatal than even intentional misconduct; because they are followed up with erroneous notions of self-interest, and are long persevered in without remorse or reserve. If Louis XIV had believed his extravagant ostentation to have been a mere gratification of his personal vanity, and his conquests the satisfaction of personal ambition alone, his good sense and proper feeling would probably, in a short time, have made it a matter of conscience to desist, or at any rate, he would have stopped short for his own sake; but he was firmly persuaded that his prodigality was for the public good as well as his own; so that nothing could stop him but misfortune and humiliation.

So little were the true principles of political economy understood, even by men of the greatest science, so late as the 18th century that Frederick II of Prussia, with all his anxiety in search of truth, his sagacity, and his merit, writes thus to D'Alembert in justification of his wars: "My numerous armies promote the circulation of money and disburse impartially amongst the provinces the taxes paid by the people to the state." Again I repeat, this is not the fact; the taxes paid to the government by the subject are not refunded by its expenditure. Whether paid in money or in kind, they are converted into provisions and supplies, and in that shape consumed and destroyed by persons that never can replace the value because they produce no value whatever. It was well for Prussia that Frederick II did not square his conduct to his principles. The good he did to his people by the economy of his internal administration more than compensated for the mischief of his wars.

Since the consumption of nations or the governments which represent them occasions a loss of value, and consequently, of wealth, it is only so far justifiable as there results from it some national advantage equivalent to the sacrifice of value. The whole skill of government, therefore, consists in the continual and judicious comparison of the sacrifice about to be incurred with the expected benefit to the community; for I have no hesitation in pronouncing every instance, where the benefit is not equivalent to the loss, to be an instance of folly, or of criminality, in the government.

It is yet more monstrous, then, to see how frequently governments, not content with squandering the substance of the people in folly and absurdity instead of aiming at any return of value, actually spend that substance in bringing down upon the nation calamities innumerable; practice exactions the most cruel and arbitrary, to forward schemes the most extravagant and wicked; first rifle the pockets of the subject, to enable them afterwards to urge him to the further sacrifice of his blood. Nothing but the obstinacy of human passion and weakness could induce me again and again to repeat these unpalatable truths, at the risk of incurring the charge of declamation.

The consumption effected by the government forms so large a portion of the total national consumption, amounting sometimes to a sixth, a fifth, or even a fourth part of the total consumption of the community, that the system acted upon by the government must have a vast influence upon the advance or decline of the national prosperity. Should an individual take it into his head that the more he spends the more he gets, or that his profusion is a virtue; or should he yield to the powerful attractions of pleasure, or the suggestions of perhaps a reasonable resentment, he will in all probability be ruined and his example will operate upon a very small circle of his neighbours. But a mistake of this kind in the government will entail misery upon millions, and possibly end in the national downfall or degradation. It is doubtless very desirable that private persons should have a correct knowledge of their personal interests; but it must be infinitely more so that governments should possess that knowledge. Economy and order are virtues in a private station; but, in a public station, their influence upon national happiness is so immense that one hardly knows how sufficiently to extol and honour them in the guides and rulers of national conduct.

An individual is fully sensible of the value of the article he is consuming; it has probably cost him a world of labour, perseverance, and economy; he can easily balance the satisfaction he derives from its consumption against the loss it will involve. But a government is not so immediately interested in regularity and economy, nor does it so soon feel the ill consequences of the opposite qualities. Besides, private persons have a further motive than even self-interest; their feelings are concerned; their economy may be a benefit to the objects of their affection; whereas the economy of a ruler accrues to the benefit of those he knows very little of, and perhaps he is but husbanding for an extravagant and rival successor.

Nor is this evil remedied by adopting the principle of hereditary rule. The monarch has little of the feelings common to other men in this respect. He is taught to consider the fortune of his descendants as secure, if they have ever so little assurance of the succession. Besides, the far greater part of the public consumption is not personally directed by himself; contracts are not made by himself, but by his generals and ministers; the experience of the world hitherto all tends to show that aristocratical republics are more economical than either monarchies or democracies.

Neither are we to suppose that the genius which prompts and excites great national undertakings is incompatible with the spirit of public order and economy. The name of Charlemagne stands among the foremost in the records of renown; he achieved the conquest of Italy, Hungary, and Austria; repulsed the Saracens; broke the Saxon confederacy; and obtained at length the honours of the purple. Yet Montesquieu has thought it not derogatory to say of him, that "the father of a family might take a lesson of good housekeeping from the ordinances of Charlemagne. His expenditure was conducted with admirable system; he had his demesnes valued with care, skill, and minuteness. We find detailed in his capitularies the pure and legitimate sources of his wealth. In a word, such were his regularity and thrift, that he gave orders for the eggs of his poultry yards, and the surplus vegetables of his garden, to be brought to market." The celebrated Prince Eugene, who displayed equal talent in negotiation and administration as in the field, advised the Emperor Charles VI to take the advice of merchants and men of business in matters of finance. Leopold, when Grand Duke of Tuscany, towards the close of the 18th century gave an eminent example of the resources to be derived from a rigid adherence to the principles of private economy in the administration of a state of very limited extent. In a few years he made Tuscany one of the most flourishing states of Europe.

The most successful financiers of France, Suger, Abbé de St. Dennis, the Cardinal D'Amboise, Sully, Colbert, and Necker, have all acted on the same principle. All found means of carrying into effect the grandest operations by adhering to the dictates of private economy. The Abbé de St. Dennis furnished the outfit of the second crusade; a scheme that required very large supplies, although one I am far from approving. The Cardinal furnished Louis XII with the means of making his conquest of the Milanese. Sully accumulated the resources, that afterwards humbled the house of Austria. Colbert supplied the splendid operations of Louis XIV. Necker provided the ways and means of the only successful war waged by France in the 18th century.

Those governments, on the contrary, that have been perpetually pressed with the want of money have been obliged, like individuals, to have recourse to the most ruinous and sometimes the most disgraceful expedients to extricate themselves. Charles the Bald put his titles and safe conducts up to sale. Thus, too, Charles II of England sold Dunkirk to the French king and took a bribe of eighty thousand pounds from the Dutch to delay the sailing of the English expedition to the East Indies, 1680, intended to protect their settlements in that quarter which, in consequence, fell into the hands of the Dutchmen. Thus, too, have governments committed frequent acts of bankruptcy, sometimes in the shape of adulteration of their coin, and sometimes by open breach of their engagements.

Louis XIV towards the close of his reign, having utterly exhausted the resources of a noble territory, was reduced to the paltry shift of creating the most ridiculous offices, making his counsellors of state, one an inspector of fagots, another a licenser of barber-wig-makers, another visiting inspector of fresh, or taster of salt, butter, and the like. Such paltry and mischievous expedients can never long defer the hour of calamities that must sooner or later befall the extravagant and spend-thrift governments. "When a man will not listen to reason," says Franklin, "she is sure to make herself felt."

Fortunately, an economical administration soon repairs the mischiefs of one of an opposite character. Sound health cannot be restored all at once, but there is a gradual and perceptible improvement; every day some cause of complaint disappears and some new faculty comes again into play. Half the remaining resources of a nation, impoverished by an extravagant administration, are neutralized by alarm and uncertainty; whereas, credit doubles those of a nation blessed with one of a frugal character. It would seem that there exists in the politic, to a stronger degree than even in the natural, body a principle of vitality and elasticity which cannot be extinguished without the most violent pressure. One cannot look into the pages of history without being struck with the rapidity with which this principle has operated. It has nowhere been more strikingly exemplified than in the frequent vicissitudes that our own France has experienced since the commencement of the revolution. Prussia has afforded another illustration in our time. The successor of Frederick the Great squandered the accumulations of that monarch, which were estimated at no less a sum than forty-two millions of dollars, and left behind him, besides, a debt of twenty-seven millions. In less than eight years, Frederick William III had not only paid off his father's debts, but actually began a fresh accumulation; such is the power of economy, even in a country of limited extent and resources.

Section II: Of the Principal Objects of National Expenditure

In the preceding section it has been endeavoured to show that since all consumption by the public is in itself a sacrifice of value, an evil balanced only by such benefit as may result to the community from the satisfaction of any of its wants, a good administration will never spend for the mere sake of spending, but take care to ascertain that the public benefit resulting in such instance from the satisfaction of a public want shall exceed the sacrifice incurred in its acquirement.

A comprehensive view of the principal public wants of a civilized community can alone qualify us to estimate with tolerable accuracy the sacrifice it is worthwhile for the community to make for their gratification.

The public consumes little else, but what have been denominated *immaterial* products, that is to say, products destroyed as soon as created; in other words, the services or agency, either of human beings, or of other objects, animate or inanimate.

It consumes the personal service of all its functionaries, civil, judicial, military, or ecclesiastical. It consumes the agency of land and capital. The navigation of rivers and seas, utility of roads and ground open to the public, are so much agency derived by the public from land, of which either the absolute property or the beneficial enjoyment is vested in the public. Where capital has been vested in the land, in the shape of buildings, bridges, artificial harbors, causeways, dikes, canals, etc., the public then consumes the agency or the rent of the land, *plus* the agency, or the interest of the capital so vested.

Sometimes the public maintains establishments of productive industry, for instance, the porcelain manufacture of Sevres, the Gobelin tapestry, the salt-works of Lorraine and of the Jura, etc., in France. When concerns of this kind bring more than their expenditure, which is but rarely the case, they furnish part of the national revenue, and must by no means be classed among the items of national charge.

Of the Charge of Civil and Judicial Administration

The charge of civil and judicial administration is made up partly of the specific allowances of magistrates and other officers, and partly of such degree of pomp and parade, as may be deemed necessary in the execution of their duties. Even if the burthen of that pomp and parade be thrown wholly or partially upon the public functionary, it must ultimately fall upon the shoulders of the public, for the salary of the functionary must be raised in proportion to the appearance he is expected to make. This observation applies to every description of functionary, from the prince to the constable inclusive consequently, a nation, which reverences its prince only when surrounded with the externals of greatness, with guards, horse and foot, laced liveries, and such costly trappings of royalty, must pay dearly for its taste. If, on the contrary, it can be content to respect simplicity rather than pageantry, and obey the laws, though unaided by the attributes of pomp and ceremony, it will save in proportion. This is what made the charges of government so light in many of the Swiss cantons before the revolution, and in the North American colonies before their emancipation. It is well-known that those colonies, though under the dominion of England, had separate governments of which they respectively defrayed the charge; yet the whole annual expenditure all together amounted to no more than 64,700l. sterling. "An ever memorable example," observes Smith, "at how small an expense three millions of people may not only be governed, but well governed."

Causes entirely of a political nature as well as the form of government which they help to determine, have an influence in apportioning the salaries of public officers, civil and judicial, the charge of public display, and those likewise of public institutions and establishments. Thus, in a despotic government, where the subject holds his property at the will of the sovereign, who fixes himself the charge of his household, that is to say, the amount of the public money which he chooses to spend on his personal necessities and pleasures, and the keeping up of the royal establishment, that charge will probably be fixed at a higher rate than where it is arranged and contested between the representatives of the prince and of the taxpayers respectively.

The salaries of inferior public officers in like manner depend partly upon their individual importance, and partly upon the general plan of government. Their services are dear or cheap to the public, not merely in proportion to what they actually cost, but likewise in proportion as they are well or ill executed. A duty ill performed is dearly bought, however little be paid for it; it is dear too, if it be superfluous or unnecessary; resembling in this respect an article of furniture that, if it do not answer its purpose or be not wanted, is merely useless lumber. Of this description, under the old régime of France, were the officers of high-admiral, high-steward of the household, the king's cup-bearer, the master of his hounds, and a variety of others, which added nothing even to the splendor of royalty, and were merely so many means of dispensing personal favour and emolument.

For the same reason, whenever the officers of government are needlessly multiplied, the people are saddled with charges which are not necessary to the maintenance of public order. It is only giving an unnecessary form to that benefit or product, which is not at all the better of it, if indeed it be not worse. A bad government that cannot support its violence, injustice, and exaction, without a multitude of mercenaries, satellites, and spies, and gaols innumerable, makes its subjects pay for its prisons, spies, and soldiers, which nowise contribute to the public happiness.

On the other hand, a public duty may be cheap, although very liberally paid. A low salary is wholly thrown away upon an incapable and inefficient officer; his ignorance will probably cost the public ten times the amount of his salary; but the knowledge and activity of a man of ability are fully equivalent to the pay he receives; the losses he saves to the public and the benefits derived from his exertions greatly outweigh his personal emolument, even if settled on the most liberal scale.

There is real economy in procuring the best of everything, even at a larger price. Merit can seldom be engaged at a low rate because it is applicable to more occupations than one. The talent that makes an able minister would, in another profession, make a good advocate, physician, farmer, or merchant; and merit will find both employment and emolument in all these departments. If the public service offer no adequate reward for its exertion, it will choose some other more promising occupation.

Integrity is like talent; it cannot be had without paying for it, which is not at all wonderful; for the honest man cannot resort to those discreditable shifts and contrivances, which dishonesty looks to as a supplemental resource.

The power which commonly accompanies the exercise of public functions is a kind of salary that often far exceeds the pecuniary emolument attached to them. It is true that in a well ordered state, where law is supreme, and little is left to the arbitrary control of the ruler, there is little opportunity of indulging the caprice and love of domination implanted in the human breast. Yet the discretion which the law must inevitably vest in those who are to enforce it, and particularly in the ministerial department, together with the honour commonly attendant on the higher offices of the state, have a real value which makes them eagerly sought for, even in countries where they are by no means lucrative.

The rules of strict economy would probably make it advisable to abridge all pecuniary allowance wherever there are other sufficient attractions to excite a competition for office, and to confer it on none but the wealthy, were there not a risk of losing, by the incapacity of the officer, more than would be gained by the abridgment of his salary. This, as Plato well observes in his *Republic*, would be like entrusting the helm to the richest man on board. Besides, there is some danger that a man who gives his services for nothing will make his authority a matter of gain, however rich he may be. The wealth of a public functionary is no security against his venality; for ample fortune is commonly accompanied with desires as ample, and probably even more ample, especially if he have to keep up an appearance both as a man of wealth and a magistrate. Moreover, supposing what is not altogether impossible, namely that one can meet with wealth united with probity, and with, besides, the activity requisite to the due performance of public duty, is it wise to run the risk of adding the preponderance of authority to that of wealth, which is already but too manifest? With what grace could his employers call to account an agent, who could assume the merit of generosity, both with the people and with the government? There are, however, some ways, in which the gratuitous services of the rich may be employed with advantage; particularly in those departments that confer more honour than power, as in the administration of institutions of public charity, or of public correction or punishment.

In France under the old régime, the government, when harassed with the want of money, was in the habit of putting up its offices to sale. This is the very worst of all expedients; it introduces all the mischiefs of gratuitous service; for the emolument is then no more than the interest of the capital expended in the purchase of the office; and has the additional evil of costing to the state as much as if the service were not gratuitously performed; for the public remains charged with the interest of a capital that has been consumed and lost.

It has been sometimes the practice to consign certain civil functions, such as the registry of births, marriages, and deaths, to the ecclesiastical body, whose emoluments, arising from their clerical duties, may be supposed to enable them to execute these without pay. But there is always danger in confiding the execution of civil duties to a class of men that pretend to a commission from a still higher than a national authority.

In spite of every precaution, the public or the monarch will never be served so well or so cheaply as individuals. Inferior public agents cannot be so narrowly watched by their superiors as private ones; nor have the superiors themselves an equal interest in vigilant superintendence. Besides, it is easy enough for underlings to impose on a superior, who has many to look after, is perhaps placed at a distance, and can give but little attention to each individually; and whose vanity makes him more alive to the officious zeal of his inferior than to the real service and utility that the public good requires. As to the monarch and the nation, who are the parties most interested in good public administration because it consolidates the power of the one and enlarges the happiness of the other, it is next to impossible for them to exert a perpetual and effectual control. In most cases, this duty must of necessity devolve on agents who will deceive them when it is their interest to do so, as is proved by abundance of examples. "Public services," says Smith, "are never better performed than when their reward comes only in consequence of their being performed, and is proportioned to the diligence employed in performing them." Accordingly, he recommends that the salaries of judges should be paid at the final determination of each suit, and the share of each judge proportioned to their respective trouble in the progress of it. This would be some encouragement to the diligence of each particular judge as well as to that of the court in bringing litigation to an end. There would be some difficulty in applying this method to all the branches of the public service; and it would probably introduce as great abuses in the opposite way; but it would at least be productive of one good; viz. preventing the needless multiplication of offices. It would likewise give the public the same advantage of competition as is enjoyed by individuals, in respect to the services they call for.

Not only are the time and labour of public men in general better paid for than those of other persons, besides being often wasted by their own mismanagement, without the possibility of an efficient check; but there is often a further enormous waste, occasioned by compliance with the customs of the country, and court etiquette. It would be curious to calculate the time wasted in the toilet, or to estimate, if possible, the many dearly-paid hours lost in the course of the last century on the road between Paris and Versailles.

Thus, in the governments of Asia, there is an immense waste of the time of the superior public servants in tedious and ceremonious observances. The monarch, after allowing for the hours of customary parade, and those of personal pleasure, has little time left to look after his own affairs which, consequently, soon go to ruin. Frederick II of Prussia, by adopting a contrary line of conduct, and by the judicious distribution and apportionment of his time, contrived to get through a great deal of business himself. By this means, he really lived longer than older men than himself, and succeeded in raising his kingdom to a first-rate power. His other great qualities, doubtless, contributed to his success; but they would not have been sufficient without a methodical arrangement of his time.

Of Charges, Military and Naval

When a nation has made any considerable progress in commerce, manufacture, and the arts, and its products have, consequently, become various and abundant, it would be an immense inconvenience if every citizen were liable to be dragged from a productive employment, which has become necessary to society, for the purposes of national defense. The cultivator of the soil works no longer for the sustenance of himself and family only, but also for that of many other families who are either owners of the soil and share in its produce, or traders and manufacturers that supply him with articles he cannot do without. He must, therefore, cultivate a larger extent of surface, must vary his tillage, keep a larger stock of cattle, and follow a complex mode of cultivation that will fully occupy his leisure between seed-time and harvest.

Still less can the trader and manufacturer afford thus to sacrifice time and talents, whereof the constant occupation, except during the intervals of rest, is necessary to the production from which they are to derive their subsistence.

The owners of land let out to farm may, undoubtedly, serve as soldiers without pay; as indeed the nobility and gentry do, in some measure, in monarchical states; but they are, for the most part, so much accustomed to the sweets of social existence, so little goaded by necessity towards the conception and achievement of great enterprises, and feel so little of the enthusiasm of emulation and *esprit de corps,* that they commonly prefer a pecuniary sacrifice to that of comfort, and possibly of life. And these motives operate equally with the owners of capital.

All these reasons have led individuals in most modern states to consent to a taxation that may enable the monarch or the republic to defend the country against external violence with a hired and professional soldiery, who are, however, too apt to become the tools of their leader's ambition or tyranny.

When war has become a trade it benefits, like all other trades, from the division of labour. Every branch of human science is pressed into its service. Distinction or excellence, whether in the capacity of general, engineer, subaltern, or even private soldier, cannot be obtained without long training, perhaps, and constant practice. The nation, which should act upon a different principle, would lie under the disadvantage of opposing the imperfection, to the perfection, of art. Thus, excepting the cases in which the enthusiasm of a whole nation has been roused to action, the advantage has uniformly been on the side of a disciplined and professional soldiery. The Turks, although professing the utmost contempt for the arts of their Christian neighbours, are compelled by the dread of extermination to be their scholars in the art of war. The European powers were all forced to adopt the military tactics of the Prussians; and when the violent agitation of the French revolution pressed every resource of science to the aid of the armies of the republic, the enemies of France were obliged to follow the example.

This extensive application of science, and adaptation of fresh means and more ample resources to military purposes, have made war far more expensive now than in former times. It is necessary now-a-days to provide an army beforehand, with supplies of arms, ammunition, magazines of provision, ordnance, etc., equal to the consumption of one campaign at the least. The invention of gunpowder has introduced the use of weapons more complex and expensive, and very chargeable in the transport, especially the field and battering trains. Moreover, the wonderful improvement of naval tactics, the variety of vessels of every class and construction, all requiring the utmost exertion of human genius and industry; the yards, docks, machinery, store houses, etc. have entailed upon nations addicted to war almost as heavy an expense in peace as in times of actual hostility; and obliged them not only to expend a great portion of their income, but to vest a great amount of capital likewise in military establishments. In addition to which, it is to be observed, that the modern colonial system, that is to say, the system of retaining the sovereignty of towns and provinces in distant parts of the world, has made the European states open to attack and aggression in the most remote quarters of the globe, and the whole world the theatre of warfare, when any of the leading powers are the belligerents.

Wealth has, consequently, become as indispensable as valour to the prosecution of modern warfare; and a poor nation can no longer withstand a rich one. Wherefore, since wealth can be acquired only by industry and frugality, it may safely be predicted that every nation whose agriculture, manufacture, and commerce shall be ruined by bad government, or exorbitant taxation, must infallibly fall under the yoke of its more provident neighbours. We may further conclude that, henceforward, national strength will accompany national science and civilization; for none but civilized nations can maintain considerable standing armies, so that there is no reason to apprehend the future recurrence of those sudden overthrows of civilized empires by the influx of barbarous tribes, of which history affords many examples.

War costs a nation more than its actual expense; it costs besides, all that would have been gained, but for its occurrence.

When Louis XIV in 1672, resolved in a fit of passion to chastise the Dutch for the insolence of their newspaper writers, Boreel, the Dutch ambassador, laid before him a memorial showing that France through the medium of Holland sold produce annually to foreign nations, to the amount of sixty millions fr. at the then scale of price; which will fall little short of one hundred and twenty millions (twenty two millions of dollars) at the present. But the court treated his representations as the mere empty bravado of an ambassador.

To conclude: The charges of war would be very incorrectly estimated, were we to take no account of the havoc and destruction it occasions; for that one at least of the belligerents, whose territory happens to be the scene of operations, must be exposed to its ravages. The more industrious the nation, the more does it suffer from warfare. When it penetrates into a district abounding in agricultural, manufacturing, and commercial establishments, it is like a fire in a place full of combustibles; its fury is aggravated, and the devastation prodigious. Smith calls the soldier an unproductive labourer; would to God he were nothing more, and not a destructive one into the bargain! He not only adds no product of his own to the general stock of wealth in return for the necessary subsistence he consumes, but is often set to work to destroy the fruits of other people's labour and toil without doing himself any benefit.

The tardy, but irresistible expansion of intelligence will probably operate a still further change in external political relations, and with it a prodigious saving of expenditure for the purposes of war. Nations will be taught to know that they have really no interest in fighting one another; that they are sure to suffer all the calamities incident to defeat, while the advantages of success are altogether illusory. According to the international policy of the present day, the vanquished are sure to be taxed by the victor, and the victor by domestic authority; for the interest of loans must be raised by taxation. There is no instance on record of any diminution of national expenditure being effected by the most successful issue of hostilities. And what is the glory it can confer more than a mere toy of the most extravagant price, that can never even amuse rational minds for any length of time? Dominion by land or sea will appear equally destitute of attraction when it comes to be generally understood that all its advantages rest with the rulers, and that the subjects at large derive no benefit whatever. To private individuals, the greatest possible benefit is entire freedom of intercourse, which can hardly be enjoyed except in peace. Nature prompts nations to mutual amity; and if their governments take upon themselves to interrupt it, and engage them in hostility, they are equally inimical to their own people, and to those they war against. If their subjects are weak enough to second the ruinous vanity or ambition of their rulers in this propensity, I know not now to distinguish such egregious folly and absurdity from that of the brutes that are trained to fight and tear each other to pieces for the mere amusement of their savage masters.

But human intelligence will not stand still; the same impulse that has hitherto borne it onwards will continue to advance it yet further. The very circumstance of the vast increase of expense attending national warfare has made it impossible for governments henceforth to engage in it without the public assent, express or implied; and that assent will be obtained with the more difficulty, in proportion as the public shall become more generally acquainted with their real interest. The national military establishment will be reduced to what is barely sufficient to repel external attack; for which purpose little more is necessary than a small body of such kinds of troops as cannot be had without long training and exercise; as of cavalry and artillery. For the rest, nations will rely on their militia, and on the excellence of their internal polity: For it is next to impossible to conquer a people unanimous in their attachment to their national institutions; and their attachment will always be proportionate to the loss they will incur by a change of domination.

Of the Charges of Public Instruction

Two questions have been raised in political economy:

1. Whether the public be interested in the cultivation of science in all its branches?

2. Whether it be necessary that the public should be at the expense of teaching those branches it has an interest in cultivating?

Whatever be the position of man in society, he is in constant dependence upon the three kingdoms of nature. His food, his clothing, his medicines, every object either of business or of pleasure, is subject to fixed laws; and the better those laws are understood, the more benefit will accrue to society. Every individual, from the common mechanic that works in wood or clay, to the prime minister that regulates with the dash of his pen the agriculture, the breeding of cattle, the mining, or the commerce of a nation, will perform his business the better, the better he understands the nature of things, and the more his understanding is enlightened.

For this reason, every advance of science is followed by an increase of social happiness. A new application of the lever, or of the power of wind or water, or even a method of reducing the friction of bodies will, perhaps, have an influence on twenty different arts. An uniformity of weights and measures, arranged upon mathematical principles, would be a benefit to the whole commercial world if it were wise enough to adopt such an expedient. An important discovery in astronomy or geology may possibly afford the means of ascertaining the longitude at sea with precision, which would be an immense advantage to navigation all over the world. The naturalization in Europe of a new botanical genus or species might possibly influence the comfort of many millions of individuals.

Among the numerous classes of science, theoretical and practical, which it is the interest of the public to advance and promote, there are fortunately many that individuals have a personal interest in pursuing, and which the public, therefore, is not called upon to pay the expense of teaching. Every adventurer in any branch of industry is urged most strongly by self-interest to learn his business and whatever concerns it. The journeyman gains in his apprenticeship, besides manual dexterity, a variety of notions and ideas only to be learnt in the workshop, and which can be no otherwise recompensed than by the wages he will receive.

But it is not every degree or class of knowledge that yields a benefit to the individual equivalent to that accruing to the public. In treating above of the profits of the man of science, I have shown the reason why his talents are not adequately remunerated; yet theoretical is quite as useful to society as practical knowledge; for how could science ever be applied to the practical utility of mankind unless it were discovered and preserved by the theorist? It would rapidly degenerate into mere mechanical habit, which must soon decline; and the downfall of the arts would pave the way for the return of ignorance and barbarism.

In every country that can at all appreciate the benefits to be derived from the enlargement of human faculties, it has been deemed by no means a piece of extravagance to support academies and learned institutions and a limited number of very superior schools, intended not as mere repositories of science and of the most approved mode of instruction, but as a means of its still further extension. But it requires some skill in the management to prevent such establishments from operating as an impediment, instead of a furtherance, to the progress of knowledge, and as an obstruction, rather than as an avenue, to the improvement of education. Long before the revolution it had become notorious that most of our French universities had been thus perverted from the intention of their founders. All the principal discoveries were made elsewhere; and most of them had to encounter the weight of their influence over the rising generation and credit with men in power.

From this example, we may see how dangerous it is to entrust them with any discretionary control. If a candidate presents himself for examination, he must not be referred to teachers who are at the same time judges and interested parties, sure to think well of their own scholars and ill of those of everybody else. The merit of the candidate should alone decide, and not the place where he happens to have studied, nor the length of his probation; for to oblige a student in any science, medicine for instance, to learn it at a particular place is, possibly, to prevent his learning it better elsewhere; and to prescribe any fixed routine of study is, possibly, to prevent his fixing a shorter road. Moreover, in deciding upon comparative merit there is much unfairness to be apprehended from the *esprit de corps* of such communities.

Encouragement may, with perfect safety, be held out to a mode of instruction of no small efficacy; I mean, the composition of good elementary works. The reputation and profit of a good book in this class do not indemnify the labour, science, and skill requisite to its composition. A man must be a fool to serve the public in this line where the natural profit is so little proportioned to the benefit derived to the public. The want of good elementary books will never be thoroughly supplied until the public shall hold out temptations sufficiently ample to engage first-rate talents in their composition. It does not answer to employ particular individuals for the express purpose; for the man of most talents will not always succeed the best, nor to offer specific premiums; for they are often bestowed on very imperfect productions, and the encouragement ceases the moment the premium is awarded. But merit in this kind should be paid proportionately to its degree, and always liberally. A good work will thus be sure to be superseded by a better, till perfection is at last attained in each class. And I must observe, by the way, that there is no great expense incurred by liberally rewarding excellence; for it must always be extremely rare; and what is a great sum to an individual is a small matter to the pockets of a nation.

These are the kinds of instruction most calculated to promote national wealth, and most likely to retrograde if not in some measure supported by the public. There are others which are essential to the softening of national manners, and stand yet more in need of that support.

When the useful arts have arrived at a high degree of perfection, and labour has been very generally and minutely subdivided, the occupation of the lowest classes of labourers is reduced to one or two operations, for the most part simple in themselves, and continually repeated: To these their whole thought and attention are directed; and from them they are seldom diverted by any novel or unforeseen occurrence; their intellectual faculties, being rarely or never called into play, must of course be degraded and bratified, and themselves rendered incapable of uttering two words of common sense out of their peculiar line of business, and utterly devoid of any generous ideas or elevated notions. Elevation of mind is generated by enlarged views of men and things, and can never exist in a being incapable of conceiving the general bearings and connections of objects. A plodding mechanic can conceive no connection between the inviolability of property and public prosperity, or how he can be more interested in that prosperity than his more wealthy neighbour; but is apt to consider all these important benefits as so many encroachments on his rights and happiness. A certain degree of education, of reading, of reflection while at work, and of intercourse with persons of his own condition, will open his mind to these conceptions, as well as introduce a little more delicacy of feeling into his conduct, as a father, a husband, a brother, or a citizen.

But, in the vast machinery of national production, the mere manual labourer is so placed as to earn little or nothing more than a bare subsistence. The most he can do is to rear his young family, and bring them up to some occupation: He cannot be expected to give them that education which we have supposed the well-being of society to require. If the community wish to have the benefit of more knowledge and intelligence in the labouring classes, it must dispense it at the public charge.

This object may be obtained by the establishment of primary schools, of reading, writing, and arithmetic. These are the groundwork of all knowledge, and are quite sufficient for the civilization of the lower classes. In fact, one cannot call a nation civilized, nor consequently possessed of the benefits of civilization, until the people at large be instructed in these three particulars; till then it will be but partially reclaimed from barbarism. With the help of these advantages alone it may safely be affirmed that no transcendent genius or superior mind will long remain in obscurity, or be prevented from displaying itself to the infinite benefit of the community. The faculty of reading alone will, for a few dollars, put a man in possession of all that eminent men have said or done, in the line to which the bent of genius impels. Nor should the female part of the creation be shut out from this elementary education; for the public is equally interested in their civilization; and they are indeed the first, and often the only teachers of the rising generation.

It would be the more unpardonable in governments to neglect the business of education, and abandon to their present ignorance the great majority of the population in those nations of Europe that pretend to the character of refinement and civilization, now that the improved methods of mutual instruction that have been tried with such complete success, afford a ready and most economical means of universally diffusing knowledge amongst the inferior classes.

Thus, none but elementary and abstract science,—the highest and the lowest branches of knowledge, are so much less favoured in the natural course of things, and so little stimulated by the competition of demand, as to require the aid of that authority which is created purposely to watch over the public interests. Not that individuals have no interest in the support and promotion of these, as well as of the other branches of knowledge; but they have not so direct an interest,—the loss occasioned by their disappearance is neither so immediate nor so perceptible; a flourishing empire might retrograde until it reached the confines of barbarism before individuals had observed the operating cause of its decline.

I would not be understood to find fault with public establishments for purposes of education in other branches than those I have been describing. I am only endeavouring to show in what branches a nation may wisely, and with due regard to its own interest, defray the charge out of the public purse. Every diffusion of such knowledge as is founded upon fact and experience, and does not proceed upon dogmatical opinions and assertions, every kind of instruction that tends to improve the taste and understanding, is a positive good; and, consequently, an institution calculated to diffuse it must be beneficial. But care must be taken that encouragement of one branch shall not operate to discourage another. This is the general mischief of premiums awarded by the public; a private teacher or institution will not be adequately paid where the same kind of instruction is to be had for nothing, though, perhaps, from inferior teachers. There is, therefore, some danger that talent may be superseded by mediocrity; and a check be given to private exertions from which the resources of the state might expect incalculable benefit.

The only important science which seems to me not susceptible of being taught at the public charge is that of moral philosophy, which may be considered as either experimental or doctrinal. The former consists in the knowledge of moral qualities, and of the chain of connection between events dependent upon human will; and forms indeed a part of the study of man which is best pursued by social converse and intercourse. The latter is a series of maxims and precepts, possessing very little influence upon human conduct, which is best guided in the relations of public and of private life, by the operation of good laws, of good education, and of good example.

The sole encouragement to virtue and good conduct that can be relied on is the interest that everybody has in discovering and employing no persons but those of good character. Men the most independent in their circumstances want something more to make them happy; that is to say, the general esteem and good opinion of their fellow creatures; and these can only be acquired by putting on the appearance at least of estimable qualities, which it is much easier to acquire than to simulate.

The influence of the sovereign or ruling body upon the manners of the nation is very extensive because it employs a vast number of people; but it operates less beneficially than that of individuals because it is less interested in employing none but persons of integrity. If to its luke-warmness in this particular be added the example of immorality and contempt for honesty and economy too frequently held out to people by their rulers, the corruption of national morals will be wonderfully accelerated. But a nation may be rescued from moral degradation by the reaction of opposite causes. Colonies are, for the most part, com-posed of by no means the most estimable classes of the mother coun-try: In a very short time, however, when the hopes of return are wholly abandoned, and the settlers have made up their minds to pass the rest of their lives in their new abode, they gradually feel the necessity of conciliating the esteem of their fellow citizens, and the morals of the colony improve rapidly. By morals, I mean the general course of human conduct and behavior.

These are the causes that have a positive influence upon national morality. To these must be added the effect of education in general, in opening the eyes of mankind to their real interests, and softening the temper and disposition.

Religious instruction ought, strictly speaking, to be defrayed by the respective religious communions and societies, each of which regards the opinions of the rest as heretical, and naturally revolts at the injus-tice of contributing to the propagation of what it deems erroneous, if not criminal.

Of the Charges of Public Benevolent Institutions

It has been much debated whether individual distress has any title to public relief. I should say none, except inasmuch as it is an unavoida-ble consequence of existing social institutions. If infirmity and want be the effect of the social system, they have a title to public relief; provided always that it be shown that the same system affords no means of pre-vention or cure. But it would be foreign to the matter to discuss the question of right in this place. All we need do is to consider benevolent institutions with regard to their nature and consequences.

When a community establishes at the public charge any institution for benevolent purposes, it forms a kind of saving bank to which every member contributes a portion of his revenue to entitle him to claim a benefit in the event of accident or misfortune. The wealthy are generally impressed with an idea that they shall never stand in need of public charitable relief; but a little less confidence would become them better. No man can reckon in his own case upon the continuance of good fortune with as much certainty as upon the permanence of wants and infirmities; the former may desert him, but the latter are inseparable companions. It is enough to know that good fortune is not inexhaustible, to infuse an apprehension that it may some day or other be exhausted: One has but to look round, and this apprehension will be confirmed by the experience of numbers, whose misfortunes were to themselves quite unexpected.

Hospitals for the sick, almshouses and asylums for old age and infancy, inasmuch as they partially relieve the poorer classes from the charge of maintaining those who are naturally dependent on them, and thereby to allow population to advance somewhat more rapidly, have a natural tendency a little to depress the wages of labour. That depression would be greater still, if such establishments should be so multiplied as to take in all the sick, aged, and infants of those classes, who would then have none but themselves to provide for out of their wages. If they were entirely done away, there would be some rise of wages, although not sufficient to maintain so large a labouring population as may be kept up with their help; for the demand for their labour would be somewhat reduced by the advance of its price.

From these two extreme suppositions we may judge of the effect of those efforts to relieve indigence, which all nations have made in some degree or other; and see the reason why the distress and relief go on increasing together, although not exactly in the same ratio.

Most nations preserve a middle course between the two extremes, affording public relief to a part only of those who are helpless from age, infancy, or casual sickness. Of the rest they endeavour to rid themselves in one of two ways; either by requiring certain qualifications in the applicants, whether of age, of specific disease, or, perhaps, of mere interest and favouritism; or by limiting narrowly the extent of the relief, giving it upon hard terms to the applicants, or attaching some degree of shame to the acceptance.

It is a distressing reflection that there are no other methods of confining the number of applicants for relief within the means available to the community, except the offer of hard conditions or the want of a patron. It were to be desired that asylums of the more comfortable class, instead of favouritism, should be open to unmerited misfortune only; and that, to prevent improper nominations, the pretensions of the candidate should be ascertained by the inquest of a jury. The rest can probably be protected from too great an influx of indigence, by no other means consistent with humanity except the observance of severe, though impartial, discipline, sufficient to invest them with some degree of terror.

This evil does not apply to the asylums devoted to invalid soldiers and sailors. The qualification is so plain and intelligible that the doors ought to be shut against none who are possessed of it; and the comforts of the institution can never increase the number of applicants. Their being nursed in the public asylums with the same domestic care and comfort as are to be found in the homes of persons in the same class of life, and indulged in repose, and some even of the whims of old age, will undoubtedly somewhat enhance the charge, that is to say, so far as it might prolong lives that otherwise might fall a sacrifice to wretchedness; but this is the utmost increase of charge; and it is one that neither patriotism nor humanity will grudge.

The houses of industry that are multiplying so rapidly in America, Holland, Germany, and France, are noble and excellent institutions of public benevolence. They are designed to provide all persons of sound health with work according to their respective capacities; some of them are open to any workman out of employ that chooses to apply; others are a kind of houses of correction, where vagrants, beggars, and offenders are kept to work for fixed periods. Convicts have sometimes been set to hard labour in their respective vocations during their confinement; whereby the public has been wholly or partially relieved from the charge of keeping up gaols, and a method contrived for reforming the morals of the criminals and rendering them a blessing, instead of a curse, to society.

Indeed, such establishments can hardly be reckoned among the items of public charge; for the moment their production equals their consumption, they are no longer an encumbrance to anybody. They are of immense benefit in a dense population where, amidst the vast variety of occupations, some must unavoidably be in a state of temporary inaction. The perpetual shiftings of commerce, the introduction of new processes, the withdrawing of capital from a productive concern, accidental fire, or other calamity may throw numbers out of employment; and the most deserving individual may, without any fault of his own, be reduced to the extreme of want. In these institutions he is sure of earning at least a subsistence, if not in his own line, in one of a similar description.

The grand obstacle to such establishments is the great outlay of capital they require. They are adventures of industry, and as such must be provided with a variety of tools, implements, and machines, besides raw material of different kinds to work upon. Before they can be said to maintain themselves, they must earn enough to pay the interest of the capital embarked, as well as their current expenses.

The favour shown them by the public authority in the gratuitous supply of the capital and buildings, and in many other particulars, would make them interfere with private undertakings were they not subject, on the other hand, to some peculiar disadvantages. They are obliged to confine their operations to such kinds of work, as sort with the feebleness and general inferiority in skill of the inmates, and cannot direct them to such as may be most in demand. Moreover, it is in most of them a matter of regulation and police to lay by always the third or fourth part of the labourer's wages or earnings as a capital to set him up on his quitting the establishment: This is an excellent precaution, but prevents their working at such cheap rates, as to drive all competition out of the market.

Although the honour attached to the direction and management of institutions of public benevolence will generally attract the gratuitous service of the affluent and respectable part of the community, yet, when the duties become numerous and laborious they are commonly discharged by gratuitous administrators with the most unfeeling negligence. It was probably by no means wise to subject all the hospitals of Paris to a general superintendence. At London, each hospital is separately administered; and the whole are managed with more economy and attention in consequence. A laudable emulation is thereby excited amongst the managers of rival establishments; which affords an additional proof of the practicability and benefit of competition in the business of public administration.

Of the Charges of Public Edifices and Works

I shall not here attempt to enumerate the great variety of works requisite for the use of the public; but merely lay down some general rules for calculating their cost to the nation. It is often impossible to estimate with any tolerable accuracy the public benefit derived from them. How is one to calculate the utility, that is to say, the pleasure which the inhabitants of a city derive from a public terrace or promenade? It is a positive benefit to have, within an easy distance of the close and crowded streets of a populous town, some place where the population can breathe a pure and wholesome atmosphere, and take health and exercise under the shade of a grove, or with a verdant prospect before the eye; and where schoolboys can spend their hours of recreation; yet this advantage it would be impossible to set a precise value upon.

The amount of its cost, however, may be ascertained or estimated. The cost of every public work or construction consists:

1. Of the rent of the surface whereon it is erected; which rent amounts to what a tenant would give to the proprietor.

2. Of the interest of the capital expended in the erection.

3. Of the annual charge of maintenance.

Sometimes, one or more of these items may be curtailed. When the soil, whereon a public work is erected, will fetch nothing from either a purchaser or a tenant, the public will be charged with nothing in the nature of rent; for no rent could be got if the spot had never been built on. A bridge, for instance, costs nothing but the interest of the capital expended in its construction and the annual charge of keeping it in repair. If it be suffered to fall into decay, the public consumes, annually, the agency of the capital vested, reckoned in the shape of interest on the sum expended and, gradually, the capital itself into the bargain; for as soon as the bridge ceases to be passable, not only is the agency or rent of the capital lost, but the capital is gone likewise.

Supposing one of the dikes in Holland to have cost in the outset, twenty thousand dollars; the annual charge on the score of interest, at five per cent, will be one thousand dollars; and if it cost six hundred dollars more in the keeping it up, the total annual charge will be sixteen hundred dollars.

The same mode of reckoning may be applied to roads and canals. If a road be broader than necessary, there is annually a loss of the rent of all the superfluous land it occupies, and, besides, of all the additional charge of repair. Many of the roads out of Paris are one hundred and eighty feet wide, including the unpaved part on each side; whereas, a breadth of sixty feet would be full wide for all useful purposes, and would be quite magnificent enough even for the approaches to a great metropolis. The surplus is only so much useless splendor; indeed, I hardly know how to call it so; for the narrow pavement in the centre of a broad road, the two sides of which are impassable the greater part of the year, is an equal imputation upon the liberality, and upon the good sense and taste of the nation. It gives a disagreeable sensation to see so much loss of space, more particularly if it be badly kept. It appears like a wish to have magnificent roads without having the means of keeping them uniform and in good condition; like the palaces of the Italian nobles that never feel the effects of the broom.

Be it as it may, on the sides of the road I am speaking of, there is a space of one hundred and twenty feet that might be restored to cultivation; that is to say, forty-eight acres to the ordinary league. Add together the rent of the surplus land, the interest of the sum expended in the first cost and preparation, and the annual charge of keeping up the unnecessary space, which is something, badly as it is kept up; you will then ascertain the sum France pays annually for the very questionable honour of having roads too wide, by more than the half, leading to streets too narrow, by three-fourths.

Roads and canals are costly public works, even in countries where they are under judicious and economical management. Yet, probably, in most cases the benefits they afford to the community far exceed the charges. Of this the reader may be convinced, on reference to what has been said above of the value generated by the mere commercial operation of transfer from one spot to another, and of the general rule that every saving in the charges of production is so much gain to the consumer. Were we to calculate what would be the charge of carriage upon all the articles and commodities that now pass along any road in the course of a year, if the road did not exist, and compare it with the utmost charge under present circumstances, the whole difference that would appear will be so much gain to the consumers of all those articles, and so much positive and clear net profit to the community.

Canals are still more beneficial; for in them the saving of carriage is still more considerable.

Public works of no utility, such as palaces, triumphal arches, monumental columns, and the like, are items of national luxury. They are equally indefensible, with instances of private prodigality. The unsatisfactory gratification afforded by them to the vanity of the prince or the people by no means balances the cost, and often the misery they have occasioned.

Chapter VII: Of the Actual Contributors to Public Consumption

A portion of the objects of public consumption have, in some very rare instances, been provided by a private individual. We see occasional acts of private munificence in the erection of a hospital, the laying out of a road, or of public gardens upon the land, and at the cost of an individual. In ancient times, examples of this kind were more frequent, though much less meritorious. The private opulence of the ancients was commonly the fruit of domestic, or provincial, plunder and peculation, or perhaps the spoil of a hostile nation, purchased with the blood of fellow citizens. Among the moderns, though such excesses do sometimes occur, individual wealth is, in the great majority of cases, the fruit of personal industry and economy. In England, where there are so many institutions founded and supported by private funds, most of the fortunes of the founders and supporters have been acquired in industrious occupations. It requires a greater exertion of generosity to sacrifice wealth, acquired by a long course of toil and self-denial, than to give away what has been obtained by a stroke of good fortune, or even by an act of lucky temerity.

Among the Romans, a further portion of the public consumption was supplied directly by the vanquished nations who were subjected to a tribute which the victors consumed.

In most modern states, there is some territorial property vested, either in the nation at large, or in the subordinate communities, cities, towns, and villages, which is leased out or occupied directly by the public. In France, most of the public lands of tillage and pasturage, with their appurtenances, are let out on lease; the government reserving only the national forests under the direct administration of its agents. The produce of the whole forms a considerable item in the catalogue of public resources.

But these resources consist, for the most part, of the produce of taxes levied upon the subjects or citizens. These taxes are sometimes national, that is, levied upon the whole nation and paid into the general treasury of the state, whence the public national expenditure is defrayed; and sometimes local, or provincial, that is, levied upon the inhabitants of a certain canton or province only, and paid into the local treasury, whence are defrayed the local expenses.

It is a principle of equity that consumption should be charged to those who derive gratification from it; consequently, those countries must be pronounced to be the best governed in respect of taxation, where each class of inhabitants contributes in taxation proportionately to the benefit derived by it from the expenditure.

Every individual and class in the community is benefitted by the central administration, or, in other words, the general government so likewise of the security afforded by the national military establishment; for the provinces can hardly be secure from external attack if the enemy have possession of the metropolis, and can thence overawe and control them; imposing laws upon districts where his force has not penetrated, and disposing of the lives and property even of such as have not seen the face of an enemy. For the same reason the charge of fortresses, arsenals, and diplomatic agents is properly thrown upon the whole community.

It would seem that the administration of justice should be classed among the general charges, although the security and advantage it affords have more of a local character. When the magistracy of Bordeaux arrests and tries an offender, the public internal security of France is unquestionably promoted. The charge of gaols and courthouses necessarily follows that of the magistracy. Smith has expressed an opinion that civil justice should be defrayed by the litigating parties; which would be more practicable than at present, were the judges in the appointment of the parties in each particular case, and no otherwise in the nomination of the public authority than inasmuch as the choice might be limited to specified persons of approved knowledge and integrity. They would then be arbitrators, and a sort of equitable jurors, and might be paid proportionately to the matter in dispute without regard to the length of the suit; and would thus have an obvious interest in simplifying the process and sparing their own time and trouble, as well as in attracting business by the general equity of their decisions.

But local administration and local institutions of utility, pleasure, instruction, or beneficence appear to yield a benefit exclusively to the place or district where they are situated. Wherefore, it should seem, that their expenses ought to fall, as in most countries they do, upon the local population. Not but that the nation at large derives some benefit from good provincial administration or institutions. A stranger has access to the public places, libraries, schools, walks, and hospitals of the district; but the principal benefit unquestionably results to the immediate neighbourhood.

It is good economy to leave the administration of the local receipts and disbursements to the local authorities; particularly where they are appointed by those whose funds they administer. There is much less waste when the money is spent under the eye of those who contribute it and who are to reap the benefit; besides, the expense is better proportioned to the advantage expected. When one passes through a city or town badly paved and ill-conditioned, or sees a canal or harbor in a state of dilapidation, one may conclude, in nine cases out of ten, that the authorities, who are to administer the funds appropriated to those objects, do not reside on the spot.

In this particular, small states have an advantage over more extensive ones. They have more enjoyment from a less expenditure upon objects of public utility or amusement; because they are at hand to see that the funds, destined to the object, are faithfully applied.

Chapter VIII: Of Taxation

Section I: Of the Effect of all Kinds of Taxation in General

Taxation is the transfer of a portion of the national products from the hands of individuals to those of the government for the purpose of meeting the public consumption or expenditure. Whatever be the denomination it bears, whether tax, contribution, duty, excise, custom, aid, subsidy, grant, or free gift, it is virtually a burthen imposed upon individuals, either in a separate or corporate character, by the ruling power for the time being, for the purpose of supplying the consumption it may think proper to make at their expense; in short, an impost in the literal sense.

It would be foreign to the plan of this work to inquire in whom the right of taxation is, or ought to be vested. In the science of political economy, taxation must be considered as matter of fact, and not of right; and nothing further is to be regarded than its nature, the source whence it derives the values it absorbs, and its effect upon national and individual interests. The province of this science extends no further.

The object of taxation is not the actual commodity, but the value of the commodity, given by the taxpayer to the tax-gatherer. Its being paid in silver, in goods, or in personal service, is a mere accidental circumstance, which may be more or less advantageous to the subject or to the sovereign. The essential point is the value of the silver, the goods, or the service. The moment that value is parted with by the taxpayer, it is positively lost to him; the moment it is consumed by the government or its agents, it is lost to all the world and never reverts to, or re-exists, in society. This, I apprehend, has already been demonstrated when the general effect of public consumption was under consideration. It was there shown that however the money levied by taxation may be refunded to the nation, its value is never refunded; because it is never returned gratuitously or refunded by the public functionaries without receiving an equivalent in the way of barter or exchange.

The same causes that we have found to make unproductive consumption nowise favourable to reproduction, prevent taxation from at all promoting it. Taxation deprives the producer of a product which he would otherwise have the option of deriving a personal gratification from, if consumed unproductively, or of turning to profit, if he preferred to devote it to an useful employment. One product is a means of raising another; and, therefore, the subtraction of a product must needs diminish, instead of augmenting, productive power.

It may be urged that the pressure of taxation impels the productive classes to redouble their exertions, and thus tends to enlarge the national production. I answer that, in the first place, mere exertion cannot alone produce, there must be capital for it to work upon, and capital is but an accumulation of the very products that taxation takes from the subject: That, in the second place, it is evident that the values which industry creates expressly to satisfy the demands of taxation are no increase of wealth; for they are seized on and devoured by taxation. It is a glaring absurdity to pretend that taxation contributes to national wealth by engrossing part of the national produce, and enriches the nation by consuming part of its wealth. Indeed, it would be trifling with my reader's time to notice such a fallacy, did not most governments act upon this principle, and had not well-intentioned and scientific writers endeavoured to support and establish it.

If, from the circumstance that the nations most grievously taxed are those most abounding in wealth as Great Britain, for example, we are desired to infer that their superior wealth arises from their heavier taxation, it would be a manifest inversion of cause and effect. A man is not rich because he pays largely; but he is able to pay largely because he is rich. It would be not a little ridiculous if a man should think to enrich himself by spending largely because he sees a rich neighbour doing so. It must be clear that the rich man spends because he is rich; but never can enrich himself by the act of spending.

Cause and effect are easily distinguished when they occur in succession; but are often confounded when the operation is continuous and simultaneous.

Hence, it is manifest that, although taxation may be, and often is, productive of good, when the sums it absorbs are properly applied, yet, the act of levying is always attended with mischief in the outset. And this mischief good princes and governments have always endeavoured to render as inconsiderable to their subjects as possible by the practice of economy, and by levying, not to the full extent of the people's ability, but to such extent only as is absolutely unavoidable. That rigid economy is the rarest of princely virtues, is owing to the circumstance of the throne being constantly beset with individuals who are interested in the absence of it; and who are always endeavouring by the most specious reasoning, to impress the conviction that magnificence is conducive to public prosperity, and that profuse public expenditure is beneficial to the state. It is the object of this third book to expose the absurdities of such representations.

Others there are, who are not impudent enough to pretend that public profusion is a public benefit; yet undertake to show by arithmetical deduction that the people are scarcely burthened at all, and are equal to a much higher scale of taxation. As Sully tells us in his Memoirs, "The ear of the prince is assailed by a set of flattering advisers who think to make their court to him by perpetually suggesting new ways of raising money; discharged functionaries, for the most part, whose experience of the sweets of office has left no other impression than the tincture of the baneful art of fiscal extortion; and who seek to recommend themselves to power and favour by commending it to the lips of royalty."

Others suggest financial projects, and ways and means for filling the coffers of the prince, as they assert, without fleecing the subject. But no plan of finance can give to the government without taking either from the people or from the government itself in some other way; unless it be a downright adventure of industry. Something cannot be produced out of nothing by a mere touch of the wand. However an operation may be cloaked in mystery, however often we may twist and turn and transform values, there are but two ways of obtaining them, namely, creating oneself, or taking from others. The best scheme of finance is to spend as little as possible; and the best tax is always the lightest.

Admitting these premises, that taxation is the taking from individuals a part of their property for public purposes; that the value levied by taxation never reverts to the members of the community after it has once been taken from them; and that taxation is not itself a means of reproduction; it is impossible to deny the conclusion that the best taxes, or, rather those that are least bad, are:

1. Such as are the most moderate in their ratio.

2. Such as are least attended with those vexatious circumstances that harass the taxpayer without bringing anything into the public exchequer.

3. Such as press impartially on all classes.

4. Such as are least injurious to reproduction.

5. Such as are rather favourable than otherwise to the national morality; that is to say, to the prevalence of habits, useful and beneficial to society.

These positions are almost self-evident; yet I shall proceed to illustrate them successively, with some few observations.
1. Of such as are most moderate in their ratio.
Since taxation does, in point of fact, deprive the taxpayer of a product which is to him either a means of personal gratification or a means of reproduction, the lighter the tax is, the less must be the privation.

Taxation, pushed to the extreme, has the lamentable effect of impoverishing the individual without enriching the state. We may readily conceive how this can happen if we recall to our attention the former position; viz. that each taxpayer's consumption, whether productive or not, is always limited to the amount of his revenue. No part of his revenue, therefore, can be taken from him without necessarily curtailing his consumption in the same ratio. This must need reduce the demand for all those objects he can no longer consume, and particularly those affected by taxation. The diminution of demand must be followed by diminution of the supply of production; and, consequently, of the articles liable to taxation. Thus, the taxpayer is abridged of his enjoyments, the producer of his profits, and the public exchequer of its receipts.

This is the reason why a tax is not productive to the public exchequer in proportion to its ratio; and why it has become a sort of apophthegm that two and two do not make four in the arithmetic of finance. Excessive taxation is a kind of suicide, whether laid upon objects of necessity, or upon those of luxury; but there is this distinction that, in the latter case, it extinguishes only a portion of the products on which it falls, together with the gratification they are calculated to afford; while, in the former, it extinguishes both production and consumption and the taxpayer into the bargain.

Were it not almost self-evident, this principle might be illustrated by abundant examples of the profit the state derives from a moderate scale of taxation, where it is sufficiently awake to its real interests.

When Turgot, in 1775, reduced to half the market-dues and duties of entry upon fresh sea fish sold in Paris, their product was nowise diminished. The consumption of that article must, therefore, have doubled. The fishermen and dealers must have doubled their concerns and their profits; and since population always increases with increasing production, the number of consumers must have been enlarged; and that of the producers must have been enlarged likewise; for an increase of profits, that is to say of individual revenue, multiplies savings, and thus generates the multiplication of capital and of families; and that very increase of production will, beyond all doubt, augment the product of taxation in other branches; to say nothing of the popularity accruing to the government from the alleviation of the national burthens.

The government agents who farm or administer the collection of the taxes very often abuse their interest and authority to construe all doubtful points of fiscal law in their own favour, and sometimes to create obscurity for the purpose of profiting by it. The effect is precisely the same as if the scale of taxation were raised *pro tanto.* Turgot adopted a contrary course, and made it a rule to lean always to the side of the taxpayer. The public contractors made a great outcry at this innovation, declaring that it was impossible for them to fulfill their engagements, and offering to collect on the government account and risk. The event, however, falsified their predictions by an actual increase of the receipts. The greater lenity in the collection proved so advantageous to production and the consumption consequent upon it that the profits, which had before not exceeded 10,550,000 liv., rose to 60,000,000 liv.; an advance which could hardly be credited if it were not attested by unquestionable evidence.

We are told by Humboldt, to whom we are indebted for a variety of valuable information, that in thirteen years from 1778, during which time Spain adopted a somewhat more liberal system of government in regard to her American dependencies, the increase of the revenue in

Mexico alone amounted to no less a sum than one hundred millions of dollars; and that she drew from that country, during the same period, an addition in the single article of silver, to the amount of 14,500,000 dollars. We may naturally suppose that, in those years of prosperity, there was a corresponding, and rather greater increase, of individual profits; for that is the source whence all public revenue is derived.

A similar course of conduct has invariably been followed by a similar effect; and it is a great satisfaction to a writer of liberal principles to be able to prove by experience that moderation is the best policy.

Upon the same principles, it will be easy to demonstrate in the next place that the taxes least mischievous are:

2. Such as are least attended with those vexatious circumstances that harass the taxpayer without bringing anything into the public exchequer.

It has been held by many that the costs of collection are no very great evil, inasmuch as they are refunded to the community in some other shape. On this head, I must refer my readers to what has been already observed. These costs are no more refunded than the net proceeds of the taxes themselves; because both the one and the other consists in reality, not of the money wherein the taxes are paid, but of the value wherewith the taxpayer produces that money, and the value which the government again procures with it; which latter is destroyed and consumed outright.

The necessities of princes have operated far more effectually than their regard to the public good, to introduce the practice of better order and economy in the financial departments of most European states during the two last centuries, than in former times. The people are generally made to bear as much as they can well stand under; so that every saving in the charge of collection has gone to swell the receipts of the exchequer.

Sully tells us in his Memoirs that for about six millions of dollars brought into the royal treasury in 1598, by means of taxation, individuals were out of pocket about thirty millions of dollars, and assures us that he had with great pains ascertained the fact, however incredible it might appear. Under the administration of Necker, upon a revenue of about one hundred and ten millions of dollars, the charges of collection amounted to no more than ten millions of dollars; yet, under his management, there were two hundred and fifty persons employed in the collection: most of them, however, had other collateral occupations.

The charge was, therefore, about ten and four-fifths per cent; yet this is much higher than the rate at which the business is done in England.

Besides the charge of collection, there are other circumstances that are burthensome to the people without being productive of gain to the public revenue. Lawsuits, imprisonment, and other preventive measures entail additional expense without procuring the smallest increase of revenue. And this addition is sure to fall on the most necessitous class of taxpayers; for the other classes pay without litigation or constraint. Such odious means of enforcing the payment of taxes are precisely the same as demanding of a man twelve dollars because he has not wherewithal to pay ten dollars. Rigour is never necessary to enforce taxation where it presses lightly on the resources of individuals; but when a state is so unfortunate as to be obliged to impose heavy burthens of two evils, the process of levy by distress is preferable to that of personal constraint. For at any rate, by seizing and selling the taxpayer's goods, and thereby raising the arrears of his taxes, he is compelled to pay no more than is due; and the whole of what he does pay goes into the public purse.

On this account it is, that works executed by the public requisition of labour, as the roads were in France under the old régime, are always a mischievous kind of taxation. The time lost by the labourers put in requisition in coming three or four leagues, perhaps, to their work, and that which is always wasted by people who get no pay, and work against their inclination, is all a dead loss to the public, with no return of revenue. Even supposing the work to be well executed, there is often more loss incurred by the interruption of the regular agricultural pursuits than gain made from the compulsory employment that has been substituted. Turgot called upon the surveyors and engineers of the respective provinces for an estimate of the average expense, one year with another, of keeping up old roads and constructing the usual number of new ones, directing them to make their calculations on the most liberal scale. The estimate of the annual expense, made in compliance with his orders, amounted to two millions of dollars for the whole kingdom: Whereas, according to the calculations of Turgot, the old *corvée* system involved a sacrifice to the nation of eight millions of dollars.

Days of rest, enjoined either by law or by custom and usage too powerful to be infringed upon, are another kind of taxation, productive of nothing to the public purse.

3. Such as press impartially on all classes.

Taxation being a burthen, must needs weigh lightest on each individual when it bears upon all alike. When it presses inequitably upon one individual or branch of industry, it is an indirect, as well as a direct, encumbrance; for it prevents the particular branch or the individual from competing on even terms with the rest. An exemption granted to one manufacture has often been the ruin of several others. Favour to one is most commonly injustice to all others.

The partial assessment of taxation is no less prejudicial to the public revenue than unjust to individual interests. Those who are too lightly taxed are not likely to cry out for an increase; and those who are too heavily taxed are seldom regular in their payments. The public revenue suffers in both ways.

It has been questioned whether it be just to tax that portion of revenues which is spent on luxuries more heavily than that spent on objects of necessity. It seems but reasonable to do so; for taxation is a sacrifice to the preservation of society and of social organization which ought not to be purchased by the destruction of individuals. Yet, the privation of absolute necessaries implies the extinction of existence. It would be somewhat bold to maintain that a parent is bound in justice to stint the food or clothing of his child, to furnish his contingent to the ostentatious splendor of a court, or the needless magnificence of public edifices. Where is the benefit of social institutions to an individual whom they rob of an object of positive enjoyment or necessity in actual possession, and offer nothing in return but the participation in a remote and contingent good, which any man in his senses would reject with disdain?

But how is the line to be drawn between necessaries and superfluities? In this discrimination there is the greatest difficulty, for the terms necessaries and superfluities convey no determinate or absolute notion, but always have reference to the time, the place, the age, and the condition of the party; so that, were it laid down as a general rule to tax none but superfluities, there would be no knowing where to begin and where to stop. All that we certainly know is that the income of a person or a family may be so confined, as barely to suffice for existence; and may be augmented from that minimum upwards by imperceptible gradation, till it embrace every gratification of sense, of luxury, or of vanity; each successive gratification being one step further removed from the limits of strict necessity, till at last the extreme of frivolity and caprice is arrived at; so that, if it be desired to tax individual income in such manner as to press lighter in proportion as that income approaches to the confines of bare necessity, taxation must not only be equitably apportioned, but must press on revenue with progressive gravity.

In fact, supposing taxation to be exactly proportionate to individual income, a tax of ten per cent for instance, a family possessed of sixty thousand dollars per annum would pay six thousand dollars in taxes, leaving a clear residue of fifty-four thousand dollars for the family expenditure. With such an expenditure, the family could not only live in abundance, but could still enjoy a vast number of gratifications by no means essential to happiness. Whereas another family, with an income of sixty dollars, reduced by taxation to fifty-four dollars per annum, would, with our present habits of life and ways of thinking, be stinted in the bare necessaries of subsistence. Thus, a tax merely proportionate to individual income would be far from equitable; and this is probably what Smith meant by declaring it reasonable that the rich man should contribute to the public expenses, not merely in proportion to the amount of his revenue, but even somewhat more. For my part, I have no hesitation in going further and saying that taxation cannot be equitable unless its ratio is progressive.

4. Such as are least injurious to reproduction.

Of the values whereof taxation deprives individuals, a great part would, undoubtedly, if left at the disposal of the individuals themselves, have gone to the satisfaction of their wants and appetites; but some part would have been laid by, and have gone to the further accumulation of productive capital. Thus, all taxation may be said to injure reproduction inasmuch as it prevents the accumulation of productive capital.

This effect is more direct and serious whenever the taxpayer is obliged to withdraw a part of the capital already embarked for the purpose of enabling him to pay the tax; which case, as Sismondi has shrewdly observed, resembles the exaction of a tithe upon grain at seed-time, instead of harvest-time. Of this kind is the tax on legacies and successions. An heir, succeeding to a property of twenty dollars and called upon for a tax of five per cent upon it, will pay it not out of his ordinary income, burthened as it is already with the ordinary taxes, but out of the inheritance, which is thereby reduced to nineteen thousand dollars. Wherefore, if it happen to be a vested capital of twenty thousand dollars and be reduced by the tax to nineteen thousand dollars, the national capital will be diminished to the amount of the one thousand dollars thus diverted into the public exchequer.

It is the same with all taxes upon the transfer of property. The owner of land worth twenty thousand dollars will get but nineteen thousand dollars for it, if the purchaser be saddled with a tax of five per cent. The seller will have a disposable capital of nineteen thousand dollars only, in lieu of land worth twenty thousand dollars; and the national capital will sustain a loss of the difference. Should the purchaser be so bad an arithmetician as to pay the full value of the land, without allowing for the tax, he will sacrifice a capital of twenty-one thousand dollars in the purchase of value to the amount of but twenty thousand dollars? In either case, the loss to the national capital will be the same; although in the latter, it will fall upon the purchaser instead of the seller.

Taxes, upon transfer, besides the mischief of pressing upon capital, are a clog to the circulation of property. But has the public any interest in its free circulation? So long as the object is in existence, is it not as well placed in one hand as in another? Certainly not. The public has a perpetual interest in the utmost possible freedom of its circulation; because by that means it is most likely to get into the hands of those who can make the most of it. Why does one man sell his land? But because he thinks he can lay out the value to more advantage in some channel of productive industry. And why does another buy it? But because he wishes to invest a capital that is lying idle, or less productively vested; or because he thinks it capable of improvement. The transfer tends to augment the national income because it tends to augment the income of the two contracting parties. If they be deterred by the expenses of the transfer, those expenses will have prevented this probable increase of the national income.

Such taxes, however, as encroach upon the productive capital of the community, and consequently abridge the demand for labour and the profits of industry within the community, possess, in a very high degree, one quality which that distinguished political economist, Arthur Young, has pronounced to be an essential requisite in taxation, namely, the facility and cheapness of collection. Since taxation presents at best but a choice of evils, a nation, heavily burthened, will probably do well in submitting to a moderate impost upon capital.

Taxes upon law proceedings and, generally, all that is paid to law officers and agents are taxes upon capital. For litigation is not proportionate to the income of the suitors, but to accident, to the complexity of family interests, and to the imperfections of the law itself.

Forfeitures are equally a tax on capital.

The influence of taxation upon production is not confined to the circumstance of diminishing one of its sources, that is to say, capital; it operates besides in the nature of a penalty, inflicted upon certain branches of production and consumption. Patents, licenses to follow any specified calling and, generally, all taxes that bear directly upon industry are liable to this objection; but when moderate in their ratio, industry will contrive to surmount such obstacles without much difficulty.

Nor is industry affected only by taxes bearing directly upon it; it is indirectly affected by such also, as bear upon the consumption of the articles it has to work upon.

The products consumed in reproduction are, for the most part, those of primary necessity; and taxes that discourage such products must be injurious to reproduction. This is more especially the case in respect to those raw materials of manufacture, which can only be consumed reproductively. An excessive duty upon cotton checks the production of all articles wherein that substance is worked up.

Brazil is a country abounding in animal productions that might be cured and exported if they were allowed to be salted. Its fisheries are very productive, and cattle so abundant that they are killed merely for the sake of the hide. Indeed, it is thence that our tanneries in Europe are in a great measure supplied. But the salt duties prevent the export of either fish or meat; and thus, for the sake of a revenue of about two hundred thousand dollars perhaps, incalculable mischief is done to the productive powers of the country, as well as to the public revenue which they might be made to yield.

In like manner, as taxation operates in the nature of a penalty to discourage reproductive consumption, it may be employed to check consumption of an unproductive kind; in which case it has the two-fold advantage of subtracting no value from reproductive investment, and of rescuing values from unproductive consumption to be employed in a manner more beneficial to the community. This is the advantage of all taxes upon luxuries.

When sums levied by taxation upon capital, instead of being simply expended by the government, are laid out upon productive objects; or, when individuals contrive to make good the deficiency out of their private savings, the positive mischief of taxation is then balanced by a counteracting benefit. The proceeds of taxation are reproductively vested when laid out in improving the internal communications, constructing harbors, or other such works of utility. Governments sometimes employ a part of the revenue thus realized in adventures of industry.

Colbert did so, when he made advances to the manufacturers of Lyons. The governments of Hamburgh, and of some other places in Germany, were in the habit of embarking their revenues in productive undertakings; and it is said that the authorities of Berne were in the habit of so employing a part of its revenues every year; but such instances are of very rare occurrence.

5. Such as are rather favourable than otherwise to the national morality; that is to say, to the prevalence of habits, useful and beneficial to society.

Taxation influences the habits of a nation in the same way as it operates upon its production and consumption, that is, by imposing a pecuniary penalty upon specified acts; and it is, moreover, possessed of the grand requisites to render punishment effectual; namely moderation and difficulty of evasion. Without reference, therefore, to the purposes of finance and revenue it is a powerful engine in the hands of government, for either corrupting or reforming the national morals, and may be directed to the promotion of idleness or industry, extravagance, or economy.

The tax of five per cent upon all lands devoted to productive husbandry, and the exemption of pleasure-grounds which existed in France before the revolution, operated, of course, as a premium upon luxury, and a penalty upon agricultural enterprise.

The tax of one per cent upon the redemption of ground-rents and rent-charges was virtually a penalty upon an act, equally advantageous to the parties and to the community at large; a fine upon the meritorious exertions of prudent land owners to pay off their encumbrances.

The law of Napoleon, exacting from each scholar educated in a private academy, a specified payment into the chests of the public universities, operated as a penalty upon that mode of education, which alone can soften national manners and fully develop the faculties of the human mind.

When a government derives a profit from the licensing of lotteries and gambling-houses, what does it else but offer a premium to a vice most fatal to domestic happiness, and destructive of national prosperity? How disgraceful is it to see a government thus acting as the pander of irregular desires, and imitating the fraudulent conduct it punishes in others, by holding out to want and avarice the bait of hollow and deceitful chance!

On the contrary, taxes that check and confine the excesses of vanity and vice, besides yielding a revenue to the state, operate as a means of prevention. Humboldt mentions a tax upon cock-fighting which yields to the Mexican government forty-five thousand dollars per annum, and has the further advantage of checking that cruel and barbarous diversion.

Exorbitant or inequitable taxation promotes fraud, falsehood, and perjury. Well-meaning persons are presented with the distressing alternative of violating truth or sacrificing their interests in favour of less scrupulous fellow citizens. They cannot but feel involuntary disgust at seeing acts, in themselves innocent, and sometimes even useful and meritorious, branded with the name and subjected to all the consequences of criminality.

These are the principal rules by which present or future taxation must be weighed with a view to the public prosperity. After these general remarks, which are applicable to taxation in all its branches, it may be useful to examine the various modes of assessment; in other words, the methods adopted for procuring money from the subject; as well as to inquire upon what classes of the community the burthen principally falls.

Section II: Of the Different Modes of Assessment, and the Classes they Press upon Respectively

Taxation, as we have seen above, is a requisition by the government upon its subjects for a portion of their products, or of their value. It is the business of the political economist to explain the effects resulting from the nature of the products put in requisition, and from the mode of apportioning the burthen, as well as upon whom the burthen of the charge really falls, since it must inevitably fall upon someone or other. The application of the above principles in a few specific instances will show how they may be applied in all others.

The public authority levies the values taken in the way of taxation, sometimes in the shape of money, sometimes in kind, according to its own wants or the ability of the taxpayer. In whatever shape it is paid, the actual contribution of the taxpayer is always of the value of the article he gives. If the government, wanting or pretending to want corn, or leather, or woolens, makes a requisition of those articles upon the taxpayer and obliges him to furnish them in kind, the tax paid amounts exactly to what the payer has expended in procuring those articles, or what he could have sold them for if the government had not taken them from him. This is the only way of ascertaining the amount of the tax, whatever price or rate the government may set upon it in the plenitude of its power.

So, likewise, the charges of collection, in whatever shape they may appear, are always an aggravation of the assessment, whether they accrue to the profit of the state or not. If the taxpayer be obliged to lose his time, or transport his goods for the purpose of paying the tax, the whole of the time lost, or expense of transport, is an aggravation of the tax.

Among the contributions that a government exacts from its subjects should likewise be comprised all the expenses which its political conduct may bring upon the nation. Thus, in estimating the expenses of war, we must include the value of equipment and pocket-money with which the military are supplied by themselves or their families; the value of the time lost by the militia; the sums paid for exemption and substitutes; the full charge of quarters for the troops; the pillage and destruction they may be guilty of; the presents and attentions lavished on them by friends or countrymen on their return; to all which must be added, the alms extorted from pity and compassion by the misery consequent upon such misrule. For, in fact, none of these values need have been taken from the members of the community under a better system of government. And although none of them have gone into the treasury of the monarch, yet have they been paid by the people and their amount is as completely lost as if they had contributed to the happiness of the human species.

Hence, we may form some notion of the extent of the national sacrifices. But, from what source are they drawn? Doubtless, either from the annual product of the national industry, land, and capital; that is to say, from the national revenue; or from the values previously saved and accumulated; that is to say, from the national capital.

When taxation is moderate, the subject cannot only pay his taxes wholly out of his revenue, but will not be altogether disabled from besides saving some part of that revenue; and although some of the taxpayers may be obliged to trench upon their capital for the payment of their taxes, the loss to the general stock is amply reimbursed by the savings, which this happy state of affairs allows others to effect.

But it is far otherwise, when military despotism or usurped authority extorts excessive contributions. Great part of the taxes is then taken from the vested and accumulated capital; and if the country be long subjected to its domination, the revenues of each successive year are progressively reduced, and the ruin and depopulation of the country will recoil upon its rulers unless their downfall be accelerated by their own folly and excesses.

Under the protecting influence of just and regular government, on the contrary, there is a progressive annual enlargement of the profits and revenues on which taxation is to be levied; and that taxation, without any alteration of its ratio, gradually becomes more productive by the mere multiplication of taxable products.

Nor is the government more deeply interested in moderating the ratio of taxation than its impartial assessment upon every class of individual revenue, and its equal pressure upon all. In fact, when revenue is partially affected, taxation sooner reaches the extreme limits of the ability of some classes, while others are scarcely touched at all: It becomes vexatious and destructive before it arrives at the highest practical ratio. The burthen is galling, not because of its weight, but because it does not rest upon all shoulders alike.

The different methods employed to reach individual revenues may be classed under two grand divisions—direct and indirect taxation; the former is the absolute demand of a specific portion of an individual's real or supposed revenue; the latter, a demand of a specific sum on each act of consumption of certain specified objects to which that income may be applied.

In neither case is the real subject of taxation that commodity on which the estimate is made, and which forms the groundwork of the demand for the tax; or of necessity that value, whereof a part is taken by the state; individual revenue is the only real subject of taxation; and the specific commodity is selected only as a more or less effective means of discovering and attacking that revenue. If individual honesty could in every case be relied on, the matter would be simple enough; all that would be requisite would be to ask each person the amount of his annual profits, that is to say, his annual revenue. The contingent of each would be readily settled, and one tax only necessary which would be at the same time the most equitable, and the cheapest in the collection. This was the method adopted at Hamburgh, before that city fell into misfortune; but it can never be practiced, except in a republic of small extent, and very moderately taxed.

As a means of assessing direct taxation proportionately to the respective revenues of the taxpayers, governments sometimes compel the production of leases by landlords, or, where there is no lease, set a value on the land and demand a certain proportion of that value from the proprietor; this is called a land-tax. Sometimes they estimate the revenue by the rent of the habitation and the number of servants, horses, and carriages kept, and make the assessment accordingly. This is called, in France, the tax on moveables. Sometimes they calculate the profits of each person's profession or calling by the extent of the population and district where it is followed. This is called, in France, the license tax. All these different modes of assessment are expedients of direct taxation.

In the assessment of indirect taxation, and such as is intended to bear upon specific classes of consumption, the object itself is alone attended to, without regard to the party who may incur the charge. Sometimes a portion of the value of the specific product is demanded at the time of production; as in France, in the article of salt. Sometimes the demand is made on entry, either into the state, as in the duties of import; or into the towns only, as in the duties of entry. Sometimes a tax is demanded of the consumer at the moment of transfer to him from the last producer; as in the case of the stamp duty in England, and the duty on theatrical tickets in France. Sometimes the government requires a commodity to bear a particular mark for which it makes a charge; as in the case of the assay-mark of silver, and stamp on newspapers. Sometimes it monopolizes the manufacture of a particular article, or the performance of a particular kind of business; as in the monopoly of tobacco, and the postage of letters. Sometimes, instead of charging the commodity itself, it charges the payment of its price; as in the case of stamps on receipts and mercantile paper. All these are different ways of raising a revenue by indirect taxation; for the demand is not made on any person in particular, but attaches upon the product or article taxed.

It may easily be conceived that a class of revenue which may escape one of these taxes will be affected by another; and that the multiplicity of the forms of taxation gives a great approximation to its equal distribution; provided always that all are kept within the bounds of moderation.

Every one of these modes of assessment has peculiar advantages and peculiar disadvantages besides the general evil of all taxation, that of appropriating a part of the products of the community to purposes little conducive to its happiness and reproductive powers. Direct taxation, for instance, is cheap in the collection; but, on the other hand, it is paid with reluctance, and must be enforced with considerable harshness and rigour. Besides, it bears very inequitably upon the individual. A rich merchant, charged only one hundred and twenty dollars for his license, makes an annual profit, perhaps, of twenty thousand dollars;

while the retailer, who can scarcely be supposed to make more than three hundred dollars, is charged for his license twenty dollars, which is the lowest rate. The revenue of the landholder is already affected by the land-tax, before it is further reduced by the tax on moveables; while the capitalist is subjected to the latter burthen only.

Indirect taxation has the recommendation of being levyable with more ease, and with less apparent vexation or hardship. All taxes are paid with reluctance because the equivalent to be expected for them, that is, the security afforded by good order and government, is a negative benefit which does not immediately interest individuals; for the benefit afforded consists rather in prevention of ill, than in the diffusion of good. But the buyer of the taxed commodity does not suspect himself to be paying for the protection of government, which probably he cares very little about; but merely for the commodity itself, which is an object of his urgent desire, although, in fact, that price is aggravated by the tax. The inducement to consume is strong enough to include the demand of the government; and he readily parts with a value that procures an immediate gratification.

It is this circumstance that makes such taxes appear to be voluntary. And, indeed, so much so were they considered by the United States before their emancipation that, although the right of the British Parliament to tax America without her consent was stoutly denied, yet she was ready to acknowledge the right of imposing taxes upon consumption, which everybody could evade if he pleased by abstaining from the articles taxed. Personal taxes are viewed in a different light, and have more of the character of ostensible spoliation.

Indirect taxation is levied piecemeal, and paid by individuals according to their respective ability at the moment. It involves none of the perplexity of separate assessments on each province, department, or individual; or of the inquisitorial inspection into private circumstances; nor does it make one person suffer for the default of another. The inconvenience of appeals and private animosities, as well as of levy by distress or imprisonment, is avoided altogether.

Another advantage of indirect taxation is that it enables the government to bias the different classes of consumption; favouring such as promote the public prosperity, as does reproductive consumption of all kinds; and checking such as tend to public impoverishment, as do all kinds of unproductive consumption; discouraging the costly and insipid indulgences of the wealthy, and promoting the simpler and cheaper enjoyments of the poor and industrious.

It has been objected to indirect taxation, that it entails a heavy expense of collection and management, and a large establishment of officers, clerks, directors, and subordinate agents; but it is observable that these charges may be vastly reduced by good administration. The excise and stamp-duties in England cost but three and a fourth per cent in the collection in the year 1799. There are few classes of direct taxation that are managed so economically in France.

It has been further objected that its product is uncertain and fluctuating; whereas, the public exigencies require a regular and certain supply: But there has never been any lack of bidders, whenever such taxes have been let out to farm; and experience has shown that the product of every class of taxation may always be nearly estimated and safely reckoned upon, except in very rare and extraordinary emergencies. Besides, taxes on consumption are necessarily various; so that the deficit of one is covered by the surplus of another.

Indirect taxation is, however, an incentive to fraud, and obliges governments to brand with the character of guilt, actions that are innocent in their nature; and, consequently, to resort to a distressing severity of punishment. But this mischief is never considerable until taxation has grown excessive, so as to make the temptation to fraud counterbalance the danger incurred. All excess of taxation is attended with this evil; that, without enlarging the receipts of the public purse, it multiplies the sufferings of the population.

It may be observed that consumption and, consequently, individual revenue, are unequally affected by indirect, as well as by direct, taxation; for the private consumption of many articles is not proportionate to the revenue of the consumer. The possessor of an annual revenue of twenty thousand dollars does not consume in the year a hundred times as much salt as the possessor of a revenue of two hundred dollars only. But this inequality may be obviated by the variety of taxes on consumption. Moreover, it is to be recollected that such taxes fall upon incomes already charged with the taxes on land and on moveables. A person whose whole income is derived from land in respect to which he is taxed in the first instance, pays on the same income a second tax under the head of moveables; and a third on every taxed article that he buys and consumes.

Although all these kinds of taxes be paid in the outset by the persons of whom they are demanded by the public authority, it would be wrong to suppose that they always ultimately fall on the original payers, who, in many instances, are not the parties really charged, but merely advance the tax in the first instance and contrive to get indemnified wholly or partially by the consumers of their own peculiar products. But the rate of indemnity is infinitely diversified by the respective circumstances of the individuals.

Of this diversity, we may form some notion by the consideration of the following general facts:

When the taxation of the producers of a specific commodity operates to raise its price, part of the tax is paid by the consumers of the commodity. If its price be nowise raised, it falls wholly upon the producers. If the commodity, instead of being thereby advanced in price, is deteriorated in quality, a portion of the tax at least must fall upon the consumer; for a purchase of inferior quality at equal price is equivalent to a purchase of equal quality and superior price.

Every addition to price must needs reduce the number of those possessed of the ability to purchase; or, at any rate, must diminish the extent of that ability. There is much less salt consumed when it sells for three cents than when it sells for one cent per pound. Now, the ratio of the demand to the means of production being lowered, productive agency in this department is worse paid; that is to say, the master manufacturer of salt, and all the subordinate agents and labourers, together with the capitalist that supplies the funds, and the landlord of the premises where the concern is carried on, must be content with smaller profits because their product is less in demand. The productive classes, indeed, naturally strive to indemnify themselves to the amount of the tax; but, they can never succeed to the full extent because the intrinsic value of the commodity that, I mean, which goes to pay the charges of production, is really diminished. So that, in fact, the tax upon an article never raises its total price by the full amount of the tax; because to do so, the total demand must remain the same; which it never can do. Wherefore, in such cases the tax falls partly upon those who still continue to consume, notwithstanding the increase of price, and partly upon the producers who raise a less product and find that, in consequence of the reduced demand, they really obtain less on the sale when the tax comes to be deducted. The public revenue gains the whole excess of price to the consumer, and the whole of the profit which the produce is thus compelled to resign. The effect is analogous to that of gunpowder, which at the same time propels the bullet and makes the piece recoil.

By laying a tax upon the consumption of woolens, their consumption is reduced, and the revenue of the wool-grower suffers in consequence. It is true, he may take to a different kind of cultivation, but we may fairly suppose that, under all the circumstances of soil and situation, the rearing of sheep was the most profitable kind of culture; otherwise, he would not have chosen it. A change in the mode of cultivation must, therefore, involve a loss of revenue. But the clothier and the capitalist will each be subjected to a portion of the loss resulting from the tax.

Each concurrent producer is affected by a tax on an article of consumption in proportion only to the share he may have in raising the product taxed.

When the owner of the soil furnishes the greatest part of the value of a product, as he does in respect to products consumed nearly in the primary state, he it is that bears the greatest part of that portion of the tax which falls on the producers. A duty of entry upon the wine imported into the towns falls heavily upon the wine-grower; but an exorbitant excise upon lace will affect the flax-grower in a degree hardly perceptible; whereas, all the other producers, the dealers, the operative and speculative manufacturers who create the far greater proportion of the value of the lace will suffer very severely.

When the value of a product is partly of foreign, and partly of domestic creation, the domestic producers bear nearly the whole burthen of the tax. A tax upon cottons in France will reduce the earnings of her cotton manufacturers by lowering the demand for their product; thus, part of the tax will fall on them. But the wages of the productive agency of the cotton-growers in America will be very little affected indeed, unless there be a concurrence of other circumstances. In fact, the tax would reduce the consumption in France ten per cent, perhaps, and demand in America one per cent only, if the demand from France were but a tenth of the general demand upon America.

The taxation of an object of consumption, if it be one of primary necessity, operates upon the price of almost all other products, and consequently falls upon the revenues of all the other consumers. An *octroi* upon meat, corn, and fuel, at their entry into a town, enhances the price of everything manufactured in it; while a tax upon the tobacco there consumed makes no other commodity dearer; the producers and consumers of tobacco alone are affected; and for a very plain reason; the producer who indulges in superfluities has to maintain a competition with another, who abstains from them; but, if he pays a tax upon necessaries, he need fear no competition; for his neighbours will be all in the same predicament.

The direct taxation of the productive classes must, *à fortiori,* affect the consumers of their products, but can never raise the prices of those products so much as completely to indemnify the producer; because, as I have repeatedly explained, the increased price abridges the demand, and the contraction of the demand reduces the profits of all the productive agency that has been exerted in the supply.

Of the concurrent producers of a specific product, some can more easily evade the effect of the tax than others. The capitalist, whose capital is not absolutely vested and sunk in a particular business, may withdraw it and transfer it elsewhere from a concern that yields him a reduced interest, or has become more hazardous. The adventurer or master manufacturer may, in many cases, liquidate his account and transfer his labour and intelligence to some other quarter. Not so the land owner and proprietor of fixed capital. An acre of vineyard or corn-land will only produce a given quantity of corn or wine, whatever be the ratio of taxation; which may take half or even three-fourths of the net produce, or rent as it is called, and yet the land be tilled for the sake of the remaining half or fourth. The rent, that is to say, the portion assigned to the proprietor, will be reduced, and that is all. The reason will be manifest to anyone who considers that in the case supposed the land continues to raise and supply the market with the same amount of produce as before; while on the other hand, the motives in which the demand originates remain just as they were. If, then, the intensity of supply and demand must both remain the same in spite of any increase or diminution of the ratio of the direct taxation upon the land, the price of the product supplied will likewise remain unchanged, and nothing but a change of price can saddle the consumer with any portion whatever of that taxation.

Nor can the proprietor evade the tax even by the sale of the estate; for the price or purchase money will be calculated according to the revenue which may be left him by taxation. The purchaser makes his estimate according to the net revenue, charges, and taxes deducted. If the ordinary interest on such investments of capital be five per cent, an estate that before would have sold for twenty thousand dollars will fetch but sixteen thousand dollars when it comes to be charged with an annual tax of two hundred dollars; for its actual product to the proprietor will not exceed eight hundred dollars. The effect is precisely the same as if the government were to appropriate to itself a fifth of the land in the country; which would make no difference at all to the consumers of its produce.

But property in dwelling-houses is otherwise circumstanced; a tax upon the ownership raises the rents; for a house, or rather the satisfaction it yields to the occupier, is a product of manufacture and not of land; and the high rate of house rent reduces the production and consumption of houses in the like manner as of cloth or any other manufactured commodity. Builders, finding their profits reduced, will build less; and consumers, finding the accommodation dearer, will content themselves with inferior lodging.

From all those circumstances, we may judge of the temerity of asserting as a general maxim that taxation falls exclusively upon any specific class or classes of the community. It always falls upon those who can find no means of evasion; for every one naturally tries to shift the burthen off his own shoulders if possible; but the ability to evade it is infinitely varied, according to the various forms of assessment and the position of each individual in the social system. Nay, more; it varies at different times even in the same channel of production. When a commodity is in great request, the holder will not part with the possession unless indemnified for all his advances of which the tax he has paid is a part: He will take nothing short of a full and complete indemnity. But, if any unlooked-for occurrence should happen to lower the demand for his product, he will be glad enough to take the tax upon himself for the sake of quickening the sale. There are few things so unsteady and variable as the ratio of the pressure of taxation upon each respective class of the community. Those writers who have maintained that it bears upon any one or more classes in particular, or in any fixed or certain proportion, have found their theory contradicted by experience at every turn.

Furthermore, the effects I have been describing, and which are equally consonant to experience and to reason, are uniform in their operation and of equal duration with the causes in which they originate. The owner of land will never be able to saddle the consumers of its produce with any part of his land-tax; not so the manufacturer. A manufactured commodity will invariably feel a diminution in its consumption in consequence of the price being raised by taxation, supposing other circumstances to be stationary; and its production will be a less profitable occupation. A person, who is neither producer nor consumer of an object of luxury, will never bear any portion whatever of the tax that may be laid upon it.—What, then, must we think of a proposition, unfortunately sanctioned by the approbation of an illustrious body, that has too much neglected this branch of science, namely, that it is of little importance whether a tax press upon one branch of revenue or another, provided it be of long standing; because every tax in the end affects every class of revenue, in like manner, as bleeding in the arm reduces the circulating blood of the whole human frame. The object of comparison has no analogy whatever with taxation. Social wealth is not a fluid, tending constantly to find a level. It rather resembles the vegetable creation, which admits of the loss of a limb without the destruction of the trunk, and in which the loss is more to be lamented, if the branch be productive, than if it be barren.—But the tree will bear cutting and hacking in every part before it becomes barren all over, or necessarily falls into decay. This is a far more apposite case; but neither will do to reason upon. Comparisons are not proofs, but mere illustrations, tending to make that intelligible which can be made out in proof without their assistance.

When speaking of taxes upon products, which I have sometimes called taxes upon consumption, although not paid entirely in all cases by the consumer, I have hitherto made no mention of the particular stage of production at which the tax may be demanded, or of the consequence of this particular circumstance, which deserves a little of our attention.

Products increase in value progressively as they pass through the hands of the different concurrent producers; and even the most simple undergo a variety of modifications before they arrive at a fit state for consumption. Wherefore, a tax does not take the proportion of the value of a product which it professes unless it be levied at the precise moment when it has arrived at the full value and has undergone all the productive modifications. If a tax be imposed on the raw material in the outset, proportioned not to its then value, but to the value it is about to receive, the producer, in whose hands it happens to be, is obliged to advance a tax out of proportion to the value in hand; which advance, besides being highly inconvenient to himself, is refunded with equal inconvenience by every successive producer till it reach the hands of the last, who is in turn but partially indemnified by the consumer. And there is this further mischief in such an advance of tax; that it prevents the class of industry which is called upon to make it from being originally set in motion without a larger capital than the nature of the business requires; and that the additional interest of the capital which must be paid, part by the consumers, and part by the producers, is so much additional taxation, without any addition of public revenue.

Thus, both theory and experience lead to the conclusion precisely opposite to that drawn by the sect of economists; and show that portion of the tax, which presses upon the consumer's revenue, to be always the more burthensome the earlier it is levied in the process of production.

Direct and personal taxes which operate to raise the price of necessaries, or such as fall immediately upon necessaries, are liable to this inconvenience in the highest degree: For they oblige each producer to advance the personal tax on all the producers that have preceded him, so that the same amount of capital will set in motion a smaller amount of industry; and the taxpayers pay the tax, *plus* a compound interest upon it, yielding no benefit to the exchequer.

Nor is this mere theory: The neglect of these principles has occasioned may serious practical errors; like that of the Constituent Assembly of France which carried to excess the system of direct taxation, especially upon land; being misled by the prevailing and fashionable doctrine of the economists;—that land is the source of all wealth, the agriculturist the only productive labourer, and France naturally and essentially an agricultural country.

It seems to me that, in the present stage of political economy, the principles of taxation will be more correctly laid down as follows:

Taxation is the taking a portion of the general product of the community which never returns to the community in the channel of consumption.

It takes from the community over and above the values actually brought into the exchequer, the charges of collection, and the personal trouble it entails; together with all those values of which it obstructs the creation.

The privation resulting from taxation, whether voluntary or compulsory, affects the taxpayer in his quality of producer whenever it operates to curtail his profits; that is to say, his income or revenue; and affects him in his character of consumer, whenever it increases his expenditure, by raising the prices of products.

And, since an increase of expenditure is precisely the same thing as a diminution of revenue, whatever is taken by taxation may be said to be so much deducted from the revenues of the community.

In a great majority of cases, the taxpayer is affected by taxation in both his characters, of producer and consumer; and, when he cannot manage to pay the public burthens out of his revenue, along with his personal consumption, he must encroach upon his capital. When this encroachment of one person is not counterbalanced by the savings of another, the wealth of the community must gradually decline.

The individual actually paying the tax to the tax-gatherer is not always the party really charged with it, at least, not the party charged with the whole that is paid. He frequently does no more than advance the tax, either wholly or partially; being afterwards reimbursed by the other classes of the community, in a very complicated way, and perhaps after a vast variety of intermediate operations; so that a great many persons are paying portions of the tax at a time when probably they least suspect it, either in the shape of the advanced price of commodities, or of personal loss, which they feel but cannot account for.

The individuals, on whose revenues the tax ultimately falls, are the real taxpayers, and contribute value greatly exceeding the sum that is brought into the exchequer, even with the addition of the charges of collection. The misconduct of the government in the matter of taxation is proportioned to this excess of the payment above the receipt.

A country heavily taxed may be considered in the same light as one labouring under natural impediments to production. With a heavy charge of production, it raises a very small product. Personal exertion, capital, and the productive agency of land are all but poorly recompensed; and more is expended in earning a less profit.

It is worthwhile on this head to recur to the principles explained in the preceding book, when describing the difference between positive and relative dearness. High price resulting from taxation is positive dearness: It indicates a smaller product raised by the efforts of a larger amount of productive agency. Besides which, taxation generally occasions a contemporary advance of commodities in comparison with silver; that is to say, raises their money price: And for this reason; because specie is not an annual, regenerative product, like those that are swallowed up by taxation. Government is not a consumer of specie, except when it happens to export it for the payment of its armies or foreign subsidies: It refunds in the purchases it makes all the specie it obtains by taxation; but the value levied is never refunded. Wherefore, since taxation paralyzes one part of the sources of production, and effects the rapid destruction of the product of the other, when its ratio is excessive, it must gradually render products more scarce in proportion to the specie which is not varied in quantity by the operation. Now, whenever the commodities to be circulated become fewer in proportion to the specie that is to circulate them, their relative value to the specie must rise; the same money will purchase a smaller quantity of products.

It might be supposed that such a superabundance of gold and silver specie ought to operate in exoneration of the public: Yet it cannot have that effect; for however plentiful it may be in proportion to other commodities, still individuals can only obtain it by giving their own products in exchange, and the raising of those products has become more difficult and more costly.

Besides, when money prices grow high, and specie is consequently reduced in relative value, it gradually takes its departure and becomes scarcer, like all other commodities: And thus a country, burthened with a taxation too heavy for its productive powers, is first drained of its commodities, and next of its specie; till it gradually reaches the extreme of penury and depopulation.

The careful study of these principles will give some insight into the mode in which the annual and really monstrous expenditure of national governments, in modern times, has habituated the subject to severer toil and exertion, without which it would be impossible that, after providing for the subsistence, comfort, and pleasures of himself and family, according to the habits of the time and place, he should be able to meet the consumption of the state, and the collateral waste and destruction it occasions; the amount of which it is impossible to ascertain, though in the larger states it is confessedly enormous.

This very profusion, though it proves the vices and defects of the political system and organization, has been attended with one advantage at any rate; it has operated to stimulate the approximation to perfection in the art of production by obliging mankind to turn the natural agents to better account. In this point of view, taxation has certainly helped to develop and enlarge the human faculties; so that, when the progress of political science shall limit taxation to the supply of real public wants only, the improvements in the art of production will prove a vast accession to human happiness. But, should the abuses and complexity of the political system lead to the prevalence, extension, increase, and consolidation of oppressive and disproportionate taxation, it is much to be feared that it may plunge again into barbarism those nations, whose productive powers are now the most astonishing; and the condition of the labouring classes, who are always the bulk of the community, may in such nations present a picture of drudgery so incessant and toilsome, as to make them cast a wistful eye upon the liberty of savage existence; which, though it offer no prospect of domestic comfort, at least promises emancipation from perpetual exertion to supply the prodigality of a public expenditure, yielding to them no satisfaction, and perhaps even operating to their prejudice.

Section III: Of Taxation in Kind

Taxation in kind is the specific and immediate appropriation of a portion of the gross product to the public service.

It has this advantage, of calling on the producer only for what he has actually in hand, in the identical shape which it happens to be under. Belgium, after its conquest by France, found itself at times unable to pay its taxes, in spite of abundant crops; the war, and the prohibition of exportation, obstructed the sale of its produce, which the government enforced by demanding payment in money; whereas, the taxes might have been collected without difficulty, had the government been content to take payment in kind.

It has the further advantage of making it equally the interest of government and of the farmer to obtain plentiful crops and improve the national agriculture. The levying of taxes in kind in China was probably the origin of the peculiar encouragement, bestowed by its government upon the agricultural branch of production. But, why favour one branch when all are equally entitled to protection, because all contribute to bear the public burthens? And why has not government an equal interest in supporting the other branches, which it takes the trouble of extinguishing?

It has likewise the advantage of excluding all exaction and injustice in the collection; the individual, when he gathers in his harvest, knows exactly what he has to pay; and the state knows what it has to receive.

This tax, which might appear at first sight to be of all others the most equitable, is nevertheless of all others the most inequitable; for it makes no allowance for the advances made in the course of production, but is taken upon the gross, instead of the net, product. Take two farmers in different branches of cultivation; the one farming tillage-land of moderate quality; his expenses of cultivation, amounting one year with another, say to sixteen hundred dollars, and the gross product of his farm, say to twenty-four hundred dollars, so as to yield him a net product of eight hundred dollars only; the other farming pasturage or woodland, yielding a gross product of precisely the same amount of twenty-four hundred dollars: With an expense of cultivation, amounting, perhaps, to but four hundred dollars, leaving him a net product, one year with another, of two thousand dollars. Suppose a tax in kind to be imposed in the ratio of one-twelfth of the annual product of land of all descriptions indiscriminately. The former will have to pay in sheaves of corn to the amount of two hundred dollars; the latter will pay, in cattle or in wood, an equal value of two hundred dollars. What is the result? The one will have paid the fourth part of a net revenue of eight hundred dollars; the other but a tenth part of a net revenue of two thousand dollars.

The revenue that each person has for his own share is the net residue only after replacing the capital he has embarked, whatever may be its amount. Is the gross amount of the sales he effects in the year the annual income of the merchant? Certainly not; all the income he gets is the surplus of his receipts above his advances; on this surplus alone can he pay taxes, without ruin to his concerns.

The ecclesiastical tithe levied in France under the old system was liable to this inconvenience in part only. It attached neither upon meadow, nor wood-land, nor kitchen-ground, nor many other kinds of cultivation; and in some places was an eighteenth, in others a fifteenth or a tenth of the gross product; so that the real was corrected by the apparent inequality.

The marechal de Vauban, in his work entitled, *Dixime Royale,* a book replete with just views, and well worth the study of those who manage national finances, proposes a tax of a twentieth of the product of the land, which, in times of great emergency, might be raised to a tenth. But this proposition was made as a substitute for a still more inequitable system: Namely, the saddling of the lands of the commonalty with the whole tax, and altogether exempting the lands of the nobles and clergy. The public-spirited writer, who had occasion, in his character of engineer, to become personally acquainted with every part of France, speaks most feelingly of the hardships resulting from the land-tax of those days. And there is no doubt that the adoption of his plan at that time would have been a vast relief to the country. But it was disregarded. Why? Because every courtier had an interest to resist it; and this fine country was left to flounder through its distresses. The consequence was a heavier loss of population from famine than from the sword in the war of the Spanish succession.

The difficulty and expense of collection, together with the abuses to which it is liable, are another objection to taxation in kind. The immense number of agents must open a fine field for peculation. The government may be imposed upon, in respect to the amount collected, upon the subsequent sale and disposal, in respect to the quantity damaged, as well as in the charges of storing, preservation and carriage. If the tax be farmed to contractors, the profits and expenses of numberless farmers and contractors must all fall upon the public. The prosecution of the farmers and contractors would require the active vigilance of administration. "A gentleman of great fortune,: says Smith, "who lived in the capital, would be in danger of suffering much by the neglect, and more by the fraud, of his factors and agents, if the rents of an estate in a distant province were to be paid to him in this manner. The loss of the sovereign, from the abuse and depredation of his tax-gatherers, would necessarily be much greater."

Various other objections have been urged against taxation in kind, which it would be useless and tedious to enumerate. I shall only take the liberty of remarking the violent operation upon relative price which must follow from so vast a quantity of produce being thrown upon the market by the agents of the public revenue, who are notoriously equally improvident as buyers and as sellers. The necessity of clearing the storehouses to make room for the fresh crop, and the ever urgent demands upon the public purse, would oblige them to sell below the level to which the price would naturally be brought by the rent of the land, the wages of labour, and the interest of the capital engaged in agriculture; and private dealers would be unable to maintain the competition. Such taxation not only takes from the cultivator a portion of his product, but prevents his turning the residue to good account.

Section IV: Of the Territorial or Land-Tax of England

In the year 1692, which was four years after the happy revolution that placed the prince of Orange upon the British throne, a general valuation was made of the income of all the land in the country; and, upon that valuation, the land-tax continues to be levied to this day; so that the tax of four shillings in the pound, upon the rents of land, is a fifth of its rent in 1692, and not of the actual rent at the present day.

It may easily be conceived how much this tax must operate to encourage improvements of the land. An estate that has been improved so as to double the rent, does not pay double the original tax; neither does it pay a less tax if it be suffered to fall into neglect and impoverishment; thus, it operates as a penalty upon negligence.

To this fixation of the tax, many writers attribute the high state of the cultivation of the land in England; and doubtless it may have done much to promote improvement. But, what would be thought of a government that should say to a tradesman in a small way of business, "You are trading in a small way upon a small capital, and consequently pay very little in direct taxes. Borrow and enlarge your capital, extend your dealings, and increase your profits as much as you can, and we will not charge you with any increase of taxes. Nay, further, when your heirs succeed to the business, and have still further extended it, they shall be assessed at precisely the same rate, and shall continue subject to the same taxes only." All this might be a vast encouragement to trade and manufacture; but would there be any equity in such a proceeding? And might they not advance without such assistance? Has not England herself presented the example of a still more rapid improvement in commercial and manufacturing industry, without any such unjust partiality? A land owner, by attention, economy, and intelligence, improves his annual income to the amount, say of one thousand dollars: If the state claim a fifth of this advance, there will still be a bonus of eight hundred dollars to stimulate and reward his exertions.

It would be easy to put cases in which the tax, becoming by its fixation disproportionate to the means of the taxpayers and the condition of the soil, might be productive of as much mischief as it has done good in other instances: Where it would operate to throw out of cultivation a class of land that, by one cause or other, had become incompetent to pay the same ratio of taxation. We have seen an example of this in Tuscany. There, a census or terrier was made in 1496, wherein the plains and valleys were rated very low on account of the frequent floods and inundations which prevented any regular and profitable cultivation; while the uplands, that were then the only cultivated spots, were rated very high. Since then, the torrents and inundations have been confined by drainage and embankment, and the plains reduced to fertility; their produce, being comparatively exempt from tax, came to market cheaper than that of the uplands, which, consequently, were unable to maintain the competition under the pressure of disproportionate taxation, and have gradually been abandoned and deserted. Whereas, had the tax been adjusted to the change of circumstances, both might have been cultivated together.

In speaking of a tax peculiar to a particular nation, I have used it merely in illustration of general and universal principles.

Chapter IX: Of National Debt

Section I: Of the Contracting Debt by National Authority, and of its General Effect

There is this grand distinction between an individual borrower and a borrowing government that, in general, the former borrows capital for the purpose of beneficial employment, the latter for the purpose of barren consumption and expenditure. A nation borrows either to satisfy an unlooked-for demand, or to meet an extraordinary emergency; to which ends, the loan may prove effectual or ineffectual: But, in either case, the whole sum borrowed is so much value consumed and lost, and the public revenue remains burthened with the interest upon it.

Melon maintains, that a national debt is no more than a debt from the right hand to the left, which nowise enfeebles the body politic. But he is mistaken; the state is enfeebled, inasmuch as the capital lent to its government, having been destroyed in the consumption of it by the government, can no longer yield anybody the profit, or in other words, the interest it might earn in the character of a productive means. Wherewith, then, is the government to pay the interest of its debt? Why, with a portion of the revenue arising from some other source, which it must transfer from the taxpayer to the public creditor for the purpose.

Before the act of borrowing, there will have been in existence two productive capitals, each of them yielding, or capable of yielding, revenue; that is to say, a capital about to be lent to government, and a capital whereon the future taxpayers derive that revenue, which is about to be applied in satisfaction of the interest upon the capital lent. After the act of borrowing, there will remain but one of these capitals; viz. the latter of the two, whereof the revenue is thenceforward no longer at the disposal of its former possessors, the present taxpayers, since it must be taken in some form of taxation or other by the government for the sake of providing the payment of interest to its creditors. The lender loses no part of his revenue; the only loser is the payer of taxes.

People are apt to suppose that, because national loans do not necessarily occasion any diminution of the national money or specie, therefore, they occasion not a loss but merely a transfer of national wealth. With a view to the more ready exposure of this fallacy, I have subjoined a synoptical table, showing what becomes of the sum borrowed, and whence the public creditor's interest is satisfied.

When a government borrows, it either does or does not engage to repay the principal. In the latter case, it grants what is called a perpetual annuity. Redeemable loans are capable of infinite variety in the terms. The principal is contracted to be repaid, sometimes gradually, and in the way of lottery; sometimes by installments payable together with the interest, sometimes in the way of increased interest with condition to expire on the death of the lender; as in the case of tontines and life annuities, whereof the latter determine on the death of the individual lender; whereas, in tontines, the full interest continues to be divided amongst the survivors until the whole of the lives have expired.

Tontines and life annuities are very improvident modes of borrowing; for the borrower remains throughout liable to the full rate of interest, although he annually repays a part of the principal. Besides, they savour of immorality; offering a premium to egotism, and a stimulus to the dilapidation of capital by enabling the lender to consume both principal and interest without fear of personal beggary.

The governments best acquainted with the business of borrowing and lending have not, of late years at least, given any engagement to repay the principal of the loan. Thus, public creditors have no other way of altering the investment of their capital except by selling their transferable security, which they can do with more or less advantage to themselves, according to the buyer's opinion of the solidity of the debtor government that has granted the perpetual annuity. Despotic governments have always found a great difficulty in negotiating such loans. Where the sovereign is powerful enough to violate his contracts at pleasure, or where there is a mere personal contract with the reigning monarch, with a risk of disavowal by the successor, lenders are loath to advance their money without a near and definite period of payment.

The appointment to posts and offices, under condition of an annual payment, or of deposit for which the government engages to pay interest, is a mode of borrowing in perpetuity in which the loan is compulsory. When once this paltry expedient is resorted to, it requires very little ingenuity to find plausible grounds for converting almost every occupation, down to the dust-man and street-porter, into patent and saleable offices.

Another mode of borrowing is by the anticipation of revenue by which is meant, the assignment by a government of revenues not yet due, with allowance in the nature of discount, the taking up money in advance from lenders who charge a discount proportionate to the risk they run from the instability of the government and possible deficiency of the revenue. Engagements of this kind contracted by a government, and satisfied either out of the revenue when collected or by the issue of fresh bills upon the public treasury, constitute what bears the uncouth English denomination of *floating* debt; the consolidated debt being that, whereon the creditor can demand the interest only, and not the principal.

National loans of every kind are attended with the universal disadvantage of withdrawing capital from productive employment and diverting it into the channel of barren consumption; and, in countries where the credit of the government is at a low ebb, with the further and particular disadvantage of raising the interest of capital. Who can be expected to lend at five per cent to the farmer, the manufacturer, or the merchant, while he can readily get an offer of seven or eight per cent from the government? That class of revenue which has been called, profit of capital, is thereby advanced in its ratio at the expense of the consumer: The consumption falls off, in consequence of the advance in the real price of products; the productive agency of the other sources of production are less in demand, and consequently worse paid; and the whole community is the sufferer with the sole exception of the capitalist.

The ability to borrow affords one main advantage to the state, namely, the power of apportioning the burthen entailed by a sudden emergency among a great number of successive years. In the present state of public affairs, and on the present scale of international warfare, no country could support the enormous expense from its ordinary annual revenue. The larger states pay in taxation nearly as much as they are able; for economy is by no means the order of the day with them; and their ordinary expenditure seldom falls much short of the income. If the expenditure must be doubled to save the nation from ruin, borrowing is usually the only resource unless it can make up its mind to violate all subsisting engagements and be guilty of spoliation of its own subjects and foreigners too. The faculty of borrowing is a more powerful agent than even gun-powder; but probably the gross abuse that is made of it will soon destroy its efficacy.

Great pains have been taken to find in the system of borrowing, as well as in taxation, some inherent advantage beyond that of supplying the public consumption. But a close examination will expose the hopelessness of such an attempt.

It has been maintained, for instance, that the debentures and securities which form a national debt become real and substantial values, existing within the community; that the capital, of which they are the evidence or representative, is so much positive wealth, and must be reckoned as an item of the total substance of the nation. But it is not so; a written contract or security is a mere evidence that such or such property belongs to such an individual. But wealth consists in the property itself, and not in the parchment by which its ownership is evidenced; therefore à *fortiori,* a security is not even an evidence of wealth, where it does not represent an actual existing value, and when it operates as a mere power of attorney from the government to its creditor, enabling him to receive annually a specified portion of the revenue expected to be levied upon the taxpayers at large. Supposing the security to be cancelled, as it might be by a national bankruptcy, would there be any the least diminution of wealth in the community? Undoubtedly not. The only difference would be that the revenue, which before went to the public creditor, would now be at the disposal of the taxpayer from whom it used to be taken.

Those who tell us that the annual circulation is increased by the whole amount of the annual disbursements of the government, forget that these disbursements are made out of the annual products and are a portion of the annual revenue, taken from the taxpayer, which would have been brought into the general circulation just the same, although no such thing as national debt had existed. The taxpayer would have spent what is now spent by the public creditor; that is all.

The sale or purchase of debentures or securities is not a productive circulation, but a mere substitution of one public creditor in place of another. When these transfers degenerate into stock-jobbing, that is to say, the making of a profit by the rise and fall of their price, they are productive of much mischief; in the first place, by the unproductive employment on this object of the agent of circulation, money, which is an item of the national capital; and, in the next, by procuring a gain to one person by the loss of another; which is the characteristic of all gaming. The occupation of the stock-jobber yields no new or useful product; consequently having no product of his own to give in exchange, he has no revenue to subsist upon, but what he contrives to make out of the unskillfulness or ill-fortune of gamesters like himself.

A national debt has been said to bind the public creditors more firmly to the government, and make them its natural supporters by a sense of common interest; and so it does, beyond all doubt. But, as this common interest may attach equally to a bad or a good government, there is just as much chance of its being an injury, as a benefit to a nation. If we look at England, we shall see a vast number of well-meaning persons, induced by this motive to uphold the abuses and misgovernment of a wretched administration.

It has been further urged that a national debt is an index of the public opinion, respecting the degree of credit which the government deserves, and operates as a motive to its good conduct, and endeavours to preserve the public opinion of which such a debt furnishes the index. This cannot be admitted without some qualification. The good conduct of government in the eyes of the public creditors consists in the regular payment of their own dividends; but in the eyes of the taxpayers, it consists in spending as little as possible. The market price of stock does, indeed, furnish a tolerable index of the former kind of good conduct, but not of the latter. Perhaps it would be no exaggeration to say that the punctual payments of the dividends, instead of being a sign of good, is in numberless instances a cloak to bad government; and, in some countries, a boon for the toleration of frequent and glaring abuses.

Another argument in favour of national debt is that it affords a prompt investment to capital, which can find no ready and profitable employment, and thus must, at any rate, prevent its emigration. If it do, so much the worse: It is a bait to tempt capital towards its destruction, leaving the nation burthened with the annual interest, which government must provide. It is far better that the capital should emigrate, as it would probably return sooner or later; and then its interest for the mean time will be chargeable to foreigners. A national debt of moderate amount, the capital of which should have been well and judiciously expended in useful works, might indeed be attended with the advantage of providing an investment for minute portions of capital in the hands of persons incapable of turning them to account, who would probably keep them locked up or spend them by driblets, but for the convenience of such an investment. This is perhaps the sole benefit of a national debt; and even this is attended with some danger; inasmuch as it enables a government to squander the national savings. For, unless the principal be spent upon objects of permanent public benefit, as on roads, canals, or the like, it were better for the public that the capital should remain inactive or concealed; since, if the public lost the use of it, at least it would not have to pay the interest.

Thus, it may be expedient to borrow when capital must be spent by a government, having nothing but the usufruct at its command but we are not to imagine that, by the act of borrowing, the public prosperity can be advanced. The borrower, whether a sovereign or an individual, incurs an annual charge upon his revenue, besides impoverishing himself to the full amount of the principal if it be consumed; and nations never borrow but with a view to consume outright.

Section II: Of Public Credit, its Basis, and the Circumstances that Endanger its Solidity

Public credit is the confidence of individuals in the engagements of the ruling power or government. This credit is at the extreme point of elevation when the public creditor gets no higher interest than he would by lending on the best private securities; which is a clear proof that the lenders require no premium of insurance to cover the extra risk they incur, and that in their estimation there is no such extra risk. Public credit never reaches this elevation, except where the government is so constituted as to find great difficulty in breaking its engagements, and where, moreover, its resources are known to be equal to its wants; for which latter reason, public credit is never very high unless where the financial accounts of the nation are subject to general publicity.

Where the public authority is vested in a single individual, it is next to impossible that public credit should be very extensive: For there is no security beyond the pleasure and good faith of the monarch. When the authority resides in the people or its representatives, there is the further security of a personal interest in the people themselves, who are creditors in their individual, and debtors in their aggregate character; and therefore, cannot receive in the former, without paying in the latter. This circumstance alone would lead us to presume that now, when great undertakings are so costly as to be effected by borrowing alone, representative governments will acquire a marked preponderance in the scale of national power, simply on account of their superior financial resources, without reference to any other circumstance.

In one light, the obligations of government inspire more confidence than those of individuals, that is to say, by the greater solidity of its resources. The resources of the most responsible individual may fail suddenly and totally, or at least to such an extent as to disable him from performing his engagements.

Numerous commercial failures, political or national calamities, litigation, fraud, or violence may ruin him entirely; but the supplies of a government are derived from such various quarters that the individual calamities of its subjects can operate but partially upon the revenue of the state. There is also another thing that facilitates the borrowing of government even more than the credit it is fairly entitled to; and that is the great facility of transfer presented to the stockholder. Public creditors always reckon upon the possibility of withdrawing by the sale of their debentures before the occurrence of embarrassment or bankruptcy; and even where they contemplate such a risk, generally consider some advance of the rate of interest a sufficient premium of insurance against it.

Moreover, it is observable that the sentiments of lenders and of mankind upon all occasions are more powerfully operated upon by the impressions of the moment than by any other motive; experience of the past must be very recent, and the prospect of the future very near, to have any sensible effect. The monstrous breach of faith on the part of the French government in 1721, in regard to its paper money and the Mississippi shareholders, did not prevent the ready negotiation of a loan of two hundred millions liv. in 1759; nor did the bankrupt measures of the Abbé Terrai in 1772 prevent the negotiation of fresh loans in 1778 and every subsequent year.

In other points of view, the credit of individuals is better founded than that of the government. There is no compulsory process against the latter for the breach of its engagements; nor do governments ever husband the national resources with nearly the care and attention of individuals. Besides, in the event of external or internal subversion, individuals may withdraw their property from the wreck much better than governments can.

Public credit affords such facilities to public prodigality that many political writers have regarded it as fatal to national prosperity. For, say they, when governments feel themselves strong in the ability to borrow, they are too apt to intermeddle in every political arrangement, and to conceive gigantic projects that lead sometimes to disgrace, sometimes to glory, but always to a state of financial exhaustion; to make war themselves, and stir up others to do the like; to subsidize every mercenary agent, and deal in the blood and the consciences of mankind; making capital, which should be the fruit of industry and virtue, the prize of ambition, pride, and wickedness.

A nation which has the power to borrow and yet is in a state of political feebleness will be exposed to the requisitions of its more powerful neighbours. It must subsidize them in its defense; must purchase peace; must pay for the toleration of its independence, which it generally loses after all; or perhaps must lend with the certain prospect of never being repaid.

These are by no means hypothetical cases; but the reader is left to make the application himself.

By the establishment of sinking-funds, well-ordered governments have found means to extinguish and discharge their redeemable debt. The constant operation of this contrivance contributes more than any-thing else to the consolidation of public credit. The mode of proceeding is simply this:

Suppose that the state borrows one hundred millions of dollars at an interest of five per cent; to pay that interest, it must appropriate a portion of the national revenue to the amount of five millions of dollars. For this purpose, it usually imposes a tax calculated to produce this sum annually. If the tax be made to produce somewhat more, say 5,462,400 dollars, and the surplus of 462,400 dollars be thrown into a particular fund, and laid out annually in the purchase of government debentures to that amount in the market, and if, in addition to this surplus, the interest likewise upon the debt thus extinguished, be annually em-ployed in such purchases, the whole principal debt will be extinguished at the end of fifty years. This is the mode in which a sinking-fund op-erates. The efficacy of this expedient depends upon the progressive power of compound interest; that is to say, the gradual augmentation of the interest of capital by the addition of interest upon the arrears of interest reckoned from certain stated periods.

It is obvious that by an annual installment of not more than ten per cent upon its own interest, the principal of a debt bearing an interest of five per cent may be extinguished in less than fifty years. However, the sale of the debentures being voluntary, if the holders will not sell at par, that is to say, at twenty years purchase, the redemption, in this way, will take somewhat longer time; but this very state of the market will be a convincing proof of the high ratio of national credit. On the other hand, if the credit decline so that the same sum will purchase a larger amount of debentures, the extinction of the debt will be effected in a shorter period. So that the lower public credit falls, the more powerful is the operation of a sinking-fund to revive it; and that fund grows less effi-cient, exactly in proportion as it becomes less requisite.

To the establishment of such a fund, has the long-continued public credit of Great Britain been attributed, and her ability still to go on bor-rowing, in spite of a debt of more than eight hundred millions sterling. And doubtless this it is, that has made Smith declare sinking-funds, which were contrived expressly to reduce national debt, the main in-struments of their increase. Had not governments the happy knack of abusing resources of every kind, they would soon grow too rich and powerful.

A sinking-fund is a complete delusion, whenever a government continues borrowing on one hand as much as it redeems on the other; and *à fortiori,* when it borrows more than it redeems, as England has constantly done since the year 1793 to the present time. Whencesoever the amount of the sinking-fund be derived, whether it be merely the product of a fresh tax, or that product augmented by the interest on the extinguished debt, if the government borrow a million for every million of debt that it pays off, it creates an annual charge of precisely the same amount as that extinguished: It is precisely the same thing as lending to itself the million devoted to the purpose of redemption. Indeed, the latter course would save the expense of the operation. This position has been fully established in an excellent work by Professor Hamilton which is quite conclusive upon the subject. The enormous burthens of the people of England, the scandalous abuse its government has made of the power of borrowing, and her substitution of paper money in place of specie, will have produced some benefit at least; inasmuch as they have assisted the solution of many problems highly interesting to the happiness of nations, and given warning to all future generations to be-ware of the like excesses.

It must be evident, that the grand requisite to the efficiency of a sinking-fund is the punctual and inviolable application of the sums ap-propriated to the purpose of redemption. Yet this has never been rigidly adhered to, even in England, where consistency and good faith to the creditors are a point of honour with the government. So that English writers put no faith in the extinction of the debt by the operation of the sinking-fund: Nay, Smith makes no scruple of declaring that national debts have never been extinguished except by national bankruptcy.

It has been sometimes a matter of speculation to inquire into the effect of a national bankruptcy upon the relative condition of individu-als, and the internal economy of the nation. In ordinary cases, when a government commits an act of bankruptcy, it adds to the revenues of the taxpayers the whole amount that it discontinues paying to the pub-lic creditors.—Nay, it goes somewhat further: For it remits likewise the charges of collection and management of the revenue and the debt. A nation burthened with one hundred millions of annual interest on its debt, whereon the charges above mentioned should amount to thirty per cent more, might by a bankruptcy remit to the taxpayers one hundred and thirty millions, while it stript its creditors of one hundred millions only.

In England the effect would be more complicated; because she does not pay the dividends on her debt wholly out of the annual proceeds of taxation; at least, not at the moment of my writing; but annually borrows a sum nearly equal to the interest of her debt. Were she to commit an act of bankruptcy, the annual loans of forty millions sterling, more or less, would be withdrawn from unproductive consumption by the public creditors, and be applicable to the purposes of reproductive consumption; for it may fairly be supposed that the capitalists who accumulate and lend to the state would look out for some profitable investment. In this point of view, the operation would tend vastly to the increase of the national capital and revenue; but the execution would be attended with very disastrous immediate consequences: for this annual amount of forty millions would be withdrawn from the class of consumers who have no other means of subsistence, and would be utterly unable to make good their losses in any other way, for want of both personal industry and of the command of capital.

A bankruptcy would probably obviate the necessity of fresh loans; but would not release an atom of the former taxation where the interest of the debt is habitually paid, not with the proceeds of taxation, but with new loans. Thus, the burthens of the people would not be alleviated, nor the charges of production reduced: Consequently there would be no sensible reduction in the price of commodities; nor would British products find a readier market either at home or abroad.

The classes liable to taxation would be diminished in numerical strength by the whole of the suppressed stockholders; and taxation less productive, although not lower in ratio. The forty millions of revenue, withdrawn from the public creditors, would pay taxes only upon the annual profit or revenue they might yield in the character of productive capital. The ruin of the public creditors would be attended with abundance of collateral distress; with private failures and insolvency without end; with the loss of employment to all their tradesmen and servants, and the utter destitution of all their dependents.

On the other hand, if she persevere in borrowing to pay the interest of the former loans, that interest and with it taxation also, must go on increasing to infinity. It is impossible to avoid a precipice when one follows a road that leads nowhere else.

The potentates of Asia, and all sovereigns who have no hopes of establishing a credit, have recourse to the accumulation of treasure. Treasure is the reserve of past, whereas a loan is the anticipation of future revenue. They are both serviceable expedients in case of emergency.

A treasure does not always contribute to the political security of its possessors. It rather invites attack, and very seldom is faithfully applied to the purpose for which it was destined. The accumulation of Charles V of France fell into the hands of his brother, the duke of Anjou; those which Pope Paul II destined to oppose the Turkish arms, and drive them out of Europe, supplied the extravagancies of Sixtus IV and his nephews. The treasures amassed by Henry IV, for the humiliation of the house of Austria, were lavished upon the favourites of the queen-mother; and, at a later period, we have seen the political power of Prussia brought into imminent hazard by those very savings which were destined by Frederick III to its consolidation.

The command of a large sum is a dangerous temptation to a national administration. Though accumulated at their expense, the people rarely, if ever, profit by it: Yet in point of fact, all value, and consequently, all wealth, originates with the people.

❖ ❖ ❖

An Essay on a Reduction of the Interest
Of the National Debt

J.R. McCulloch; 1816

Section First

Connection between Agriculture, and Commerce and Manufacturing Industry.—Proof of a flourishing state of the former, being a consequence of the prosperity of the latter.

That the modern improvements in farming and machinery have greatly diminished the quantity of human labour, and expense necessary for working lands, is universally admitted. The surplus produce of the soil, or that part which remains to be disposed of, after supporting the labourers employed in its production, has been thereby doubly increased. In the first place, by the diminution of the number of labourers; and in the second place, by the greater actual amount of the produce itself. Those philosophers who assert that population is alone the source of national wealth and happiness, may indeed maintain, that the first of these ways, in which the disposable produce has been increased, is a positive loss to the state. The absurdity of these dogmas has, however, been clearly demonstrated; but upon their own principles, they are compelled to admit the superior advantages of improved and scientific agriculture, from the undoubted fact of its affording a greater actual quantity of produce,—an object of the utmost importance, according to the views of all political economists, however different in other respects they may be. The object of this Section is to develop the means by which this surplus is procured; and to show, that if the arts ministering to the comforts and the luxuries of man, had not given employment to a great portion of people, a portion adequate to consume all the extra produce remaining after the support of the cultivators, that extra produce could not possibly have existed nearly to the same extent.

If the ground belonging to a state is divided into small portions, like that of Sparta after the institutions of Lycurgus, and Rome in the early ages of the commonwealth, it can only be cultivated as far as manual labour will go. Capital cannot be formed in such a society as this, and there can be no encouragement for the mechanical arts. The expensive machines used in modern agriculture, such as the thrashing-mill, fanners, etc. will be entirely unknown, and the beneficial effects resulting from the division of labour will be scarcely felt. No expensive improvement, or that would not yield an immediate return, will be thought of. Marshes will not be drained; canals, bridges, and roads will not be formed. The miserable cultivators, forming in such a state of society the whole body of the people, will be too much distressed with thoughts of providing for their present wants, to pay any attention to schemes of general or prospective improvement. A perpetual sameness, like that of China, or at most, a nearly imperceptible progress, is all that can be here expected, and is all that will take place. Such nations may produce excellent soldiers, but it is only in countries like Athens or England, that the energies of man, as well as that of the soil, will be developed in their full extent. The diversity of the objects of pursuit will there give ample room for gratifying the diversity of dispositions; while the applause consequent on any invention that either extends the power of man over the physical world, or gratifies his intellectual faculties, will ensure the continuity of discovery.

After the Roman empire had been overthrown, and the feudal system had been established in Europe, its inhabitants were essentially agricultural; but the lands being divided into large portions, while the right of primogeniture was everywhere maintained, the number of cultivators was necessarily very limited, and the productive energies of the land were not called forth to nearly the same extent as in countries where the influence of Agrarian laws fixed the quantity of land to be possessed by each person to a few acres. The crimes, the ignorance, the superstition, and the barbarity of this period, are known to all. Among the causes that brought forth the present order of things from such a chaos, the first place is due to commerce. This will not admit of a doubt, if we either consult history, or reflect on the present state of those nations of Europe, such as Poland, into which it has been only partially introduced, or of Spain, from which it has been excluded. The poverty and impotence of both, with the depopulation of the latter, are notorious. From these facts, and an infinity of others that might be mentioned, we are warranted in concluding, the cultivation of commerce and manufactures to be the great cause of national prosperity. In the words of Mr. Malthus, "They infuse fresh life and activity into all the classes of the state, afford opportunities for the inferior orders to rise by personal merit and exertion, and stimulate the higher orders to depend for distinction upon other grounds than mere rank and riches. They excite invention, encourage science and the useful arts, spread intelligence and spirit, inspire a taste for conveniences and comforts among the labouring classes; and, above all, give a new and happier structure to society, by increasing the proportion of the middle classes; that body on which the liberty, public spirit, and good government of every country must mainly depend."[1]

It has been often stated, and is indeed expressly mentioned by the great political economist just quoted, that if the people who are employed in expensive manufactures for the gratification of the rich, and the luxurious, were employed in the cultivation of poor waste land, a greater quantity of food and articles of the first necessity would be thereby produced. This is indeed true; but these people, without this very passion of the rich for luxuries, would not in fact be employed at all. A sentence or two will render this evident. A gentleman we shall suppose possesses a farm, in a highly polished and manufacturing country, five hundred acres in extent: In order to live like his neighbours, and to be enabled to command those comforts which his station of life requires, the whole productive energies of his farm must be called into action, the surplus is sent to the manufacturers, and he gets their wares in return; but suppose him to live in a country in a different state of society where these manufactures and arts are unknown, or only slightly introduced, and where people in his station are contented with the mere necessaries of life, what would be the consequence? It would be precisely this, the cultivation of a few acres would suffice to satiate all his wants, and the residue would lie desolate and waste; for he never would bestow labour in raising that which nowise conduced to his comfort or advantage. Let us cease, therefore, to inveigh against the luxury of the rich, as it gives effectual support to the agriculture and the population of nations.[2]

Section Second

Effects of a relatively high price of Labour injurious to Commerce, and consequently to Agriculture.

In the last Section, we have shown that an improved system of agriculture is a consequence, not a cause, of great commercial and manufacturing prosperity. Whatever, therefore, tends to cramp or counteract the manufacturing spirit, is decidedly hurtful and prejudicial to agriculture itself. Let us examine if a high relative price of provisions would have that effect.

It is clear, that a high relative price of provisions directly affects manufactures, in so far as, by raising the price of labour, it tends to enhance the cost of the goods, and in that way makes them compete in the market with disadvantage.

During the discussions on the Corn Bill, the effect of which was, both by its advocates and by its opposers, understood to be to raise the price of corn, and consequently of labour, in as far as the one is dependent on the other, its injurious operation on the manufacturing interest in this respect was generally admitted. It was, however, alleged, that our immense capital, the excellence of our machinery, and the skill and industry of our artisans, were of themselves sufficient to give a decided superiority to our manufactures. That these are immense advantages cannot be denied; but it may be fairly doubted, whether they will have the effects here ascribed to them.

Independently of other considerations, it is an axiom in political economy, that capital naturally transfers itself to those countries in which it may be employed to the greatest advantage. If an English manufacturer, from the high price of labour, caused by a high price of corn, and by the influence of an oppressive taxation on the other necessaries of life, should only be able to clear five per cent on that capital, which, in a like establishment in the Netherlands would enable him to clear fifteen per cent his *amor patrice* must indeed be pretty strong, if he do not think of changing his residence. But supposing that he keeps his capital and his industry at home, it is more than probable, that in a short space of time he would be beat out of the market. If the Flemish manufacturer brings forward goods of equal value with the latter, his profits will be thrice as much,[3]—his expense in other things will also be less,—and he will thus have great facilities for creating capital, and for improving machinery. Though the goods of the Flemish manufacturer should be of an inferior quality, it would not alter their relative profits, as in that case they would be manufactured at a still less expense. The difference of the value of the products derived by each from the capitals invested would be precisely the same. The advantages, therefore, on the side of the foreign manufacturers, are very great, and must, without a fall on the expense of manufacturing in Britain, ultimately turn the scale in their favour.[4]

These general principles, which of themselves serve to determine the question, receive additional confirmation from the particular state of the continent and of America. During the time that British manufactures were excluded from a considerable portion of the one, and of the other, by the operation of Bonaparte's decrees, and of the non-intercourse act, the absence of foreign competitors gave an immense impulse to the infant establishments for manufacturing on both sides of the Atlantic. Some of them, such as the muslin manufacture in France, may now be considered as firmly established, and able to stand a competition, on the principle of free trade, with any rival. The manufacture of hardware, and all kinds of iron-work, is understood to have been commenced in America with considerable success, and its effects have been already experienced in Birmingham and Sheffield.

It is surely not necessary to expose the absurdity of believing in the power of bounties to preserve permanently the foreign market against all other disadvantages. In no part of his most excellent work, has Dr. Smith been more fortunate, than in exposing this futile resource of the mercantile system. A bounty is, in fact, a bonus given to foreigners, to entice them to purchase our products, and must therefore be a positive loss to the nation at large.[5] A drawback, another of these expedients for forcing exportation, though it takes nothing from the purse of the nation, and is not therefore directly injurious, is indirectly so, since, by affording goods cheaper to foreigners than to our own citizens, it tends to increase the relative expense of living at home, and to encourage the emigration of capital.

It is true, that prohibitions on the import of foreign goods may, to a certain extent, preserve the home market to our manufacturers, to whatever rate the cost of manufacturing may arise. He has, however, to learn the very first principles of commerce, who does not know the ultimately injurious effects of any such prohibitions. They overturn the very foundations of a free trade, which has been proved beyond all controversy to be not more for the advantage of mankind in general, than for that of particular nations. They give a direct encouragement to smuggling, the demoralizing and pernicious consequences of which are well-known. They lessen the foreign market for manufactures, since, if you will not take the produce of their industry, they have nothing to exchange for that of yours. Lastly, they ruin the home market itself, by encouraging the emigration of people, possessed of fixed incomes, and of capitalists.[6]

The expense of living in Britain, compared with that of France, has already induced a great number of people having fixed incomes to emigrate, and it is solely owing to the unsettled state of the continent, and to the apprehension of some convulsion, that many more have not followed their example. The stimulus given to industry by the expenditure of the incomes of these people is not only lost, and thrown into the opposite scale, but their families brought up in France forget they are Britons. France will be to them their mother country; and not merely the produce of their capitals, but the capital itself, will be transferred to that nation. It has been proposed to put a stop to this emigration, by laying a heavy tax on persons who reside abroad. This would, however, increase the evil it intended to cure; it would cause an immediate transference of capital, which, as matters now stand, will be only done by degrees.

The consequence resulting from the statements of this Section, combined with the first, is, that whatever tends to increase the price of labour, compared with that of other countries, is directly hostile to commerce, and indirectly hostile to agriculture.

Section Third

Tendency and probable Effects of the late Corn Bill prejudicial to Commerce, and therefore ultimately prejudicial to Agriculture itself.

If the principles developed in the two first Sections be indisputable, and if the conclusion be legitimately brought out, it will follow, that the late Corn Bill is, as a permanent legislative measure, tending to keep up and increase the price of grain, decidedly pernicious; and, on the other hand, if it has not that effect, that it is nugatory, and cannot afford the agricultural interest that relief they are well entitled to lay claim to.[7]

Because the Corn Bill has not as yet had much effect on the market, it has been concluded that it will never have any; if we reflect, however, on the immense importations that were made during the time it was in agitation, and on the excellent crop of last harvest, we shall be convinced that these conclusions are rash and hasty in the extreme.

In supposing that the price of corn will continue to labour under its present depression, with the Corn Bill to regulate importation, it is tacitly assumed, that we shall have a continuance of harvests equally favourable with the last, and that poor land will continue to be cultivated at an expense greater than it can possibly repay, or at best with a very small profit, by no means equal to cover the risk attending such investments of capital. The first of these assumptions is extremely precarious, and the last is all but absurd. Independently of all theoretical conclusions, it is known to every person who has lately traveled through the country, that great tracts of land have been already converted into pasturage, and that a vast deal more will be sown down this season, while liming, fallowing, and expensive improvements of that nature, are nearly relinquished even on good soils. It is impossible therefore to suppose, that this rapid diminution of the supply of corn, shall not have the effect of raising its price, otherwise than by supposing a proportional decrease of the population, which cannot take place in so limited a period, or an immense decrease of manufacturing employment, and a much greater spirit of economy in the people.

It will be readily allowed, that it is by no means an easy matter to change the general habits and the manners of living in any people. It would be still more difficult to bring about a change, were it desirable to do so, in the habits of the lower orders of the English. If manufacturers will not employ them, they have a resource in the poor's house; a fund is by law set aside for their support, and when that is the case, it would be folly to imagine that any diminution of employment would cause a corresponding diminution of consumption.

If these views of the probable effects of the Corn Bill are incorrect, it will not certainly injure the commercial prosperity of the country; but neither will it administer any relief to the wide-wasting misery that is preying on the agricultural classes.—We proceed to consider their condition in the next Section.

Section Fourth

Progress of Agriculture since 1763. Effects of a permanent fall in the Price of Provisions on the Agriculturists in the present circumstances of the Country.

During the early part of last century, there was a considerable exportation of corn from Britain; but after the peace of 1763, owing to the increase of the population by the extension of commerce, the quantity of the exported grain gradually diminished, notwithstanding of the encouragement of a bounty—of a high duty on importation—and of the improvements in agriculture. After 1765, in which year the balance on the side of exportation amounted to 77,388 quarters, the clamours caused by the rapidly increasing price of corn, against the duty on importation, became exceedingly general, and in 1773 foreign wheat was allowed to be imported, on paying a nominal duty of sixpence whenever the price was forty-eight shillings a quarter.[8] It is therefore falsely maintained, that the alteration of the corn laws at that period was the cause of the rise in the price of corn; for that very rise preceded, and was the avowed cause of, their alteration.[9]

In that period of national prosperity, subsequent to the humiliation occasioned by the disastrous conclusion of the American war, and previous to the commencement of the French war the agriculture of the country, as is justly remarked by Mr. Wilson, advanced with a rapidity of improvement unknown in any former period. Our commerce, however, as is the case in all improving countries, and consequently our population, increased still faster; notwithstanding, therefore, of the stimulus given to agriculture, our imports increased; and, in 1791, an act was passed, fixing the price of the quarter of wheat at fifty-two and sixpence when the duty on importing should cease.

The encouragement given to agriculture during the late war was still more excessive. The obligation on the Bank of England to pay its notes in specie having been dispensed with in 1797, a very great additional quantity of them was immediately brought into circulation.[10] If they were not depreciated they were at least multiplied, and this was an infallible way to raise the money price of corn, and of every other commodity. Country banks were established in every village, and the utmost facility was given to the procuring of discounts, and hence to the getting a command of capital. These causes, combined with the high prices of

1800 and of 1801, caused agriculture to advance with a prodigious increase; our population had however outstripped it; and, in 1804, a duty
of twenty-four and threepence was imposed on the quarter of wheat
imported when the home price was below sixty-three shillings, and of
two and sixpence if between sixty-three shillings and sixty-six shillings
when it ceased. In addition to the direct encouragement thus given to
agriculture, it was still farther promoted from the increase of our population, and of our trade, by our almost entirely engrossing the commerce of the world. The produce of the East and of the West was at our
sole disposal; and though the consumption of the continent was much
diminished, yet, such as it was, we alone could supply it. The exchange,
too, from whatever cause it happened, having become greatly against
us, had exactly the same effect as if an additional duty had been laid on
importation. The combined effects of these different stimulants on agriculture, was quite astonishing and unprecedented. Lands that will not
now afford any rent, were improved at an immense expense, and let
from one pound to two pounds per acre. Vast sums were expended in
draining worthless bogs, or in ameliorating the surface of subsoils naturally cold and wet; and in practice it now seemed to be believed, that
"to make two stalks of corn grow where none grew before," was not
only a solid claim to be considered as the "greatest benefactor of mankind," but the surest method of acquiring a fortune.

On the return of peace, after the downfall of Bonaparte, this country was found to be in a state very different indeed from the rest of the
world. The quarter of wheat, which had been selling here at one hundred and twenty-five shillings[11] had not, in France, sold at above forty
shillings,[12] and in Poland not higher than thirty-two shillings.[13] The protecting law of 1804, fixing the rate of importation at sixty-three shillings
a quarter, was therefore quite insufficient for the support of the farmers, and a new one was passed in 1815, prohibiting the use of foreign
corn till the home price was eighty shillings a quarter, and of corn from
Canada till it was sixty-seven shillings a quarter. The avowed object of
this measure was to keep up the price of corn to eighty shillings and
consequently, in as far as it could effect its object, to render the expense of living in Britain, and the wages of labour, twice as high as on
the continent. We have already demonstrated, how pernicious it would
ultimately have been to agriculture itself if it had had that effect: We
have shown, that it would have sapped the very foundations of our
national grandeur, and that, therefore, the cure would have been much
worse than the disease.

Let us now examine a few of the answers that have been made to the complaints of the agriculturists.

To the complaints made by the agriculturists, of their loss of capital, and of the fall in the value of their produce, the following general and definite answer has been made. The nominal amount of your capital is indeed diminished, and you now receive only fifty pounds for that produce for which you formerly received a hundred pounds, but all the articles you purchased with the hundred pounds will experience a similar fall; in short, the terms of a proportion have been all divided by the same number, which, though it reduces their nominal amount, affects not their relative value. Let us examine how far this seemingly conclusive answer is well-founded.

In the first place, though it is undoubtedly true, that the wages of labour will be reduced by a fall in agricultural produce, we must not imagine that this reduction can be instantaneous. A great demand for manufacturing labour may counteract a considerable decrease in the demand for agricultural labour, till such time as the energies of the principle of population shall have equalized the number of inhabitants with the means of acquiring subsistence, and then, and then only, a fall in the wages of labour would take place, though there should still be a considerable demand for manufacturers. The price of all kinds of grain has fallen fully a half in Britain during the last two years; but although the demand for manufacturing has not been much increased, the wages of work people has not experienced a corresponding decrease. According to Sir F. M. Eden, in a labourer's family of the ordinary size, the expense of house rent, fuel, soap, candles, tea, sugar, and clothing, generally equals that of bread and meal; and the expense of milk, butter, cheese, potatoes, etc. may be considered as half as much. Several of these articles, it is evident, are but indirectly and slowly affected by a fall in the price of corn; and on others, such as fuel, soap, tea, sugar, clothing, etc. it is scarcely at all perceptible. The price of corn is not, therefore, the sole regulating principle of wages; it is certainly one of the greatest, but others besides it have a very considerable effect. We will elucidate the effect of this reasoning, by a case which is exceedingly general: Suppose a farmer in 1812 to have employed six ploughmen, paying each twenty-two pounds of wages besides victuals, and that in 1815 these wages are reduced to eighteen pounds, while the value of the produce of their labour is reduced by half, it is evident that, by this change of things, the farmer loses forty-two pounds per annum; for the wages of the ploughmen should have been reduced to eleven pounds, if they had been altogether regulated by the price of corn. Again, if we consider how many mechanics a farmer must employ, we shall be much more convinced of the truth of the above statements. Although we should suppose the manual labour of a saddler, for instance, to be somewhat reduced, that will have but very little effect on the goods the farmer must purchase from him: The duty on leather will, in this case, be a complete bar to their sensible reduction.

In the second place, let us consider how a continued depression in the price of corn is likely to affect landlords and farmers in their consumption of the necessaries, the conveniences, and the luxuries of life.

Suppose a family of seven persons, when the quartern loaf sells at a shilling expends 1l. 1s. weekly in the purchase of bread and meal, the amount of this expenditure in a year would be 54l. 12s. Let us further suppose, that the revenue of this family is derived from a farm let at three hundred pounds per annum, on the hypothesis of the quartern loaf selling at a shilling; and let us examine the change produced in the circumstances of this family by the quartern loaf falling to 6d. It is in this case plain, that the family would save 27l. 6s. in the purchase of bread, but they would, on the other hand, lose a hundred and fifty pounds of rent; on a balance, therefore, they suffer a loss of 122l. 14s. That the fall in the wages of labour may not, however be overlooked, we shall suppose that the farmer is enabled to pay 22l. 14s. over and above the half rent, which otherwise would have been a rack-rent, and in this way the actual loss of the family is a hundred pounds per annum. The consequence deducible from this statement is, that when the quartern loaf sold at a shilling, this family had 245l. 8s. to expend on the necessaries and the luxuries of life, over and above their consumption of bread; but when the quartern loaf is reduced to sixpence, it has only l45l. 8s. to expend on these articles.

Let us now consider the effects of the fall in the price of corn, on the principal articles on which this diminished income must be expended, in order that we may accurately determine the relative situation of this family, and consequently of *all the agricultural families of Britain.*

In its necessary expenditure, house rent will occupy a prominent place; but house rent is not speedily affected by a reduction of the income of the tenants; for though where such a reduction takes place, they may wish to remove to smaller houses, it is clear that this cannot be generally done, without supposing a depopulation, which can only take place by degrees.[14] Butcher meat, an article of great importance in household economy, will not be proportionally reduced: When the price of bread is low, people eat more flesh meat than at other times, and this necessarily tends to keep up its price. Surely no person will maintain, that clothes would be nearly a third reduced in price by the fall in the price of corn that we have been contemplating: In fact, a considerable time must elapse before this fall could have any sensible effect on them;[15] in as far, therefore, as regarded their purchase, the change would be peculiarly prejudicial. Tea, which has now become an article of the first necessity, would not be at all affected by this change in the price of corn; it may just as probably increase in price while the other is falling, as there is no bond of connection between them.[16] Neither ale nor porter could proportionally decline, since the fall in the price of corn affects only the malt, which, on an average of the last five years, has hardly been equal to the duty. All the fall that could take place in a gallon of whisky, must be in the fluctuating part of the price, which is not at present more than two shillings or two and sixpence while the duty is about eight and fivepence: The same may be said of rum, brandy, and wine, the duties on which are 11s. 7½d., 18s. 10½d., and 7s. 7d. per gallon, respectively. It were easy to multiply examples of this nature; but they must suggest themselves to the mind of every person, and must compel us to conclude, that this fall in the price of bread, has altered the circumstances of this family, and of all others similarly situated, very much to the worse, and that they must now be contented with half the necessaries and luxuries of life they formerly enjoyed.

Having thus shown in detail, that a fall in the price of corn cannot, as matters now stand, affect the other necessaries and comforts of life, in any way approaching to an equal proportion, let us bestow a few words on another answer that has been made to the complaints of the farming interest. Your profits, it is said, were immense during the last fifteen years; your capitals either are, or ought to have been, vastly increased; and therefore, though they may not now be equally productive with what they were of late years, still, upon the whole, your relative situation will be as good, if not better than it was in 1794. However specious in appearance this reasoning may be, it is at bottom little better than declamation. It is universally known, that a season of high profits is not that in which men are most disposed to save, especially if there is a reasonable prospect of its continuance. The great body of men only value an increase of income, merely as it enables them to live better: They acquire to spend, not to hoard. That this was eminently the case during the last twenty years cannot be denied. The way of living among the middling classes, whether manufacturers or agriculturists, was totally changed. It is idle to talk of the folly of this conduct; it was the natural consequence of an increase of revenue, and the most prudent individuals were dragged along by the general torrent. That part of their profits which was not consumed in an increased expenditure, was swallowed by oppressive taxes. For several years back, a direct impost of ten per cent, has affected all landed property, and all professional incomes above a hundred and fifty pounds, and, in many instances, it was even more than that rate.[17] The taxes on all the necessaries of life were doubled, or tripled, and an insuperable bar was in this way put to the possibility of either a landlord or a farmer accumulating profits, and to the possibility of these necessaries falling in price, when corn might happen to fall, without a corresponding reduction of taxation.

The facts just stated are incontrovertible; and therefore, from the most complete evidence, we conclude, that a diminution of imposts to such an extent as would allow the necessaries of civilized life on which they are imposed, to be sold at a corresponding money price with that of corn, is the only possible means of permanently relieving our agriculturists.[18] It would, at the same time, give an immense impulse to our manufactures, and would ensure our national prosperity for many years to come.

We proceed to develop the manner in which this reduction might be effected.

Section Fifth

A Reduction of the National Expenditure, the only possible means of procuring the advantage of all Parties. Necessity and justice of reducing the Interest of the National Debt.

Ever since the time that Charles the Seventh of France began to maintain a body of troops in constant pay, the system of keeping up large standing armies has been continually gaining ground. As soon as one powerful state led the way, the rest, in order to preserve their independence, were obliged to follow the example. Much has been said about the abuses to which this institution has led, but these are the necessary consequences of that spirit of domination and inclination for power, which is natural to states as well as to individuals. Till such time as these passions are eradicated, standing armies, to a certain extent, seem essentially requisite for the security of nations. In the present state of the world, there seems little prospect that any considerable diminution of them can be rationally expected. There is too much jealousy of each other, too many fretful apprehensions, and too many fears that are well-grounded, among the nations of Europe, to allow us to expect that they either will, or can safely make any great reduction in their military establishments. This country, from its insular situation, and from the omnipotence of its Navy, is indeed somewhat differently situated. It would, however, be very dangerous policy, to trust to those advantages alone for protection, and to pay no attention to the affairs of the continent.

In the European system, no addition can be made to the power of any single state, but what affects more or less that of all the rest. To say that Britain should look calmly on, and see one state swallow up all the rest, would be downright infatuation; she would most certainly meet the fate with which Polyphemus threatened Ulysses. If, however, it is justifiable, and essentially necessary to repress the progress of usurpation and of aggrandizement, when its tendency is evidently to destroy the balance that should subsist among the great powers of Europe, it must also be necessary to keep up a force adequate to effect those objects, and to ensure the general happiness and tranquility. Taking these general principles into view, and reflecting on the present situation of the continent, it does not seem reasonable to expect that, with the most pacific ministry, a very great reduction could be made in our land forces.

The arguments against a very great reduction of the Navy, are still stronger than against that of the Army. The Navy is the arm on which Britain ought mainly to depend, in any contest into which she may be drawn. It is besides essentially different from the Army in this, that it does not require a long service to learn all the movements necessary for a soldier, while a series of years is required to form a thorough seaman. Considering these facts, and considering how jealous the nations of Europe, as well as the United States, are of our maritime preponderance, it would certainly be highly impolitic greatly to reduce our Navy, in a peace establishment.

But, although it is not possible to make a very great reduction in our forces, such a reduction ought certainly to be made to a greatly further extent than seems to be in the contemplation of government. The advantages of peace, in a pecuniary point of view, would be next to nothing, if we were then to keep up as many troops as in time of war. We ought not to be totally unprepared for whatever events may occur, but there is no occasion for maintaining armaments nearly commensurate with those that opposed almost the whole world.

The necessity of keeping up a respectable force for the safety of the country, combined with the deadly effects of an enormous taxation, points out the strong and paramount necessity of being economical in all other respects. A rigid investigation should be made into the different ways in which the public money is disposed of. Sinecures of all descriptions should be abolished, not so much, perhaps, for the saving that might hence arise, though that would be very considerable, as because they interest a powerful body in the perpetuation of abuses. The salaries of public officers, and the civil list, should also be greatly diminished, and be made to quadrate with the situation of the country. Mr. Ricardo's masterly pamphlet has drawn aside the veil from the transactions of the Bank of England, and has shown what the public has an undoubted right to demand from that quarter.

Assuming that the government is justly compelled to be much more economical, both in the military and the civil departments, and supposing that the expenditure is thereby lessened twelve or fifteen millions, the effect of this would be to allow the half of the property tax proposed to be continued to be taken off, and about seven or ten millions of other taxes. We must not deceive ourselves, by thinking that this great reduction, greater we are afraid than will be speedily realized, would be anything like adequate relief to our distresses. We must reflect, that our peace establishment would still be fourteen or seventeen millions, besides being oppressed with the interest of the national debt, amounting to about thirty-four millions, and with ten or eleven millions more, raised to be expended in the worse than quixotic attempt of paying it off.[19] The taxes would still be excessive; and such a reduction would neither enable the manufacturer to stand a competition with foreigners, now that peace has restored a free intercourse among nations, nor would it enable the landholder to enjoy the comforts and necessaries of life. The one and the other must decline, and finally be ruined, unless such a reduction shall be made in the imposts on the necessaries of life, as will enable the people of Britain to procure them at a rate not greatly different from the nations of the continent.

To the question, How shall this reduction be effected? We answer, By reducing the interest of the national debt.

Such a reduction is at once highly expedient, and substantially just.

To insist at large on its expediency, would be to restate all that is previously stated. We have shown that a flourishing commerce is the only lasting, the only proper, and the only sure basis of national prosperity. We have shown, that a high relative price of provisions, and of the necessaries of life, is both decidedly injurious to, and ultimately destructive of commerce; we have shown as a consequence of these principles, the absurdity, and the positive mischief, of attempting to keep up the price of corn in any one country by factitious regulations; we have portrayed the distress of the agriculturists, and we have found that the influence of taxation, by preventing the money price of a great part of the necessaries of life falling in proportion to that of corn, is the real source of their misery—directly, as it affects the articles which they must purchase themselves; indirectly, as it is injurious to the manufacturers, on whom they must ultimately depend. It is certain that whatever measure would permanently relieve, to a considerable extent, the distress of these different classes, which constitute almost all that is valuable in a state, would be highly expedient.

What are the objections to so salutary a measure?

The fundamental objection is, that no reduction can be made on the interest of the national debt, without a manifest breach of faith with the public creditors, and without shamefully violating a solemn compact. If this objection is well-founded, it ought certainly to preclude all hopes of relief from that quarter; we may be poor, miserable, and borne down to earth by the weight of our burdens, but that will not excuse our committing an act of flagrant injustice. Before proceeding, therefore, we must consider whether this objection is of that overwhelming nature.

It is admitted by all modern political economists, that money has no particular value other than its value in exchange; if therefore the quantity of money, or circulating medium in a country, be increased or depreciated in a greater ratio than the things against which it is exchanged, its value in exchange will become less, and it will require a greater portion of money to procure the same quantity: This was the case in Britain from 1797 to 1813. If, on the other hand, the circulating medium should recover from its depreciation, and become scarce, while the quantity of exchangeable products was not equally diminished, a larger quantity of them than formerly would be procured for the same nominal amount of money: This has been the case in Britain for the last two years.

In the one case, the relative value of money was diminished; in the other, it was increased.

If the late Corn Bill should be repealed, and we have already shown the necessity of doing so, there can be no doubt but the price of corn in Britain would scarcely, at any time, rise higher than sixty-three shillings a quarter, the price at which importation was permitted, at a duty of two and sixpence by the act of 1804. A hundred pounds, it is evident, would then purchase nearly the double of the corn which it would have done in 1813; it would of consequence be doubly valuable in respect to corn. If, as Mr. Wilson imagines, the Corn Bill shall not raise the price of corn, exactly the same conclusion follows.[20] It is further obvious, that, in respect of manufactures, the hundred pounds would purchase a greater quantity of them, in as far as their nominal price might fall by a reduction in the nominal price of corn.

When value is rendered for value, there is no injustice;[21] but money is only so far valuable, as it enables us to command the necessaries and the luxuries of life. If the stockholder therefore is paid with half the sum that he lent, *when this half sum will purchase as many of these articles as the whole sum did before,* no injustice is done him; on the contrary, he is dealt with on the clearest principles of equity.

These are no crude and inconsiderate conclusions; they are confirmed in their full extent by the highest authority which can be quoted on subjects of this nature. Mr. Malthus, in his pamphlet entitled *Grounds of an Opinion, etc.* expresses himself on this subject as follows: "If the price of corn were now to fall to fifty shillings a quarter, and labour and other commodities nearly in proportion, there can be no doubt *that the stockholder would be benefited unfairly,* at the expense of the industrious classes of society, and consequently at the expense of the wealth and prosperity of the whole country.

"During the twenty years beginning with 1794 and ending with 1813, the average price of British corn per quarter was about eighty-three shillings; during the ten years ending with 1813, ninety-two shillings; and during the last five years of the twenty, a hundred and eight shillings. In the course of these twenty years, government borrowed near five hundred millions of real capital, for which, on a rough average, exclusive of the sinking-fund, it engaged to pay about five per cent. But if corn shall fall to fifty shillings a quarter, and other commodities in proportion, instead of an interest of about five per cent the government would really pay *an interest of seven, eight, nine, and for the last two hundred millions, ten per cent.*

"To this extraordinary generosity towards the stockholders, I should be disposed to make no kind of objection, if it were not necessary to consider by whom it is to be paid; and a moment's reflection will show us, that it can only be paid by the industrious classes of the society and the landlords, that is, by all those whose nominal incomes will vary with the variations in the measure of value. The nominal revenues of this part of the society, compared with the average of the last five years, will be diminished by half; and out of this nominally reduced income, they will have to pay the same nominal amount of taxation.

"The interest and charges of the national debt, including the sinking-fund, are now little short of forty millions a year;[22] and these forty millions, if we completely succeed in the reduction of the price of corn and labour, are to be paid in future from a revenue about half the nominal value of the national income in 1813.

"If we consider with what an increased weight the taxes on tea, sugar, malt, leather, soap, candles, etc. would in this case bear on the labouring classes of society, and what *proportion* of their incomes all the active industrious middle orders of the state, as well as the higher orders, must pay in assessed taxes, and the various articles of the customs and excise, the pressure will appear to be absolutely intolerable. Nor would even the *ad valorem* taxes afford any real relief. The annual forty millions must at all events be paid; and if some taxes fail, others must be imposed that will be more productive.

"These are considerations," Mr. Malthus justly observes, "sufficient to alarm even the stockholders themselves. Indeed, if the measure of value were really to fall as we have supposed, there is great reason to fear that the country would be absolutely unable to continue the payment of the present interest of the national debt: *And even if the price of corn be kept up by restrictions to eighty shillings a quarter, it is certain that the whole of the loans made during the war just terminated, will, on an average, be paid at an interest very much higher than they were contracted for; which increased interest can, of course, only be furnished by the industrious classes of society.*"

These conclusions are further supported by the reasoning in the very able papers in the *Edinburgh Review*, Nos. 34 and 36, on the depreciation of currency. The Reviewers justly complain of the injustice that would be done to the public creditors, and people having fixed incomes, by paying them with paper depreciated fifteen or twenty per cent. If, however, the public creditor lent the country depreciated paper, he could not object to being paid in the same kind; if he is paid in paper *that is not equally depreciated with what he lent,* he gets an undue advantage at the expense of the nation.

The question of the justice being thus satisfactorily disposed of, the stockholders argue, that if you reduce their claims on the state, you ought in like manner to reduce the claims of every individual in the country on each other, and make the measure quite general. In answer to this it may be said, that if no injustice is done you, you have no right to complain though favours are extended to others. Had your money been employed in trade, or lent to private persons, it cannot be doubted but in this space of time you must have met with many losses, from all which you have been exempt; and considering the matter generally, your capital so reduced will be larger than if it had been lent to private persons. This reduction of the claims of one individual on another could not benefit you, and why should you seek to extend what you term a calamity?[23]

It is in vain to tell us about the distress and confusion resulting from this measure; it must of necessity be very limited. There can be none, no, not even the smallest comparison, between the distress and misery produced by cutting off a half or a fourth, from the *nominal* income of a body of men such as the stockholders, or of adding a half or a fourth to the *real* taxes, that bear so enormously hard on the industrious manufacturers and agriculturists: This is the true state of the matter, and let us therefore be no longer insulted, with whining complaints, about the miseries that would be suffered by the poor stockholders!

Losing any hopes of interesting our sympathy, the stockholders tell us, that in our future wars we need not again attempt to borrow, and that no one will hereafter be found to lend us a farthing. It will perhaps be generally thought, that, were the matter to turn out as they represent it, no great disadvantage would ensue. It has been the facility of borrowing, and the funding system, that more than anything else, has frequently induced this country to make war on insignificant and trivial grounds, and it has encouraged a profligate and unmeasured expenditure in our internal economy. But waving these considerations, the consequence alluded to by the stockholders would by no means follow: The reverse, it is obvious, would be the fact; our credit would increase, as our debt would then bear some relation to our income, which is hardly the case at present.

The principle of the measure is therefore perfectly unobjectionable, and no breach of national faith would be made by carrying it into execution; the greatest difficulty is in fixing the rates at which the reduction should be made.

This could not altogether depend on the price of corn, for that does not alone regulate the price of all other commodities. The reduction must be made in a ratio compounded of the price of corn when the loan was made, of the reduced price of corn, and of the effect of the fall in the price of corn on manufactures. It would, however, be unfair to assume the prices of the individual years, when money was lent as a proper criterion of its value; for they might have been years of scarcity, such as 1800, or of great plenty, like 1802: It would be proper to take average periods of perhaps five years. These different considerations take effect in the following manner.

Mr. Malthus does not think that if the late Corn Bill had been rejected, the price of corn in Britain would have been above sixty shillings a quarter, and in this opinion he seems to be perfectly well-founded, considering the prices in France and Poland. The average price of wheat in Britain, for the five years ending 1813, was a hundred and eight shillings a quarter; this, compared with sixty shillings, the price at which it is now selling,[24] is eighty per cent higher; and this percentage should, in strict justice, be deducted from the interest of all the loans made to the country in that period, if everything else on which money is expended fell in proportion to corn. Allowing, however, most liberally for the cost of manufactured goods, and other necessaries and luxuries of life, the price of which corn does not greatly effect, we shall still have forty per cent to deduct from the interest of the two hundred millions lent to the country in these five years. In like manner, the average price of corn for the five years ending December 1815, was ninety-one shillings a quarter, and this compared with sixty-shillings and one half allowed as before, gives 25 5/6 per cent to be deducted from the interest of the very large sum borrowed in the last two years.

If we reduce the interest of all the loans made during the war, after some such method as this, the result will be having to the public of about eight or ten millions annually, and reducing the sinking-fund in the same proportion, the total saving would be about eleven or twelve millions. Mr. Malthus makes the reduction amount to eight millions; but an immense debt has been contracted since his pamphlet was printed. If we do not make this reduction, we in fact add eleven or twelve millions to the *real burdens* of the people; and we reduce the manufacturers, and the agriculturists of Britain, the soul and support of the nation, to be little better than mere purveyors for the stockholders.

The stockholders themselves would be among the first to feel the beneficial effects of this measure of reduction. They would be gainers, in as far as they paid less taxes on the necessaries of life; they would have an increased security for their real debts; and they would not have the heart-sickening reflection, of enriching themselves by the misery and distress of the country.

We have shown the indissoluble connection between commerce and agriculture, and that a continuance of the present system of taxation must necessarily be fatal to both. Let the stockholders beware of accelerating that dreadful crisis; let them not insist for seven or ten per cent, when, in justice, they can only claim five; let them accommodate themselves to the new state of things in which the country is placed; let them not seek to set their interests in opposition to those of the great body of the people; let them reflect on the possibility of a national bankruptcy; let them reflect on the certainty of the total ruin in which they would then be involved; and let them at length open their eyes to their real situation, and that of the country.

❖ ❖ ❖

Notes

1. *Observations on the Corn Laws*, p. 29.

2. I may cite the authority of Mr. Malthus himself in corroboration of what is here advanced; for he admits, "That where the property of land is divided into large shares, these arts and manufactures are absolutely necessary to the existence of any considerable population." *Essay*, vol. i. p. 272.

3. A deduction of two or three per cent will require to be made for a few years, till the machinery of the Flemish shall be brought to a par with that of the English manufacturer.

4. Dr. Smith says, that in Holland the heavy taxes upon the necessaries of life had ruined their principal manufactures, and were likely to discourage gradually their fisheries and shipbuilding. The Doctor's anticipations were confirmed in the fullest extent. *Wealth of Nations*, vol. iii. p. 392. Edit. Lond. 1802.

5. *Wealth of Nations*, book iv. chap. 5; and Say's *Traite D'Economie Politique*, liv. i. c. 17.

6. The cause that Dr. Smith assigns for great capitalists remaining in Holland, though heavily taxed, does not exist to anything like an equal extent in Britain. *Wealth of Nations*, vol. iii. p. 393.

7. L'alternative est terrible. Ou c'est l'agriculture et les proprietaires qui sont mines si les grains ne montent pas: ou bien c'est le commerce et les manufactures s'ils montent.—Say De l'Angleterre et des Anglais. p. 38.

8. Governor Pownal, in his speech on the Corn Bill of 1773, addressed the Speaker as follows: "Sir, We should guard against being avaricious of high prices; for if your corn is not cheap comparatively, it can never be an object of commerce. This is a point which should be well attended to; for unless you can be cheap, you will never be traders in corn." He might have added—nor in manufactures, nor in anything else.

9. In 1771, the balance on the side of wheat exported was reduced to 7,579 quarters; and the balance on the side of oats imported that year, amounted to 177,094 quarters. In 1772, the balance in the wheat trade was 18,515 quarters on the side of importation; and in 1778, 1774, and 1775, that balance still increased. The loss of a great part of our colonial trade, and the stagnation of our commerce and manufactures, occasioned by the ruinous war with America, having diminished the consumption, the balance was high on the side of exportation in 1778, 1779, and 1780; and, if this circumstance was any proof of national prosperity, Great Britain must then have been at the pinnacle of her grandeur; in the same way Poland would, at this day, be the most flourishing country in Europe. What must we think of premises from which such conclusions are necessarily drawn?

10. In 1797, the Bank of England had 11,191,720 pounds in circulation; in 1798, 13,334,752 pounds; in 1800, 15,841,932 pounds; and in 1814, 27,840,780 pounds. They have diminished considerably last year.

11. In 1812; one hundred and nine shillings in 1813.

12. Malthus' *Grounds of an Opinion, etc.* p. 13.

13. The same. *Observations on the Effects, etc.* p. 17.

14. This is not hypothetical reasoning: In Edinburgh at this moment, the rent of inferior houses is rising, while that of finer houses is falling.

15. Ce n'est pas le prix d'une seule denree, fut-ce meme le bled, qui a un grand effet sur les prix des choses qu'on fait; c'est le prix de tout, et le prix de tout est exageree en raison des charges publiques qui, sous milles formes diverses, atteignent le producteur et se combinent dans toutes ses depenses." *L'Angleterre, etc.* p. 40.

16. The duty on tea, is an *ad valorem* duty exactly doubling the price; if, therefore, tea should happen to rise in price when corn is falling, the duty too would rise.

17. This requires some explanation. Every income derived from heritable property, *whatever might be its amount*, paid ten per cent. Professional incomes below fifty pounds were not taxable, and incomes of that sort above fifty pounds, and under one hundred and fifty pounds, were entitled to a deduction of one shilling for every twenty shillings under that sum. In this way, a farm let at two hundred pounds per annum, paid twenty-seven pounds and ten shillings of property tax, as the tenant was assumed to make the half of the rent of profit, and a farm let at three hundred pounds paid forty-five pounds. From this statement it is obvious, that a tenant paid a higher rate of income tax, not according as his income increased, but as it diminished! The amount of property tax levied on an average of the three years preceding January 1813, was 13,281,519 pounds, and the whole average amount of taxes, permanent and annual, raised during these three years, was 64,860,192 pounds. If the property tax be ten per cent on the whole income, the rate of entire taxation has been nearly fifty per cent on the income of each individual. Hamilton, *On National Debt*, second edition, p. 18.

18. "At present the land owner and farmer are distressed because grain is cheap, while everything else is dear. The price of everything which the landed interest buy, is made up in more than one half of taxes. Were these removed, they never could feel the injury arising from cheap corn; for, in a very short time, that would be balanced by the lowering of all other prices in proportion. In the present unnatural state of things, prices may lower a little, till they reach the part which consists of taxes, but then their fall must necessarily be arrested." *Edinburgh Review*, No. 50. art. Finances.

19. If we were to have no wars for forty-five or fifty years to come, it is calculated, that, by the effects of compound interest, the sinking-fund would by that time equal the debt. To imagine that we shall have a continuance of peace for the fourth part of the time is ridiculous; but admitting it were to continue during the whole period, long ere its termination the nation would be so impoverished by this taxation, and by the emigration of capitalists, as not to be able to pay one-fourth of the sums necessary to produce the effect. The theory of compound interest cannot be applied to any extent in practice. Does any man in his senses believe Dr. Price, when he talks about a penny increasing to one hundred and fifty millions of globes

of gold? Or Mr. Morgan, when he talks about one hundred and seven millions of globes? The sinking-fund is in fact a tub to the whale; an opiate to smooth the avenues to national bankruptcy,

20. "With regard to the future prices of grain, there is reason to conclude that, with a production now so far extended as to be fully equal to our consumption, no parliamentary interference can keep up the prices in any degree higher than they were in those years of our greatest national prosperity, 1792, 1793, and 1794." See *Enquiry, etc.* p. 42. And again, at p. 85, Mr. Wilson thinks, "that it may now be held ascertained, that the prices of corn cannot be raised by any legislative measure." We have already given our reasons for considering these conclusions of Mr. Wilson as extremely doubtful.

21. Provided it is of the same kind. If I borrow three pounds from any person, I may, in fair justice, pay him with two pounds, if money since the time I borrowed has increased in value one-third; I am not entitled, however, to pay him with anything else, a hat for instance, though equally valuable, because he may not be able easily to exchange it for those articles for which he might have exchanged money.

22. They are now forty-five or forty-six millions.

23. It is not said, that in the present state of things it would be unjust to reduce the claims of individuals on each other, were it possible to ascertain the date and other essential circumstances of their claims with any accuracy; to do this would evidently be impracticable, and consequently the measure could not be applied to them.

24. It is not, in fact, selling at so much; the average price of wheat in London market 26th February last, was only fifty-four shillings a quarter, and on an average of the last twelve months it has not been higher: If wheat shall continue at fifty-four shillings or fifty-five shillings we give a considerable advantage to the stockholders in making the reduction, on the hypothesis of its selling at sixty shillings.

ABOUT THE PUBLISHER

Coventry House Publishing is a traditional publisher of adult fiction and non-fiction titles. Founded in Dublin, Ohio in 2012, we're beginning a long tradition of serving readers and authors across the country, one book at a time.

We pride ourselves on the quality, meaningful work we publish. Our primary genres of focus include business & economics, sports & recreation, education & social science, and fiction & entertainment. Please visit our website, www.coventrybooks.com, for more information about our featured books and authors.